T0254496

Formal Methods in Artificial Intelligence

Cambridge Tracts in Theoretical Computer Science

Managing Editor: Professor C. J. van Rijsbergen, Computing Science Department, University of Glasgow

Editorial Board:
S. Abramsky, Department of Computing Science, Imperial College of Science and Technology, London
P. H. Aczel, Department of Computer Science, University of Manchester
J. W. de Bakker, Centrum voor Wiskunde en Informatica, Amsterdam
J. A. Goguen, Programming Research Group, University of Oxford
J. V. Tucker, Department of Mathematics and Computer Science, University College of Swansea

Titles in the Series

FORMAL METHODS IN ARTIFICIAL INTELLIGENCE

ALLAN RAMSAY

Department of Computer Science, University College, Dublin

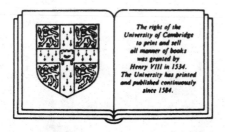

CAMBRIDGE UNIVERSITY PRESS

Cambridge

New York   Port Chester

Melbourne   Sydney

CAMBRIDGE UNIVERSITY PRESS
Cambridge, New York, Melbourne, Madrid, Cape Town, Singapore, São Paulo, Delhi

Cambridge University Press
The Edinburgh Building, Cambridge CB2 8RU, UK

Published in the United States of America by Cambridge University Press, New York

www.cambridge.org
Information on this title: www.cambridge.org/9780521424219

First published 1988
Reprinted 1989
First paperback edition 1991
Re-issued in this digitally printed version 2009

A catalogue record for this publication is available from the British Library

Library of Congress Cataloguing in Publication data
Ramsay, Allan, 1953 –
Formal Methods in Artificial Intelligence.
(Cambridge Tracts in Theoretical Computer Science; 6)
Bilbiography: p.
Includes index.
1. Artificial Intelligence – Methodology. 2. Logic, symbolic and
Mathematical. 3. Reasoning. I. Title. II. Series.
0335.R35   1988   006.3   88-9524

ISBN 978-0-521-35236-9 hardback
ISBN 978-0-521-42421-9 paperback

CONTENTS

PREFACE

Over the last few years, more and more AI research papers have used "logical" formalisms for their knowledge representation languages. Well-known AI techniques, such as the use of "frames" and defaults, have been treated with the tools of logic. At the same time, techniques from formal logic have been borrowed by AI researchers for their own ends, often in applications far removed from the context in which they were originally developed.

Much of this work has been very useful and constructive. As a result of the increasing emphasis on formal analysis of languages for knowledge representation, we now have a much better feel for the tasks that particular languages are good (or bad) for. We are also more aware of the problems that can arise if you just invent notations without ensuring that they will behave the way you want. It has become apparent that the concerns that motivated the development of formal logic in mathematics are just as important for AI. We need to know that our knowledge representation languages are well-behaved, and we need to know about their computational properties.

At the same time, it looks as though some of the papers using such formalisms are merely disguising the poverty or unoriginality of the work being reported. It seems as though you can make your program respectable if you describe it using a dense logical notation, even if it doesn't actually do anything interesting.

The prevalence of both sorts of logic-based work in AI causes problems to the newcomer to the field, and even to experienced practitioners who don't happen to have a strong background in mathematical logic. How can you work out whether someone is using a notation to good effect, or whether they are just trying to blind you? And if they are using it for a good reason, what does it mean anyway? The aim of this book is to bring together the major *useful* applications of logic in

AI in one place, with as consistent a notation as possible and with no prejudices for or against particular schools of thought. Since I am not, in this book, arguing for any specific theory which I have invested a great deal of time and effort in, I hope I can report objectively on the most widely used theories. It is almost certain that some of my own views will creep in, particularly in the specific framework I shall be using to try to unify the various theories, but at least I am not currently arguing for one language at the expense of another. My intention is to enable my readers to conduct the arguments for themselves, not to tell them the answer.

The material is fairly dense. It is also organised in a way that reflects its origins in a two-term course for graduate AI students. The book starts with a broad overview of what logic is about, and of what it is that makes a language a logic. The next two chapters cover classical logic, with comparatively little discussion of its relevance to AI. The aim of these two chapters is to establish the specific notation used in the remainder of the book, and to present the major meta-results about soundness, completeness and decidability. Some of the proofs of meta-theorems in this part of book are rather intricate. It is quite possible to read the rest of the book despite skipping these proofs, particularly the ones towards the end of Chapter 3. Of course if you do decide to skip them, you won't *really* be in a position to understand some of the debate about the merits or otherwise of particular languages; but it won't mean that you can't follow the rest of the book at all. Chapter 4 deals with theorem proving for classical logic. It is just about possible to read Chapter 4 without reading any of what comes before or after it; and to read what comes before and after without reading Chapter 4. Chapters 5, 6, 7 and 8 discuss ways in which classical logic is inadequate for describing the phenomena which AI systems have to deal with. The topics covered in these chapters are all concerned with ways of *extending* classical logic so that it is possible to describe new phenomena, or make new distinctions. These chapters do build on one another, and it would not be a good idea to try to read them in isolation, or in some other order. Finally Chapter 9 deals with two formalisms which are predicated on the assumption that classical logic is just plain *wrong*.

Acknowledgements

In writing this book, I have had a great deal of help from a lot of people. I am particularly grateful to everyone to whom I have ever taught logic, especially Helen Chappel and Ho Mun Chan, on whom I tried out the first few drafts; to Ros Barrett, for checking the text and improving my presentations; and to Fairouz Kamereddine for her comments on the penultimate draft.

Allan Ramsay, Brighton, 1988.

Note: the book contains a lot of notation, much of which will be new to most readers. All of it is introduced as it is required. All of it, that is, apart from the symbol ▦. This is a punctuation mark indicating the end of a proof.

CHAPTER ONE

LOGIC: PROOFS AND MODELS

The main aim of this book is to show how artificial intelligence (AI) can be enriched by incorporating recent advances in formal logic. Most of what we shall be looking at concerns extensions of classical logic to cover topics such as reasoning about time, reasoning about knowledge, or reasoning with uncertain knowledge. We do not intend to write a general introduction to logic, since there are already plenty of good introductory logic texts. On the other hand, we do need to make the nuances of our particular ways of thinking about classical theory clear, and to present some important meta-results in order to be able to compare it properly with the extensions and alternatives we will be considering in the remainder of the book. We therefore start with a discussion of classical logic.

1.1 Representation plus entailment

There are a number of ways of characterising what logic is about - the study of valid arguments, the study of consistent sets of statements, the foundations of mathematics, and so on. Different people will take different views as to which of these is the best way of thinking about the subject, and some people may even reject some of them. As far as AI researchers are concerned, it is perhaps most appropriate to think of it as being about knowledge representation languages in which the notion of entailment can be captured. In other words, it is about the study of languages in which we can state facts and rules, and for which we have a means of determining what other facts follow from the ones we have stated. The main thing that distinguishes logical languages from other representation languages is that the rules of entailment and the rules governing the interpretation of statements are presented with great precision. Sufficient precision, in fact, to enable us to derive rigorous proofs about properties of the language itself. We take this precision to be the defining characteristic that makes a language a *logic*, and we will be concentrating in this book on just such languages. In chapters 2 and 3 we will look in detail at two languages studied within classical logic, and we will show that these languages possess a number of desirable properties, but that both are inadequate or disappointing in some way or other. This should both give the reader a feel for the way such proofs about a language work, and also provide a reference point for considering the advantages and disadvantages of the alternative theories we look at later on.

In order to study a language, we have to be able to recognise whether or not a string of symbols is in fact an acceptable sentence in it; and for strings of symbols which are sentences, we have to know how to work out what they mean. For languages which are to be used for knowledge representation, it is also useful for us to be able to find out whether some sentence follows from some other set of sentences, so that we can perform inferences. All the languages we will be looking at are specified by three sets of rules. We need *syntactic rules*, to tell us what sequences of symbols are meaningful expressions of the language; *semantic rules*, to tell us how to interpret such meaningful expressions; and *inference rules*, to tell us about the relations between them. The syntactic rules are generally very uninteresting. We need to have them, since the meanings of expressions are specified systematically in terms of their syntactic structure, and the inference rules also apply to expressions by virtue of their syntactic structure. Furthermore, proofs about what can and cannot be expressed, or about what can and cannot be proved, are nearly all couched in terms of the various ways expressions can be built up from smaller expressions, so that the syntactic rules are particularly important when we come to try to prove things about languages. They are, then, important but not interesting (there may be an analogy here with work on computer processing of natural language, which sometimes seems to concentrate on syntactic processing to the exclusion of semantics. The point is that although it may be the semantics we are actually interested in, the only way we can get at it is via the syntax). The semantics of logical languages are generally given in terms of a *model*. We will see an exception to this when we come to consider Lorentzen's (1959) *game theoretic semantics* in Chapter 9, but apart from this one exception we will always provide the semantics via a model. The particular details of what a model is will vary from language to language, but the general notion is fairly simple. A model is no more than a collection of objects which have relationships to one another. The objects may be almost any kind of entity you care to mention - things in the real world, mathematical abstractions, ideas in people's minds, even the symbols of the language itself.

The relations between them may also be of a wide variety of types. The only requirement is that we should be able to systematically relate expressions of the language to entities and relations in the model.

Once we have the notion of a model, we can distinguish between two sorts of truth in a language. There is a weak version of truth, which we might call *truth in a model*. We will see that sentences of the second language we will be considering, called FOPC for *first-order predicate calculus*, are basically built up out of names for individuals, names for variables, names for relations, and logical operators. Models of FOPC consist of sets of individuals and relations between them. To a first approximation, a sentence of FOPC is true in a model just when the relations it names hold between the individuals it names. There is quite a lot of extra detailed wrapping to be put round this notion, but the basic idea is as we see it here. As languages get more complex, the structure of a model will get more complex, but truth in a model will essentially remain the same, namely that the relations referred to hold between the individuals referred to.

The simple notion of truth in a model is useful, but it is not really what we need. Logic is generally used in situations where we know a certain amount about how the world is, including various general rules, and we need to find out whether various statements about which we do not have direct information are also true. To take a trivial example, we might know that all cats get sleepy when it's very hot, that Cherry is a cat and that it is very hot, and we might want to know whether Cherry is sleepy. We have no direct information about the statement we are interested in, but it clearly follows from the facts and rules that we do have direct access to. The way we arrive at this conclusion is by realising that in all models in which the first three statements are true, the fourth one must also be. The notion of a statement being true in all models, or in all models in which some other set of statements are also true, is of central interest in logic. It is the way in which we validate our inference rules, and hence the basis of all inferences of new knowledge from old. We will generally reserve the term true for truth in a model, and call sentences which are true in all models (in which some other set of sentences are true) *valid* (with respect to the given set of sentences). Validity will also become more complex in detail as we move to more complex languages, but the general idea will remain the same.

As well as semantic rules, we have rules of inference. The rules of inference are formal patterns which allow us to infer sentences from other sentences. They are themselves derived from our intuitions about what the symbols of a given language are supposed to mean, and from the concrete way in which these intuitions are expressed in the semantic rules. However, when they are employed in the course of a proof, the reasons why they are accepted as rules of inference, and the meanings of the expressions they are applied to, are completely irrelevant. Rules of inference are entirely formal rules which say that if you have a collection of expressions which fit a specified pattern then you can add some new expression to them.

It is common to refer to the semantic rules of a language as its *model theory* and the inference rules as its *proof theory*. It is clearly important to ensure that the proof and model theories coincide as closely as possible. Ideally, everything which was valid according to the semantics of the language would be provable via the inference rules, and everything which was provable would be valid according to the semantics. We say that a language is *complete* if its inference rules are powerful enough to enable us to prove everything which is valid according to its semantics, and that it is *sound* if everything which is provable via the inference rules is valid. All the languages we will look at in this book are sound. A language whose rules of inference permitted you to draw conclusions which were not valid would be virtually useless, since you would then have no reason to trust any conclusions which you arrived at using those rules, and hence there would be very little point in using them. It is less important for languages to be complete. It's reassuring if they are, since it gives you confidence that you really have got the right set of inference rules, but the fact that you know that there may be things that are valid but which you cannot prove should not make it impossible for you to rely on the results of any inferences which you do manage to make.

We will return to the precise details of the relations between validity and provability for two important languages in Chapters 2 and 3, where we will prove a number of *meta-theorems*, i.e theorems which tell us about properties of languages. Before we do that, we will see how they illuminate the difference between two of the traditional ways of viewing logic.

1.2 Alternative views

Books on logic are more or less forced to start by trying to give a definition of what logic actually is. This is rather a funny situation. Most books start by giving an overview of how the subject matter being considered is going to be attacked, of what particular topics are going to be dealt with, and so on, but it is not customary to feel compelled to explain what the subject itself is actually about. The reason why logic is an exception is that there are at least two widely held, and differing, views on what it is really about. These views eventually converge, but they provide different starting points and different interpretations of the significance of the results on which the convergence occurs. We can express them informally as follows. On one view, exemplified in Hodges' (1969) introduction, logic is about the study of consistent and inconsistent sets of beliefs. It is about the conditions under which it is reasonable to hold a collection of beliefs simultaneously, and about when belief in some set of sentences seems to entail belief in some other sentence. On this view, the central focus of the subject is on the reasons for supposing that it is unacceptable for anyone to believe all of *cats get sleepy when it's hot, Cherry's a cat, it is hot* and *Cherry is not sleepy* at the same time, or that anyone who believed the first three of these ought to feel compelled to believe *Cherry is sleepy*. This view of logic, namely that it is about the consistency or otherwise of sets of sentences, puts the semantic rules first. It says that the inference rules are interesting only insofar as they provide a way of calculating which sentences are consistent with one another. The other view, which can be clearly seen in Robbin (1969) and Kleene (1967), emphasises the function of logic as the support for argumentation. The notion of a proof is central, and most of the results which are considered to be important concern the range of things for which proofs are available. The semantics from this point of view is a reference point for investigating properties of proofs - can all valid sentences be proved, can any invalid ones, and so on. Both approaches explore the relations between the proof and model theories, so it is hardly surprising that the results they come up with are the same. The difference is between those people who want to show that the proof theory conforms to the model theory and those who want to show that the model theory supports the proof theory. It clearly ought to make no serious difference to the results they come up with, but it may lead to different emphases, and it may lead them to provide slightly different versions of the language. We will remark on the differences in the ways a language may be presented after we have actually seen some details.

CHAPTER TWO

PROPOSITIONAL CALCULUS

The first language we will look at in detail is the *propositional calculus*. This is not a particularly useful language, since it lacks expressive power, but it has the advantage of being extremely simple. It therefore serves well as a vehicle for introducing the sorts of proof that are required when we want to prove meta-theorems about more realistic languages. The style of proof is similar to what we will need later, but the content is much less complex. The hope is that it will serve well as a model for the later proofs, not that we will be able to use it as a knowledge representation language for AI.

The propositional calculus is, as its name suggests, about propositions and relations between propositions. It is a formalisation of the sort of reasoning that is needed for inferring from the rule *if it is raining then people carry their umbrellas raised* and the fact *people are not carrying their umbrellas raised* the conclusion *it is not raining*. The main restriction on the propositional calculus is that there is no way of substituting particular entities which are known to satisfy some property into rules which refer to all items that satisfy it. In more concrete terms, it is not possible to express within the propositional calculus the chain of inference that leads from *if it is raining then everyone will have their umbrella up, John is a person, John does not have his umbrella up* to *it is not raining* because there is no way of substituting the name of the individual *John* into the general rule about *everyone*. This limitation does restrict the expressiveness of the propositional calculus, but it does not render it entirely useless.

We will consider three versions of propositional calculus, reflecting variations on the two general approaches to logic discussed above. The first version, known as a *Hilbert system*, is appropriate for the view that logic is about proofs. The second and third versions, a *Gentzen system* and a *tableau (or Beth) system* respectively, are appropriate for the view that it is about consistency and entailment.

2.1 Propositional calculus (Hilbert system)

2.1.1 *Propositional calculus (Hilbert system): vocabulary and syntax*

We will call our first version of the propositional calculus $Prop_{hilbert}$. The syntax of $Prop_{hilbert}$ is extremely simple. It consists of a set of names for propositions, a single logical operator or connective, and a single rule for combining simple expressions via the logical operator to get more complex ones, using brackets to indicate the way expressions have been built up where there is any possibility of ambiguity. All the languages we will be looking at use round brackets (and) and square brackets [and] wherever necessary to structure expressions correctly. No significance attaches to the choice of whether to use round or square ones, it is just a matter of readability. We will generally use curly brackets { and } to denote sets of objects, either enumerating them as in $\{x_1, x_2, x_3\}$ or defining them by a property they are expected to have as in {x: x > 4} (to be read as "the set of x such that x is greater than 4"). If we need brackets for anything else we will generally use angle brackets < and >. We will make no further mention of brackets unless we are going to use them for some special purpose - in particular it is to be assumed from now on that the standard round and square brackets can be used wherever necessary for clarity, but that they will always have to be matched up correctly (an opening square bracket cannot be paired with a closing round one, and vice versa). We will frequently call the expressions of $Prop_{hilbert}$ (and other languages when we come to consider them) *formulae*.

$Prop_{hilbert}$ is to be a Hilbert system, i.e. a system which is tailored for talking about what can and cannot be proved within the language, rather than for actually saying things and exploring entailments. To this end we want the language to be as simple as possible - we want to have as few logical connectives and as few inference rules as we can get away with. It turns out that all we need are the following:

(i) an infinite set of names for propositions. We choose to use p, q, and r, plus the infinite collection $p_1, p_2, ...$

These basic proposition letters are intended to be interpreted as the names for concrete propositions such as *it is raining, people have their umbrellas up* or *Cherry is asleep*. The inferences which we want to capture are ones that depend simply upon the way these propositions are connected together, rather than on any relationships between the concepts they refer to.

(ii) a name, †, for a distinguished proposition which is known to be false. You can think of this as some proposition which you know is false, such as 1=2, or you can simply read it as "the false".

(iii) the connective →, which is intended to be read as "implies", or "if ... then ...". → can be used to combine simple proposition letters, as in p → q, or complex formulae, as in (p → q) → (p → (r → q)). In any formula of the form A → B, A is referred to as the *antecedent* and B as the *consequent*.

(iv) a single rule for combining expressions together. If A and B are arbitrary expressions, then so is A → B (with brackets included if necessary to maintain clarity).

We use A, B, C and A_1, A_2, ... to stand for arbitrary expressions of the language. It is important to recognise the difference between p, q, r and p_i, which are particular propositions of the language, and A, B, C and A_i, which are *meta-variables* which we use for talking about general expressions. A, B, C, A_1, ... are not part of the vocabulary of $Prop_{hilbert}$. They are a notation we use for talking about general properties of expressions which do belong to $Prop_{hilbert}$. Thus if we say "If A and B are expressions", we mean that they might be replaced by any of the particular proposition letters or by complex formulae built up from them by rule (iv). We sometimes use A, B ... to write *expression schemas*, i.e. patterns which a variety of actual formulae would match, so that A → B is a schema which would match p → q, p → r, (p → q) → [(r → s) → †], and so on.

$Prop_{hilbert}$ is a very impoverished looking language. The surprising thing about it is that it turns out to be sufficient for expressing anything which can be said in any language whose semantics are based on the valuation approach given below. It is thus well designed for use by people who want to prove meta-theorems about particular formalisms. The other versions of propositional calculus that we consider in this chapter are more useful for if you want to state facts and rules, and to use these for solving specific problems by proving theorems within the formalism. $Prop_{hilbert}$ is not, in fact, quite the simplest language we could have chosen, but it is simple enough.

2.1.2 *Propositional calculus (Hilbert system): semantics*

As with every single language that we will look at in this book, the semantics for $\text{Prop}_{\text{hilbert}}$ is given by explaining the meaning of the basic formulae (in this case the proposition letters and †), and then by explaining how the meanings of complex expressions depend on the meanings of their components.

The semantics of $\text{Prop}_{\text{hilbert}}$ are given in terms of two objects called T and F. It is evident that we intend these to correspond to the intuitive notions of truth and falsity, but nothing whatsoever depends on this. They could be 1 and 0, or 2999 and the name Cherry, or one of them could be an orange and the other a banana, or even the letters "T" and "F". It makes no difference, just so long as they are two different objects. The semantics of the basic letters and † are given by providing a function V, called a *valuation*, whose domain is the set of letters plus † and whose range is the set {T, F} (in other words, it takes as argument either one of the basic letters or † and returns either T or F). There are clearly an infinite number of such functions. The only constraint is that V(†) must be F.

V defines the meaning of the basic expressions, i.e. the proposition letters and the symbol †. The next move is to show how we build up the meaning of compound expressions from the meanings of the basic ones that appear in them. We will want some way of denoting the meanings of expressions in general. It does not seem to be quite correct to denote the meaning of an expression like p → (p → q) by V(p → (p → q)), since V is simply a function which maps basic proposition letters and † to {T, F}. We will generally use the notation $[\![\text{EXPR}]\!]_T$ to denote the meaning assigned to EXPR by the theory of meaning T. $[\![\ ... \ ]\!]$ are *meta-symbols*, for making statements *about* expressions of a language, rather than symbols of any of the particular languages we will be looking at. Whenever possible we will omit the subscript indicating the particular theory of meaning.

For $\text{Prop}_{\text{hilbert}}$, the semantics of basic expressions is clear. The basic expressions of $\text{Prop}_{\text{hilbert}}$ are the proposition letters and the symbol †. If P is either of these, $[\![P]\!]_V$ is just V(P).

Once we have the semantics for the basic expressions, we can provide it for complex ones. There is only one possible way of building a complex expression in $\text{Prop}_{\text{hilbert}}$, namely by combining two simpler ones with →. We extend the semantics of $\text{Prop}_{\text{hilbert}}$ by saying that if A and B are expressions then $[\![A \rightarrow B]\!]_V$ is calculated as follows. If $[\![A]\!]_V$ is T and $[\![B]\!]_V$ is F then $[\![A \rightarrow B]\!]_V$ is F, otherwise it is T. This particular choice for the meaning of → may seem counter-intuitive. We are saying that A → B is true so long as B is never false when A is true. It is important to bear in mind that we are not attempting to characterise the idea of *causality* in our treatment of →. Causality is a complex notion which is beyond the scope of this book. For almost the whole of the current book we simply take A → B to indicate that A *materially implies* B, i.e. that it is not the case that B is false and A is true. This is a useful notion, but it must not be confused with the suggestion that A *causes* B.

The notion of a valuation can be given a very concrete realisation in terms of a *truth table*. A truth table is an enumeration of the way the valuation of a complex expression varies with the valuations of the simpler expressions it is made up from. For Prop$_{hilbert}$, the only truth table we need to consider is the one for expressions made by combining simpler expressions via →:

Fig. 2.1 Basic truth table for Prop$_{hilbert}$

A	B	A → B
T	T	T
T	F	F
F	T	T
F	F	T

We can construct truth tables for complex expressions by systematically building the tables for their components and then referring to the basic table given in Fig. 2.1. The truth table for A → (B → A), for instance, is constructed by first building the truth table for B → A for all values of A and B, and then combining these values in accordance with Fig. 2.1.

Fig. 2.2 Truth table for A → (B → A)

A	B	B → A	A → (B → A)
T	T	T	T
T	F	T	T
F	T	F	T
F	F	T	T

The final column in Fig. 2.2 is built by considering the first and third columns as though they were the first two columns in Fig. 2.1.

There are three particularly interesting schemas for Prop$_{hilbert}$. We can use these to show that this system is as expressive as any possible system whose semantics can be given either via a 2-valued valuation function or via simple truth tables, so that Prop$_{hilbert}$ is all we really need to consider as far as propositional logic is concerned. The following truth tables show that Prop$_{hilbert}$ can capture the important notions of negation, conjunction and disjunction.

Fig. 2.3 Truth table for A → †

A	†	A → †
T	F	F
F	F	T

We see that $[\![A \to \dagger]\!]_v$ is F when $[\![A]\!]_v$ is T, and T when $[\![A]\!]_v$ is F. This is exactly what we would expect the behaviour of the negation of A to be. We can therefore write ¬A as an abbreviation for A → † to include an operator for negation in Prop$_{\text{hilbert}}$. It is important to note that ¬A is not itself an expression of Prop$_{\text{hilbert}}$. It is an abbreviation which must be expanded to A → † before we can say that we have such an expression.

Fig. 2.4 Truth table for ¬A → B

A	B	¬A	¬A → B
T	T	F	T
T	F	F	T
F	T	T	T
F	F	T	F

$[\![\neg A \to B]\!]_v$ is T unless both $[\![A]\!]_v$ and $[\![B]\!]_v$ are F. This is the expected behaviour of one of the interpretations of the English word *or* (*or* in English sometimes carries the implication that exactly one of the contributing sentences is true, as in the obvious reading of *I shall either come and see you or go to London*. Logical theories generally choose to work with an interpretation of *or* which says that at least one of the alternatives is true, but that it may be that they both are). We can therefore introduce A ∨ B as an abbreviation for ¬A → B (which is in turn an abbreviation for (A → †) → B) to capture the notion of *inclusive-or*. A ∨ B is often called the *disjunction* of A and B.

Fig. 2.5 Truth table for ¬(¬A ∨ ¬B)

A	B	¬A	¬B	¬A ∨ ¬B	¬(¬A ∨ ¬B)
T	T	F	F	F	T
T	F	F	T	T	F
F	T	T	F	T	F
F	F	T	T	T	F

$[\![\neg(\neg A \vee \neg B)]\!]_V$ is T if both $[\![A]\!]_V$ and $[\![B]\!]_V$ are T, otherwise it is F. This is what we would want for a formula which captured the behaviour of *and*. We introduce A & B to stand for $\neg(\neg A \vee \neg B)$ (or in other words for $([((A \rightarrow \dagger) \rightarrow \dagger) \rightarrow (B \rightarrow \dagger)] \rightarrow \dagger)$). A & B is the *conjunction* of A and B.

The truth tables above show that we can construct expressions of $Prop_{hilbert}$ which behave in exactly the same way as negation, disjunction and conjunction. Our first meta-theorem shows that we can construct expressions of $Prop_{hilbert}$ to capture any behaviour we like. This is what justifies our claim above that $Prop_{hilbert}$ is sufficient for expressing anything which can be said in a language whose semantics is based on a 2-valued valuation function.

Theorem 2.1: Adequacy of $Prop_{hilbert}$

Suppose @ is a new operator which combines a set of formulae $A_1 ... A_k$ to make a new formula $A' = @(A_1, ..., A_k)$. Then there is a formula A'' of $Prop_{hilbert}$ such that for any V, $[\![A'']\!]_V = [\![A']\!]_V$ (note: not that for any V we can make such a formula, but that there is one formula A'' such that $[\![A'']\!]_V = [\![A']\!]_V$ for every possible V).

Proof:
Consider the truth table for A'. We can only do this in a rather general way, since we do not actually know what A' is. We do know, however, that any row of this truth table must consist of a series of T's and F's underneath the basic proposition letters appearing in the expression, followed by either a T or an F under the expression itself. Suppose the final column contains a T. We can construct an expression whose valuation would be T exactly when the proposition letters in A' have the valuations indicated in the other columns. This expression is made up by conjoining either the letters or their negations depending on whether their value in this row is T or F. If we combine all the expressions we get by making expressions for rows with T in the final column into a single disjunction, we will get a single expression of $Prop_{hilbert}$ whose valuation is T for every V for which $[\![A']\!]_V$ is T, and F for all others, as required
▦

To see how this would work in practice, consider the following truth table for an operator called @.

Fig. 2.6 Truth table for target

A	B	C	@(A, B, C)
T	T	T	T
T	T	F	T
T	F	T	F
T	F	F	T
F	T	T	F
F	T	F	F
F	F	T	F
F	F	F	T

The proof of Theorem 2.1 indicates that we need to make up expressions for the first, second, fourth and eighth rows of this table. The relevant expressions are A & (B & C), A & (B & ¬C), A & (¬B & ¬C) and ¬A & (¬B & ¬C). Joining these together leads to [A & (B & C)] V ([A & (B & ¬C)] V ([A & (¬B & ¬C)] V [¬A & (¬B & ¬C)])). This has the required truth table, and is an expression (with abbreviations) of Prop$_{hilbert}$.

2.1.3 *Propositional calculus (Hilbert system): inference rules*
Prop$_{hilbert}$ is such a simple language that it only has one inference rule, namely that for any expressions A and B, from A and A → B you can infer B. This is no more or less than you would expect if → is to capture the notion of implication. In addition to this inference rule, which is known as *modus ponens* or MP, there are a number of *axioms*, or expressions which are accepted as being true under any valuation whatsoever. There are a number of possible choices which are all equivalent. For no particular reason other than that they seem fairly acceptable and that they suffice for our purposes we choose the following set:

PH1: A → (B → A)
PH2: [A → (B → C)] → [(A → B) → (A → C)]
PH3: ¬(¬A) → A.

The first thing we must do is check that these are indeed valid. Axioms which could possibly be false would be very dangerous. We consider them one at a time.

Validity of PH1:
The only way for $[\![PH1]\!]_V$ to be F for some valuation V would be for $[\![A]\!]_V$ to be T and $[\![B \rightarrow A]\!]_V$ to be F; but for $[\![B \rightarrow A]\!]_V$ to be F, $[\![B]\!]_V$ would have to be T and $[\![A]\!]_V$ would have to be F. In other words for $[\![PH1]\!]_V$ to be F, $[\![A]\!]_V$ would have to be both F and T, which is impossible. So $[\![PH1]\!]_V$ must be T for any valuation V.

Validity of PH2:
Similarly, for $[\![PH2]\!]_V$ to be F, $[\![A \rightarrow (B \rightarrow C)]\!]_V$ would have to be T and $[\![(A \rightarrow B) \rightarrow (A \rightarrow C)]\!]_V$ would have to be F. This would mean that $[\![A \rightarrow B]\!]_V$ had to be T and $[\![A \rightarrow C]\!]_V$ had to be F, so that $[\![A]\!]_V$ was T and $[\![C]\!]_V$ was F. Going back to $[\![A \rightarrow B]\!]_V$, we see that since $[\![A]\!]_V$ is T so must $[\![B]\!]_V$ be. But then $[\![B \rightarrow C]\!]_V$ would be F (since $[\![C]\!]_V$ is F), and hence $[\![A \rightarrow (B \rightarrow C)]\!]_V$ would be F, contrary to the assumption earlier on. We thus see that there is no coherent way for V to assign values individually to A, B and C which make $[\![PH2]\!]_V$ come out as F.

Validity of PH3:
To check the validity of PH3, we first expand it out to:

PH3': $([(A \rightarrow \dagger) \rightarrow \dagger] \rightarrow A)$

For $[\![PH3']\!]_V$ to be F we would have to have $[\![A]\!]_V$ equal to F and $[\![(A \rightarrow \dagger) \rightarrow \dagger]\!]_V$ equal to T. We know that V($\dagger$) must be F, so for $[\![(A \rightarrow \dagger) \rightarrow \dagger]\!]_V$ to be T it must be the case that $[\![A \rightarrow \dagger]\!]_V$ is also F. The only way for this to happen would be for $[\![A]\!]_V$ to be T and V($\dagger$) to be F. We know that V($\dagger$) is bound to be F, but we already argued that $[\![A]\!]_V$ must be F, in which case it cannot be T as well.

We see, then, that our chosen axioms are all valid. There is no way to find a V and choices of particular expressions to replace A, B and C which could lead to any of $[\![PH1]\!]_V$, $[\![PH2]\!]_V$ or $[\![PH3]\!]_V$ being anything but T.

The inferential component of Prop$_{\text{hilbert}}$ is completed by defining the notion of a proof. A *proof* of a conclusion C from hypotheses $H_1 \ldots H_k$ is a sequence of expressions $E_1, \ldots E_n$ obeying the following conditions:

(i) C is E_n.
(ii) Each E_i is either an axiom, or one of the H_j, or is a result of applying the inference rule MP to E_k and E_l where k and l are less than i.

The following example proof should make the definition clear.

Fig. 2.7 Example proof

Proof of r from p, p → q, and q → r:

1 p   (hypothesis)
2 p → q   (hypothesis)
3 q   (from 1 and 2 by MP)
4 q → r   (hypothesis)
5 r   (from 3 and 4 by MP)

It is perfectly reasonable to have a proof of a conclusion from an empty set of hypotheses, in which case we generally just say that we have a proof. A formula which can be proved from an empty set of premises is often called a *theorem*.

We can now see the difference between a proof *within* a language, such as the one in Fig. 2.7, and a proof of a meta-theorem *about* a language, such as the proof of Theorem 2.1. Proofs within a language are constructed according to the precisely specified inference rules of the language, and are used for investigating the consequences of knowledge expressed within that language. Once we have chosen to use a logical language for knowledge representation, we construct proofs of theorems within the language in order to extract the implicit consequences of what we have said about the world. Proofs of meta-theorems are generally written in some combination of English and mathematical notation, including special symbols such as ⟦ ... ⟧. The steps in the proof of a meta-theorem are not formally justified, since the language in which the proof is written does not normally have a precise formal semantics and set of inference rules. They are just carefully constructed persuasive arguments. It would be hard, for instance, to disagree with any of the steps of the proof of Theorem 2.1, despite the fact that they are not given in any formal language. It is, indeed, hard to see how proofs of meta-theorems could be made more rigorous. We might try to develop a formal language for stating and proving meta-theorems, but we would then have to provide meta-theorems about *it* to show that it was an appropriate language for the task. At some point the process of developing languages for discussing other languages has to stop, and we have to use natural language and commonsense to show that our first, most basic formal language is indeed appropriate.

We will in general leave it to the reader to work out when we are talking about theorems within a language and when we are talking about meta-theorems about it, since it is usually fairly obvious. There is just one case where the distinction can be somewhat blurred. It is quite often possible to show that a

proof of some conclusion must exist, without actually providing the details. In
such a situation we write, for instance, p, p → q, q → r ⊢ r. The symbol ⊢ is not
part of Prop$_{hilbert}$ itself, or of any of the other languages we shall be looking at. It
is another meta-symbol, like ⟦ ... ⟧, to be used for talking about properties of
languages, rather than for making statements within them. As with ⟦ ... ⟧, we
ought to subscript it, as in ⊢$_{Prophilbert}$, but since we very seldom talk about more
than one language at a time we shall in general not bother. The statement

p, p → q, q, q → r ⊢$_{Prophilbert}$ r

is strictly speaking a meta-theorem about Prop$_{hilbert}$. We could prove it either by
constructing a proof of r from p, p → q, q, q → r within Prop$_{hilbert}$, or by arguing
informally, from general properties of the language, that there must be such a
proof. Most approaches to automatic theorem proving actually work the second
way, exploiting general properties of the language in question to show that proofs
must exist, without actually constructing them, rather than by genuinely
constructing proofs within the language.

The inferential component of Prop$_{hilbert}$ is rather awkward to use. It is stated in
a rather minimal way to facilitate proving meta-theorems about it, but the
corollary of this is that it is not particularly easy to prove theorems within it. For
instance, the easiest proof of A → A in Prop$_{hilbert}$ is as follows:

```
1  [A → ((A → A) → A)] → [(A → (A → A)) → (A → A)] (PH2)
2  [A → ((A → A) → A)]                              (PH1)
3  [A → (A → A)]  →  (A → A)                        (MP on 1, 2)
4  (A → (A → A))                                    (PH1)
5  (A → A)                                          (MP on 3, 4)
```

This is a painfully long proof, given how obvious the conclusion seems to be.
Other seemingly obvious proofs can be even worse - the proof of the converse of
PH3, namely A → ((A → †) → †)) takes about 15 steps, with expressions with
over 20 →'s in them. The following meta-theorem is critical for making it
possible to derive non-trivial proofs in Prop$_{hilbert}$.

Theorem 2.2: Deduction Theorem (DT) for Prop$_{\text{hilbert}}$

If $A_1, ..., A_n \vdash B$ then $A_1, ..., A_{n-1} \vdash A_n \to B$

Proof:
The proof proceeds by a fairly common technique known as *structural induction*. To prove that all objects of some kind have a particular property, we find some way of assigning a size to objects of this kind. We then try to assume that there is some particular object of the relevant kind which does not have the property. If there are any objects for which the property fails, there must be some which are the smallest for which it fails (where smallest is defined relative to the assigned measure). We then try to derive a contradiction by considering one of these smallest objects which fail to satisfy the property, either showing that there must in fact be smaller ones or by showing that really the property does hold for it. In the present case, the objects we are considering are proofs and the measure is the number of expressions in the proof. To prove that the Deduction Theorem holds, we try to derive a contradiction from the supposition that it fails. Suppose that it fails. If so, then there must be a shortest proof for which it fails. Suppose this proof is the sequence $E_1 ... E_k$, which derives E_k from the hypotheses $A_1 ... A_n$. If we look back at the definition of what it means to be a proof, there are only three possible ways for E_k to be the last formula in a proof.

(i) E_k is an axiom. In this case,

1 E_k	(axiom, by assumption)
2 $E_k \to (A_n \to E_k)$	(PH1)
3 $A_n \to E_k$	(MP on 1, 2)

is a proof of $A_n \to E_k$ from no hypotheses. It is clear that if we have $\vdash A_n \to E_k$ then we have $A_1, ..., A_{n-1} \vdash A_n \to E_k$, so this first possibility, that E_k is an axiom, is ruled out.

(ii) E_k is one of $A_1 ... A_n$, say A_i. As in case (i),

1 E_k	(premise)
2 $E_k \to (A_n \to E_k)$	(PH1)
3 $A_n \to E_k$	(MP on 1, 2)

is a proof of $A_n \rightarrow E_k$ from A_i. We therefore have $A_i \vdash A_n \rightarrow E_k$, and hence A_1, ..., $A_{n-1} \vdash A_n \rightarrow E_k$. The second possibility is thus also ruled out.

(iii) E_k results from E_i and E_j for some i and j less than k, where E_i is $E_j \rightarrow E_k$. E_i and E_j are clearly the conclusions of shorter proofs than the complete proof leading up to E_k. As such, our assumption that this full proof is the shortest for which the Deduction Theorem fails means that we know that $A_1 ... A_{n-1} \vdash A_n \rightarrow E_j$ and $A_1 ... A_{n-1} \vdash A_n \rightarrow (E_j \rightarrow E_k)$. In other words, we know there are proofs, which we will call PROOF1 and PROOF2, of $A_n \rightarrow E_j$ and $A_n \rightarrow (E_j \rightarrow E_k)$ from $A_1 ... A_{n-1}$. The following is a proof of $A_n \rightarrow E_k$ from $A_1 ... A_{n-1}$.

1 $A_1 ... A_{n-1} \vdash A_n \rightarrow E_j$ (PROOF1, assumed)
2 $A_1 ... A_{n-1} \vdash A_n \rightarrow (E_j \rightarrow E_k)$ (PROOF2, assumed)
3 $A_1 ... A_{n-1} \vdash [A_n \rightarrow (E_j \rightarrow E_k)] \rightarrow [(A_n \rightarrow E_j) \rightarrow (A_n \rightarrow E_k)]$ (PH2)
4 $A_1 ... A_{n-1} \vdash (A_n \rightarrow E_j) \rightarrow (A_n \rightarrow E_k)$ (MP on 2, 3)
5 $A_1 ... A_{n-1} \vdash A_n \rightarrow E_k$ (MP on 1, 4)

It is now clear that the sequence of expressions we get by joining PROOF1, PROOF2 and the above proof of $A_{n-1} \rightarrow E_k$ provide us with a proof of $A_{n-1} \rightarrow E_k$ from $A_1 ... A_{n-1}$, contrary to the assumption that $E_1 ... E_k$ is a proof for which the Deduction Theorem fails.

We have now considered all three ways that E_k could be the last formula in a shortest proof for which the Deduction Theorem fails, and shown that for all of them the theorem in fact holds. We thus see that there cannot be a shortest proof for which the theorem fails, and hence there cannot be any such proof ▦

The Deduction Theorem (DT) enables us to show the existence of proofs which would otherwise have been extremely difficult to find. The following demonstration that there is a proof of $A \rightarrow \neg\neg A$ provides a good illustration.

1 $A, A \rightarrow \dagger \vdash \dagger$ (MP on 1, 2)
2 $A, \vdash (A \rightarrow \dagger) \rightarrow \dagger$ (DT)
3 $\vdash A \rightarrow ((A \rightarrow \dagger) \rightarrow \dagger)$ (DT)
4 $\vdash A \rightarrow \neg\neg A$ $(A \rightarrow \dagger \equiv \neg A)$

The following proof that $\vdash \dagger \to A$ for any A is also worth noting, since it both provides a common neat step for generating more complex proofs, and also emphasises the dangers inherent in working with inconsistent sets of axioms.

1 $\dagger, A \to \dagger \vdash \dagger$
2 $\dagger \vdash (A \to \dagger) \to \dagger$ (DT)
3 $\dagger \vdash [(A \to \dagger) \to \dagger] \to A$ (PH3)
4 $\dagger \vdash A$ (MP on 2, 3)
5 $\vdash \dagger \to A$ (DT)

We will also need the following two results later on.

1 $A \to B, B \to \dagger, A \vdash A$
2 $A \to B, B \to \dagger, A \vdash A \to B$
3 $A \to B, B \to \dagger, A \vdash B$ (MP on 1,2)
4 $A \to B, B \to \dagger, A \vdash B \to \dagger$
5 $A \to B, B \to \dagger, A \vdash \dagger$ (MP on 3, 4)
6 $\vdash (A \to B) \to [(B \to \dagger) \to (A \to \dagger)]$ (DT times 3)
7 $\vdash (A \to B) \to (\neg B \to \neg A)$ (Abbreviation)

1 $A \to B, \neg A \to B, \neg B \vdash A \to B$
2 $A \to B, \neg A \to B, \neg B \vdash (A \to B) \to (\neg B \to \neg A)$ (as above)
3 $A \to B, \neg A \to B, \neg B \vdash \neg B \to \neg A$
4 $A \to B, \neg A \to B, \neg B \vdash \neg B$ (MP on 1, 2)
5 $A \to B, \neg A \to B, \neg B \vdash \neg A$ (MP on 3, 4)
6 $A \to B, \neg A \to B, \neg B \vdash \neg A \to B$
7 $A \to B, \neg A \to B, \neg B \vdash B$
8 $A \to B, \neg A \to B, \neg B \vdash B \to \dagger$
9 $A \to B, \neg A \to B, \neg B \vdash \dagger$
10 $A \to B, \neg A \to B \vdash (B \to \dagger) \to \dagger$ (DT)
11 $A \to B, \neg A \to B \vdash [(B \to \dagger) \to \dagger] \to B$ (PH3)
12 $A \to B, \neg A \to B \vdash B$ (MP on 10, 11)
13 $\vdash (A \to B) \to [(\neg A \to B) \to B]$ (DT times 2)

We have now seen some examples of proofs in $\text{Prop}_{\text{hilbert}}$, and some more examples of demonstrations using the Deduction Theorem that proofs exist. There are two further questions we might want to ask about the inferential component of $\text{Prop}_{\text{hilbert}}$. We would like to be reassured that it will not permit us to infer conclusions which can be false when their supporting hypotheses are true, and we would also like to know that if some conclusion is always true whenever every member of a given set of hypotheses is true, then there is a proof of the conclusion from the hypotheses. In other words, we would like to show that it is *sound* and *complete*. As we remarked in Chapter 1, a logical system which was not sound would be rather useless, since you would be able to prove things that were not true. Completeness is not quite as important, but it can be useful.

Theorem 2.3: Soundness of Prop$_{hilbert}$

If A_1 ... $A_n \vdash A$ then $[\![A]\!]_V = T$ for any valuation function V for which all the $[\![A_i]\!]_V$ are T.

Proof:
Just as for the Deduction Theorem, we derive the proof by imagining that there is some set of hypotheses and some conclusion for which the theorem fails. We then suppose that we have some particular smallest example, where smallest is defined in terms of the length of the proof which gets you from the assumptions to the conclusion. Again we have to consider the three ways that A could be the last expression in a proof.

(i) A is an axiom. We have already checked that all the axioms are valid, so $[\![A]\!]_V$ is always T.

(ii) A is one of A_1 ... A_n. Again it is obvious that $[\![A]\!]_V$ will be T if $[\![A_1]\!]_V$ = T and ... and $[\![A_n]\!]_V$ = T.

(iii) A is the result of applying MP to two formulae which have been derived earlier in the proof, say B and B $\rightarrow$ A. These were derived earlier in the proof, so each of them is the result of a shorter proof. By our assumption that A is the result of a shortest unsound proof, we know that $[\![B]\!]_V$ and $[\![B \rightarrow A]\!]_V$ must both be T for any V for which each of the $[\![A_i]\!]_V$ is T. But then the semantic rule for interpreting $\rightarrow$ indicates that $[\![A]\!]_V$ must also be T, since if $[\![B]\!]_V$ is T and $[\![A]\!]_V$ is F then we know that $[\![B \rightarrow A]\!]_V$ is F.

We have now considered all three ways that A could be the result of a shortest proof for which soundness fails and shown that for all of them it in fact holds. There therefore cannot be a shortest unsound proof, and hence there can be no unsound proofs at all ▦

The following theorem is an important consequence of Theorem 2.3.

Theorem 2.4: Consistency of Prop$_{hilbert}$

There is no proof of †.

Proof:
This follows directly from Theorem 2.3, since if there were a proof of † then we would have to have V(†) equal to T for every V, whereas in fact it must always be F ▦

The next theorem is a sort of converse to Theorem 2.3. Whereas Theorem 2.3 says that anything which can be proved is valid, so that Prop$_{hilbert}$ is guaranteed to be safe, the Completeness Theorem says that anything which is valid can be proved. This means that Prop$_{hilbert}$ is all we need, at least as far as propositions are concerned, since it is powerful enough to fully capture the notion of entailment.

Theorem 2.5: Completeness of Prop$_{hilbert}$

If A is valid then ⊢ A.

Proof (step 1):
We first prove a rather odd looking result. Given a valuation V, we define the *prime*, A', of a formula A, to be A if $[\![A]\!]_V$ is T and ¬A if $[\![A]\!]_V$ is F. We can extract all the proposition names appearing in A. Suppose they are p_1 ... p_n. Then our initial result is

p_1' ... p_n' ⊢ A'

As usual, we prove it by induction. This time the measure we are going to use is the number of →'s appearing in A. In other words, we are going to assume that if there is any A at all for which the result fails, there must be a smallest one with respect to counting →'s, and from this we are going to derive a contradiction. There are three cases.

(i) A is in fact just p_i. In that case A' is the same as p_i', so clearly p_i' ⊢ A'.

(ii) A is †. Then A' is ¬†, or † → †. We proved earlier on that for any A, ⊢ A → A, and this is just a special case of that result.

(iii) A is B → C for some B and C. B and C each contains fewer →'s than A, so by our assumption the result holds for each of them. We now have to consider the relation between A', B' and C'. We know from the semantic rule for → that $[\![A]\!]_V$ is F if $[\![B]\!]_V$ is T and $[\![C]\!]_V$ is F, and that otherwise it is T. This means that A' = ¬A if B' = B and C' = ¬ C, and that otherwise A' = A. Hence to show our result, we have to show that (a) B, ¬C ⊢ ¬A, (b) B, C ⊢ A, (c) ¬B, C ⊢ A and (d) ¬B, ¬C ⊢ A. The proofs of these are all very similar. We will just prove (a) and (d), leaving (b) and (c) for the reader.

Proof of (a): ¬A is (B → C) → †

```
1  B, C → †, B → C ⊢ B
2  B, C → †, B → C ⊢ B → C
3  B, C → †, B → C ⊢ C              (MP on 1, 2)
4  B, C → †, B → C ⊢ C → †
5  B, C → †, B → C ⊢ †              (MP on 3, 4)
6  B, C → † ⊢ (B → C) → †           (DT)
```

Proof of (d):

```
1  B → †, C → †, B ⊢ B
2  B → †, C → †, B ⊢ B → †
3  B → †, C → †, B ⊢ †              (MP on 1, 2)
4  B → †, C → †, B ⊢ † → C          (already proved)
5  B → †, C → †, B ⊢ C              (MP on 3, 4)
6  ⊢ (B → †) → [(C → †) → (B → C)]  (DT times 3)
```

Proof (step 2):
For the second part of the proof, we consider a valid formula A containing proposition letters p_1 ... p_n. Since A is valid, $[\![A]\!]_{V1}$ is T for any valuation V1, so A' is always just A. We pick some valuation V1 such that $V1(p_n)$ is T, so that with respect to this valuation pn' is just pn. Then by the result of part 1 of the proof, we know that p_1' ... p_{n-1}' p_n ⊢ A.

We can pick another valuation V2 which is just like V1 except that $V2(p_n)$ is F, so that for V2 the prime, p_n', of p_n is $\neg p_n$. Part 1 now gives us that $p_1' ... p_{n-1}'$ $\neg p_n \vdash A$.

The Deduction Theorem allows us to replace these by $p_1' ... p_{n-1}' \vdash p_n \to A$ and $p_1' ... p_{n-1}' \vdash \neg p_n \to A$.

We also have, from an earlier result, $p_1' ... p_{n-1}' \vdash (p_n \to A) \to [(\neg p_n \to A) \to A]$.

Applying MP twice, we get: $p_1' ... p_{n-1}' \vdash A$.

We have now eliminated all mention of p_n. We can do the same thing again for p_{n-1}, p_{n-2}, and so on until we have eliminated them all. At that point we have the result we wanted, namely that there is a proof of A:

$\vdash A$

Furthermore, we have not just shown that there is a proof of A, we have shown how to derive it. All you have to do is work through the steps of the proof of completeness for the particular valid formula under consideration, and you will end up with a correct proof ▦

The final theorem that we can prove about $Prop_{hilbert}$ concerns our ability to find a proof if one exists. For more powerful formalisms, it turns out to be impossible to write a program which can be guaranteed to find a proof if one exists, and which can also be guaranteed to return in a finite time if there is no proof. The simplicity of $Prop_{hilbert}$, however, allows us to prove the following theorem.

Theorem 2.6: Decidability of $Prop_{hilbert}$

There is a mechanical procedure which can decide for any A whether or not $\vdash A$.

Proof:
We prove it by outlining such a procedure. We can build the truth table for a formula by enumerating all possible values for its constituent proposition letters and then applying the semantic rules to discover the corresponding values for the main expression. We can then check for the validity of this main expression, simply by looking to see if any combination of values for the proposition letters occurring in it gives a value of F. Both of these stages are perfectly straightforward to implement, though they may lead to consideration of quite a large number of cases (2^n, where n is the number of proposition letters that have to be considered). From Theorems 2.3 and 2.5 we know that a formula has a

proof if and only if it is valid, so checking for validity provides a mechanical way of finding out whether or not a formula is provable. The steps outlined in the proof of Theorem 2.5 can be followed to construct the proof, if required, though usually all we want to know is whether or not a proof exists, not what it looks like ▦

It is worth remarking at this point on the ease with which we proved Theorem 2.6. As we look at more complex formal systems, we find that fewer and fewer positive results like Theorems 2.1 to 2.6 hold, and that in fact we start getting negative results of the form *There is no object O satisfying property P*. Positive proofs, such as Theorem 2.6, of the form *There is an object O satisfying property P* can be proved by finding an O with the required property. This can take some ingenuity, but at least the form of the proof is straightforward - to prove that there is an O satisfying P, find one. Negative proofs tend to be more indirect, since what we have to do is to derive a contradiction from the supposition that there is such an object.

These meta-results about $Prop_{hilbert}$ are valuable for showing that the calculus does what we want. Adequacy means that it is expressive enough, soundness means that it does not allow us to jump to unsafe conclusions, completeness means that if a conclusion is entailed by a set of premises there will be a proof, and decidability means that if there is a proof we can find it. $Prop_{hilbert}$, however, is not a very natural formalism for people to work with. If the aim of logic is to get precise characterisations of the way inference systems behave, and to investigate the limits on what can be said and what can be proved, then $Prop_{hilbert}$ is a very suitable system. If, on the other hand, we want to give people a tool for formalising and checking their arguments, it is not at all appropriate (as the complexity of some of the earlier proofs within the system demonstrates). For this reason, many logicians prefer to work with a slightly different presentation which we will call $Prop_{gentzen}$.

2.2 Propositional calculus (Gentzen system)

$Prop_{hilbert}$ was constructed with a minimal collection of logical operators, axioms and inference rules. This meant that the proofs of the meta-theorems were comparatively simple, since there were not too many cases to be considered, but that proofs were hard to construct because we had so little machinery to use. $Prop_{gentzen}$ is designed to be as easy to use as possible. It has the same syntax and vocabulary as $Prop_{hilbert}$, except that it contains the operators we derived for $Prop_{hilbert}$ (i.e. ¬, &, ∨) as standard operators, and a much larger set of inference rules for introducing and eliminating the operators.

There are a number of presentations of this sort of system. We will be calling systems of this kind *Gentzen systems*, or *natural deduction systems*, and will present them in terms of *sequent rules*. The particular version we will be considering is given in Gentzen (1969) - various minor variants are also discussed in the literature.

A sequent consists of two collections of formulae, separated by a sequent arrow written as =>. A sequent is interpreted as a statement to the effect that either at least one of the formulae to the left of the => are false or at least one of those to the right is true. It is important to note that the => is not an operator of $Prop_{gentzen}$ in the way that $\rightarrow$, $\neg$, & and V are. It is used for making statements about what hypotheses a chain of inference is based on, and for couching inference rules so that the steps in a chain of inference can actually be performed. The inference rules come in two groups, one for introducing logical operators and one for rearranging sequents. A sequent rule is written as a collection of sequents above a horizontal line, and a single sequent below it. The interpretation is that if you have a collection of sequents that matches what is above the line, you can replace them by the single sequent below it. In the following set of rules, Γ and Δ are arbitrary sets of formulae, either of which may be empty.

Introduction rules for $Prop_{gentzen}$

$$\frac{\Gamma, A => \Delta}{\Gamma, A \& B => \Delta} \ (L \ \&) \qquad \frac{\Gamma1 => A, \Delta1 \quad \Gamma2 => B, \Delta2}{\Gamma1, \Gamma2 => A \& B, \Delta1, \Delta2} \ (R \ \&)$$

$$\frac{\Gamma1, A => \Delta1 \quad \Gamma2, B => \Delta2}{\Gamma, \Gamma2 \ A \lor B => \Delta1, \Delta2} \ (L \ \lor) \qquad \frac{\Gamma => A, \Delta}{\Gamma => A \lor B, \Delta} \ (R \ \lor)$$

$$\frac{\Gamma1 => A, \Delta1 \quad \Gamma2, B => \Delta2}{\Gamma1, \Gamma2, A \rightarrow B => \Delta1, \Delta2} \ (L \rightarrow) \qquad \frac{\Gamma, A => B, \Delta}{\Gamma => A \rightarrow B, \Delta} \ (R \rightarrow)$$

$$\frac{\Gamma => A, \Delta}{\Gamma, \neg A => \Delta} \ (L \ \neg) \qquad \frac{\Gamma, A => \Delta}{\Gamma => \neg A, \Delta} \ (R \ \neg)$$

Structural rules for Prop$_{gentzen}$

Reordering:

$$\frac{\Gamma, A, B \Rightarrow \Delta}{\Gamma, B, A \Rightarrow \Delta} \text{ (LR)} \qquad\qquad \frac{\Gamma \Rightarrow A, B, \Delta}{\Gamma \Rightarrow B, A, \Delta} \text{ (RR)}$$

Weakening:

$$\frac{\Gamma \Rightarrow \Delta}{\Gamma, A \Rightarrow \Delta} \text{ (LW)} \qquad\qquad \frac{\Gamma \Rightarrow \Delta}{\Gamma \Rightarrow A, \Delta} \text{ (RW)}$$

Contraction:

$$\frac{\Gamma, A, A \Rightarrow \Delta}{\Gamma, A \Rightarrow \Delta} \text{ (LC)} \qquad\qquad \frac{\Gamma \Rightarrow A, A, \Delta}{\Gamma \Rightarrow A, \Delta} \text{ (RC)}$$

$$\frac{\Gamma1 \Rightarrow A, \Delta1 \qquad \Gamma2, A \Rightarrow \Delta2}{\Gamma1, \Gamma2 \Rightarrow \Delta1, \Delta2} \text{ (CUT)}$$

Each of these rules can be checked to see that it conforms to the interpretation of sequents as collections of formulae where either something on the left is false or something on the right is true. The rules are supplemented by axioms of the form A => A, which are also clearly valid on the intended meaning of =>.

Proofs in Prop$_{gentzen}$ are constructed by working from sequents of the form A => A, via the rules above, to a sequent consisting of just the desired formula on the right. Applications of contraction and reordering are usually left out when writing down proofs. A few examples should indicate what is going on.

(1) Prop$_{gentzen}$ proof of PH1:

$$\frac{\dfrac{\dfrac{A \Rightarrow A}{A, B \Rightarrow A} \text{ (LW)}}{A \Rightarrow (B \rightarrow A)} \text{ (R} \rightarrow\text{)}}{\Rightarrow A \rightarrow (B \rightarrow A)} \text{ (R} \rightarrow\text{)}$$

(2) $\text{Prop}_{\text{gentzen}}$ proof of PH2:

$$
\cfrac{
\cfrac{
\cfrac{A \Rightarrow A \qquad B \Rightarrow B}{A, A \to B \Rightarrow B}
\qquad
\cfrac{
\cfrac{B \Rightarrow B \qquad C \Rightarrow C}{B, B \to C \Rightarrow C}
\qquad A \Rightarrow A
}{A, B, [A \to (B \to C)] \Rightarrow C}
}{
\cfrac{
\cfrac{
\cfrac{A, A \to B, [A \to (B \to C)] \Rightarrow C}{A \to B, [A \to (B \to C)] \Rightarrow A \to C} \ (R \to)
}{[A \to (B \to C)] \Rightarrow (A \to B) \to (A \to C)} \ (R \to)
}{\Rightarrow [A \to (B \to C)] \to [(A \to B) \to (A \to C)]} \ (R \to)
} \ (R \to)
}{} \ (\text{CUT})
$$

(3) $\text{Prop}_{\text{gentzen}}$ proof of PH3:

$$
\cfrac{
\cfrac{
\cfrac{
\cfrac{A \Rightarrow A}{\Rightarrow \neg A, A} \ (R \neg)
}{\neg \neg A \Rightarrow A} \ (L \neg)
}{\Rightarrow \neg \neg A \to A} \ (R \to)
}{}
$$

These are in fact just the axioms of $\text{Prop}_{\text{hilbert}}$. Furthermore, the effect of the inference rule MP of $\text{Prop}_{\text{hilbert}}$ corresponds to the following derivation:

$$
\cfrac{A \Rightarrow A \qquad B \Rightarrow B}{A, A \to B \Rightarrow B} \ (L \to)
$$

We thus see that anything which can be proved in $\text{Prop}_{\text{hilbert}}$ can also be proved in $\text{Prop}_{\text{gentzen}}$. A direct consequence of this is the following.

Theorem 2.7: Completeness of $\text{Prop}_{\text{gentzen}}$

Anything which is valid is provable in $\text{Prop}_{\text{gentzen}}$.

Proof:
Immediately from Theorem 2.5 and the fact that any derivation in $\text{Prop}_{\text{hilbert}}$ can be mimicked in $\text{Prop}_{\text{gentzen}}$ ▦

We also have the other main meta-theorems for $\text{Prop}_{\text{gentzen}}$ (soundness, consistency, decidability). These all follow from the fact that we can show how to derive in $\text{Prop}_{\text{gentzen}}$ anything which is derivable in $\text{Prop}_{\text{hilbert}}$ and vice versa, so that in an important sense the two systems are equivalent. There is one further meta-theorem which only really applies to $\text{Prop}_{\text{gentzen}}$ and which will have some significance later.

Theorem 2.8: Cut Elimination Theorem

Any theorem which can be proved in $\text{Prop}_{\text{gentzen}}$ has a proof which does not contain a use of the Cut rule.

Proof:
The proof of this is rather long-winded, since we need to consider all the possible ways in which a proof could have a cut as its last step, and show that for each of them the cut can be replaced by some other step or steps. The proof does not introduce any major new ideas, and we therefore omit it here. The interested reader will find it in Gentzen (1969) ▦

2.3 Propositional calculus (tableau system)

The main advantage of working with $\text{Prop}_{\text{gentzen}}$ is that it provides a framework within which direct proofs are comparatively easy to construct. Tableau based presentations of propositional calculus such as our third version, $\text{Prop}_{\text{beth}}$, are designed to support proofs by contradiction. The basic idea behind proof by contradiction is that since every proposition is either true or false, if we show that something cannot be false then it must be true. In $\text{Prop}_{\text{beth}}$, which has the same syntax and vocabulary as $\text{Prop}_{\text{gentzen}}$, proofs are constructed in terms of an object called a *semantic tableau*. This is an attempt to enumerate the ways the world could be, given the hypotheses of the proof, and to show that in all of them the negation of the desired conclusion must be false, so that the conclusion itself must be true. A tableau is a tree of formulae, built up according to the following rules.

(rule i) If A_1, A_2 ... A_n are the premises of a proof, then

$$A_1$$
$$A_2$$
$$...$$
$$A_n$$

is a tableau.

(rule ii) If some branch of a tableau contains a formula A_i which is of the form B_i & C_i, then the tree formed by adding B_i and C_i on the end is a tableau. For instance,

p   becomes   p
q & r   q & r
                                        q
                                        r

(rule iii) If A_i in some branch of a tableau is of the form $B_i \vee C_i$, then the tree formed by adding B_i and C_i as different sub-branches is a tableau, e.g.

r   becomes   r
p $\vee$ q   p $\vee$ q
                                       _____
                                       p   q

(rule iv) If A_i is $B_i \rightarrow C_i$, then the tree is extended by adding new branches containing $\neg C_i$ and B_i, so that

r   becomes   r
p $\rightarrow$ q   p $\rightarrow$ q
                                       _____
                                       $\neg$p   q

(rule v) If A_i is $\neg B_i$ for some non-atomic B_i, then the tree is extended by adding $\neg C_i \vee \neg D_i$ if B_i is C_i & D_i, $\neg C_i$ & $\neg D_i$ if B_i is $C_i \vee D_i$, C_i & $\neg D_i$ if B_i is $C_i \rightarrow D_i$, or C_i itself if B_i is $\neg C_i$.

Each branch of a tableau represents a partial description of the world which is consistent with the original set of premises. In the last example, for instance, the two branches represent descriptions where either $\{r, p \rightarrow q, \neg p\}$ are all true or $\{r, p \rightarrow q, q\}$ are. Any branch which contains both A and $\neg$A for some A is clearly not a feasible description of the world. We say that such a branch is *closed*. If all the branches of some tableau are closed (in which case we say the tableau itself is closed), then there are no feasible descriptions of the world which are consistent with the premises on which it is based. We thus see that we can generate proofs by contradiction by adding the negation of the goal to the premises, and showing that the tableau based on this collection of formulae is closed. This shows that the negation of the goal cannot be true when the premises are all true, and hence that whenever the premises are all true the goal itself must also be. *Tableau proofs* are written out by numbering formulae as they are added to the tree. These numbers are then used to show where subsequent formulae derive from, and are also used instead of explicit marks to ensure that no formula is expanded more than once. We will consider some examples.

Tableau proof 1: to show that r follows from p, q, (p → [q → r]).

We start with the basic tableau consisting of the premises and the negation of the goal, namely

```
1            ¬r
2             p
3             q
4      p → (q → r)
```

This develops as follows:

We see that all the branches of this tree are closed, so that all possible descriptions which are consistent with the premises and the negation of the goal are in fact incoherent. Note that adding extra facts to the premises cannot change this, since any descriptions which are consistent with the extra facts must extend one of the descriptions we already have, and these are already known to be incoherent.

Tableau proof 2: to show that $[A \rightarrow (B \rightarrow C)] \rightarrow [(A \rightarrow B) \rightarrow (A \rightarrow C)]$ follows from an empty set of premises for any A, B, C.

The basic tableau is based on the negation of the goal, since there are no premises.

1   $\neg([A \rightarrow (B \rightarrow C)] \rightarrow [(A \rightarrow B) \rightarrow (A \rightarrow C)])$
$\overline{}$ (expand 1 by (iv))

2   $[A \rightarrow (B \rightarrow C)] \,\&\, \neg[(A \rightarrow B) \rightarrow (A \rightarrow C)]$
$\overline{}$ (expand 2 by (ii))

3                $A \rightarrow (B \rightarrow C)$

4            $\neg[(A \rightarrow B) \rightarrow (A \rightarrow C)]$
$\overline{}$ (expand 4 by (v))

5           $(A \rightarrow B) \,\&\, \neg(A \rightarrow C)$
$\overline{}$ (expand 5 by (ii))

6                $A \rightarrow B$

7              $\neg(A \rightarrow C)$
$\overline{}$ (expand 7 by (v))

8               $A \,\&\, \neg C$
$\overline{}$ (expand 8 by (ii))

9   A

10               $\neg C$
$\overline{}$ (expand 3 by (iv))

    11 $\neg A$ 12 $B \rightarrow C$
    $\overline{}$ $\overline{}$ (expand 12)

    CLOSED   13 $\neg B$ 14 C
                $\overline{}$ (expand 6) $\overline{}$

             15 $\neg A$ 16 B   CLOSED
             $\overline{}$ $\overline{}$

             CLOSED   CLOSED

Tableau proof 3: A → ¬¬A follows from an empty set of premises.

1   ¬(A → ¬¬A)
         ————————— (expand 1)
2   A & ¬¬¬A
         ————————— (expand 2)
3   A
4   ¬¬¬A
            ——————— (expand 4)
5   ¬A
            ———————

         CLOSED

Prop$_{beth}$ is also equivalent to Prop$_{hilbert}$, in that anything which is provable in one is provable in the other. It therefore satisfies all the meta-theorems. From one point of view, the three systems we have seen for the propositional calculus are all basically the same, since they all have the same expressive powers and the same things are provable in them. From another they are significantly different. Prop$_{hilbert}$ is given as a purely formal set of rules for manipulating sets of symbols which are given a meaning from outside by the notion of a valuation or a truth table. This view regards logic very much as the study of formal languages as entities which have properties to be discovered - what can you say in them, what can you prove in them, what is the relationship between what things mean and what can be proved, and so on. Prop$_{gentzen}$ is an attempt to give precise form to the patterns of reasoning which are recognised as being valid. The move to a formalisation of these patterns of reasoning inevitably leads to their becoming slightly less natural. There is, however, no doubt that proofs in Prop$_{gentzen}$ and the other natural deduction systems are more readable, and give a better view of exactly how the conclusion depends on the premises, than proofs in the other systems. Prop$_{beth}$ works directly with the intended semantics of the language to show how to rule out certain combinations of formulae as being incompatible, and hence to construct indirect proofs by contradiction. Prop$_{beth}$ is again fairly easy to work with, but the fact that the semantics are so closely tied up with the forms of the inference steps makes it rather hard to stand back and consider meta-theorems of the kind we proved for Prop$_{hilbert}$. All three styles of presentation have been used for the languages we shall consider later on. There are good reasons for this. In particular, as we shall see in Chapter 4, different styles fit neatly with different types of theorem prover. We shall therefore follow the approaches taken by the authors of the systems we will be looking at, rather than trying to force all the subsequent material into one of the frameworks where some of it may fit but some may be very awkward.

We said at the beginning of the discussion of propositional calculus that it is not expressive enough to be really useful as a language for knowledge representation. Our main reasons for discussing it were to demonstrate what the richer languages we would look at later would look like, and to give proofs of the various meta-theorems for a comparatively simple language so that the reader would have something to act as a guide when we want to prove the same sort of thing for more complex cases. The problem with the propositional calculus is that it simply lacks the vocabulary for making generalisations over sets of individuals. Without this, it is very difficult to write down any but the simplest rules about the world. We cannot, for instance, make statements about properties possessed by all members of some class, or about the way entities might react to situations, or indeed about almost any of the things that we know from experience we are going to need if we are to make any progress in AI. In the next chapter, therefore, we move up a step to a language in which we can make statements about properties possessed by sets of individuals, namely the first-order predicate calculus (FOPC) that was mentioned at the beginning of the chapter. We will discuss this in terms of a Hilbert-style presentation, proving the main meta-theorems and reviewing its role in AI.

CHAPTER THREE

PREDICATE CALCULUS

3.1 Predicate calculus

3.1.1 *Predicate calculus: syntax and vocabulary*

The move from propositional calculus to predicate calculus is intended to enable us to talk about named individuals, properties that such individuals may have, and rules about all entities with specified properties. We therefore need to change the basic vocabulary so that it has terms for individuals and properties, and logical operators for making general statements about sets of individuals. The basic vocabulary of FOPC consists of the following:

(i) an infinite set of *constants* (which should be thought of intuitively as names for individuals). The set we choose are the letters a, b, c and a_1, a_2, a_3 ...

(ii) an infinite set of *variables* $\_x$, $\_y$, $\_z$, $\_x_1$, $\_x_2$, $\_x_3$, ... We will always distinguish between variables and constants by starting variables with the underscore character $\_$

(iii) an infinite set of *predicate names* $p_{0,1}$, $p_{0,2}$, $p_{0,3}$, ..., $p_{1,1}$, $p_{1,2}$, $p_{1,3}$, ..., $p_{2,1}$, $p_{2,2}$, $p_{2,3}$, ..., $p_{3,1}$, $p_{3,2}$, $p_{3,3}$, ..., ...

(iv) the symbol †.

We sometimes want to make general comments about places where either constants or variables may appear. We will use the word *term* to stand for an object which may be a constant or a variable, and use t_1, t_2, ... to stand for terms. Note that t_1 and so on are not themselves elements of the vocabulary of FOPC, they are a convenience for talking about such elements. Similarly, we will use P, Q, R, P_1, P_2, ...

for making general statements about predicate letters, and A, B, C, A_1, A_2, ... for general statements about formulae.

The primitive formulae of FOPC are built up out of predicate letters and terms. Each predicate letter is supposed to stand for a relation between some fixed number of entities. This number is given by the first subscript of the predicate name, so that $p_{1,1}$ refers to a property of one object, and $p_{3,1}$ refers to a three-place relation. The primitive formulae represent statements to the effect that the named relation does indeed hold between some specific set of entities. They are therefore of the form $p_{i,j}(t_1, ..., t_j)$. 0-place predicates may be written without the brackets. † is taken to be a 0-place predicate which never holds. The following are all acceptable primitive formulae: $p_{0,7}()$, $p_{0,7}$, †$()$, †, $p_{2,3}(\_x_1, a_3)$, $p_{4,209}(\_y, b, a_{88}, b)$.

We have two ways of making complex formulae from simpler ones.

(i) We can proceed exactly as for $Prop_{hilbert}$, simply combining them via →. The abbreviations for ¬, & and v are derived as before. Thus $p_{2,3}(a,b)$ → $p_{1,4}(a)$ and ¬$p_{2,6}(a,b)$ → † are both acceptable. The latter may be abbreviated, as before, to $p_{2,6}(a,b)$.

(ii) We can make a *universal generalisation* (or *generalisation* for short) of a formula by writing ∀ (the *universal quantifier*), followed by some variable name, in front of it. ∀$\_xp_{1,1}(\_x)$, ∀$\_yp_{1,1}(\_x)$ and ∀$\_z$ $p_{3,4}(\_z,\_z,\_x)$ are all formulae. We say that the presence of ∀$\_x$ in a generalisation of a formula A *binds* any occurrences of $\_x$ in A which are not already bound by other occurrences of ∀$\_x$. Any variable which appears in a formula and which is not bound by an occurrence of ∀ is said to be *free* in that formula. Thus in ∀$\_x(p_{2,1}(\_x, \_y))$, $\_x$ is bound by the quantifier and $\_y$ is free. In $p_{2,1}(\_x, \_y)$ → ∀$\_x(p_{1,1}(\_x))$, both the occurrence of $\_y$ and the first occurrence of $\_x$ are free, though the second occurrence of $\_x$ is bound. In ∀$\_x[p_{1,1}(\_x)$ → ∀$\_x(p_{2,1}(\_x, \_x))]$, the first occurrence of $\_x$ is bound by the first quantifier but the other two are bound by the second. A formula without any free variables is called a *sentence*.

These rules tell us which expressions are formulae of FOPC. What we need now is a definition of what these formulae mean, and a set of inference rules for investigating entailments between formulae.

3.1.2 *Predicate calculus: semantics*

Since FOPC is intended to be for talking about individuals and relations between them, its semantics needs to be couched in terms of sets of individuals and relations between them. The notion of a set of individuals is fairly straightforward. We will call a set of individuals a *world*. It is possible to get into philosophical tangles trying to give a definition of what a relation is. We want to keep things as simple as possible for our definition of the semantics of FOPC, and hence we want a simple definition of what a relation is. We choose to work with an *extensional* definition, namely that an N-place relation is a set of N-tuples, which are the set of combinations of individuals for which the relation holds. This may seem initially to be rather a perverse definition - the relation of being a sibling, for instance, seems to be something different from the set of all pairs of people who have the same parents. It turns out that for most straightforward uses of the notion of a relation, the extensional definition works quite well, and that it is not at all clear what to replace it with where it does not. We will therefore accept the view that the relation *greater than* is the set {<1 0>, <2 1>, <2 0>, <3 2>, <3 1>, <3 0>, <4 3>, ...}, and that the relation *parent of* is the set {<adam cain>, <adam abel>, <eve cain>, <eve abel>, ...}. A relation is a relation *over* a world W if the individuals which occur in its N-tuples are all members of W.

We can now give the semantics of FOPC relative to a world, as follows.

A *model* for FOPC consists of a world W plus a valuation function V such that for every constant c of FOPC, V(c) is a member of the world, and for every predicate letter $p_{i,j}$ of FOPC V($p_{i,j}$) is an i-place relation over W. V(†) must be the empty relation {}.

The semantics of FOPC concerns the conditions under which a formula A is true in a model <W, V>. We use the notation <W, V> ⊨ A to indicate that A is true in <W, V>, and we will sometimes say that <W, V> *satisfies* A or that <W, V> *is a model of* A (as usual, we ought really to subscript the meta-symbol ⊨ in order to indicate that the model satisfies the formula according to the semantic rules of that language; and as usual we will omit the subscript unless there is any serious possibility of confusion). If Γ is a set of sentences, we write <W, V> ⊨ Γ to mean that <W, V> ⊨ A for every A in Γ. The conditions, for FOPC, for <W, V>

to satisfy A are as follows:

(i) If A is a primitive formula containing no variables, i.e. A is $p_{i,j}(a_k, ...,$
$a_n)$ for some i, j, k, n, then $<W, V> \vDash A$ if and only if the i-tuple $<V(a_k),$
$..., V(a_n)>$ is a member of $V(p_{i,j})$. In other words, a primitive formula
containing no variables is true in a model if the relation given as the
valuation of its predicate letter holds between the individuals which are the
valuations of its constants. Note that there is only one possible 0-tuple,
namely <>, and hence only two possible 0-ary relations, namely the set
containing this 0-tuple and the empty set. Thus the 0-ary predicates have a
very similar semantics to that of $Prop_{hilbert}$, since their semantics is based
on a two-valued valuation function (remember that we said that it did not
matter what the two values were, so long as they were distinct. {} and
{<>} will be as good as anything else). The valuation of the predicate
letter † is always taken to be {}. Since the primitive formula based on †
contains an empty set of terms as its arguments, † will be true in a model
precisely if <> is in V(†), which it clearly is not since we have required
V(†) to be the empty set.

(ii) If A is a formula of the form $B \rightarrow C$, then $<W,V> \vDash A$ if either it is not
the case that $<W, V> \vDash B$, or it is the case that $<W, V> \vDash C$. This is
exactly analogous to the definition of the valuation of a formula of the
form $B \rightarrow C$ in $Prop_{hilbert}$. Note, in particular, that since ¬A is the same as
$A \rightarrow †$, $<W,V> \vDash ¬A$ will hold if and only if $<W,V> \vDash A$ does not hold,
since we know from (i) above that $<W,V> \vDash †$ never holds. It is easy,
though tedious, to show that taking $B \vee C$ and $B \& C$ to be abbreviations
for $¬B \rightarrow C$ and $¬(¬B \vee ¬C)$ respectively, $<W,V> \vDash B \vee C$ holds if and
only if at least one of $<W,V> \vDash B$ and $<W,V> \vDash C$ holds, and $<W,V> \vDash B$
$\& C$ holds if and only both $<W,V> \vDash B$ and $<W,V> \vDash C$ hold.

(iii) The major change we need is to accommodate the semantics of
generalised statements. There are two ways of dealing with this. The way
we choose requires us to introduce the notion of substituting one term for
another in an expression. The basic idea is very straightforward - you just
copy the components of the given expression one by one, except when you
come to the term which is to be substituted, in which case you write the
new one instead. Thus substituting _y for _x in $\forall\_x \ \forall\_z(p_{2,4}(\_x,\_z) \rightarrow$
$p_{1,5}(\_x))$ would produce $\forall\_y\forall\_z(p_{2,4}(\_y,\_z) \rightarrow p_{1,5}(\_y))$. We will denote the
result of substituting t' for t in A by $A|_{<t',t>}$. We can now give the

semantics of ∀_xA by saying that <W,V> ⊨ ∀_xA if no matter which constant, say b, we substitute for _x in A, <W,V> ⊨ A|_{<b,_x>} holds. This definition only applies if _x is the only free variable in A. If there are other free variables, we simply do not know whether <W,V> ⊨ ∀_xA or not. This does not mean that A cannot itself be a universally quantified formula, say ∀_yB, since if _x is the only free variable in ∀_yB then ∀_yB|_{<b,_x>} will not contain any free variables and hence the definition will work for it as well.

The alternative way of giving a semantics for ∀_xA involves extending the valuation function V so that it allocates individuals in W to variables as well as to constants, and then to say that <W,V> ⊨ ∀_xA if <W,V> ⊨ A holds and that for all valuations V' which give everything except _x the same value, <W,V'> ⊨ A also holds. There is not much practical difference between the two ways of providing a semantics for ∀_xA. The main difference is that the second version allows us to consider a situation in which there are more objects in the world than there are constants in the language, and in which all the objects which are values of constants have some property but that some of the ones which are not don't. In this case the first semantics would say that <W,V> ⊨ ∀_xA held, whereas the second one would say it did not. We shall return to this point much later on. The only other way in which the two approaches differ is that the approach we have chosen fails to give a semantics to formulae containing free variables. Neither of these differences is particularly important at present. We have chosen the first approach on the grounds that it makes our task of proving meta-theorems about FOPC slightly easier, though they are also provable with the second.

We note finally, before moving on to the inference rules of FOPC, that if we have <W,V> ⊨ ¬∀_xA, then there must be some constant, say b, for which <W,V> ⊨ A|_{<_x,b>} fails, which in turn can only happen if <W,V> ⊨ ¬A|_{<_x,b>} holds. We are therefore justified in defining a new form E_xA, which is an abbreviation for ¬∀_x¬A, to capture the notion that there is some item with a specified property, but that we do not know what its name is. E is the *existential quantifier*, and E_xA is the *existential quantification of A with respect to _x*.

3.1.3 *Predicate calculus: axioms and inference rules*
The axioms and inference rules of FOPC are the same as those of Prop_{hilbert}, supplemented by two axioms and a rule for quantified statements:

PC1: A → (B → A)

PC2: [A → (B → C)] → [(A → B) → (A → C)]

PC3: ¬¬(A) → A.

PC4: ∀_xA → A|_{<a,x>}, where t is either a constant or does not occur inside a sub-formula of A of the form ∀_xB.

PC5: ∀_x(A → B) → (A → ∀_xB) if _x is not free in A

PC4 is used for getting rid of quantifiers when they are applied to formulae which do not contain the quantified variable, so that, for instance, we can infer P(a,b) from ∀_xP(a,b) via MP and PC4. PC5 ought to seem reasonable, since if _x is not free in A then for any constant a, A|<a,x> must be just the same as A. This means, looking back at the semantics of ∀_xA, that ∀_xA must be true exactly when A itself is true, so that A → ∀_xB must surely be true whenever ∀_x(A → B) is.

The inference rules of FOPC are as follows:

(MP) From A → B and A, infer B.

(GEN) From A, infer ∀_xA.

MP is just the same rule of modus ponens that we had for Prop$_{hilbert}$. GEN, the rule of generalisation, has no effect if _x does not appear free in A. Its main effect is to say implicitly that any free variable should be regarded as universally quantified.

The definition of a proof is exactly as it was for Prop$_{hilbert}$, namely a sequence of formulae each of which is a premise or an instantiation of an axiom, or is derived from earlier formulae via one of the inference rules, so long as when GEN is used the variable being generalised on does not appear free in any of the premises. As with Prop$_{hilbert}$, raw proofs are rather difficult to construct. We will therefore first show that the Deduction Theorem holds for FOPC, and then show some results.

Theorem 3.1: Deduction Theorem for FOPC

If $A_1, ..., A_n \vdash B$

then $A_1, ..., A_{n-1} \vdash A_n \rightarrow B$

Proof:

The proof is exactly the same as for Theorem 2.2, except that we have an extra case to check. The analyses for the cases where B is an axiom, a premise or the result of MP go through exactly as before, and there is no point in repeating them. The only new case to be considered is when B is the result of applying GEN, in other words when B is $\forall\_xB_i$ for some B_i derived earlier in the proof. We have the inductive hypothesis that the proof of B is the shortest proof for which DT fails, so it must be the case that

$$A_1, ..., A_{n-1} \vdash A_n \rightarrow B_i.$$

We also know that $\_x$ does not occur free in $A_1, ..., A_n$, since if it had done then we could not have applied GEN to get B. We can therefore apply GEN to get

$$A_1, ..., A_{n-1} \vdash \forall\_x(A_n \rightarrow B_i).$$

We have an axiom schema of the form $\forall\_x(A \rightarrow B) \rightarrow (A \rightarrow \forall\_xB)$, which we can instantiate to $\forall\_x(A_n \rightarrow B_i) \rightarrow (A_n \rightarrow \forall\_xB_i)$ and add to our proof. Applying MP to this and the last formula we derived, we get

$$A_1, ..., A_n \vdash A_n \rightarrow \forall\_xB$$

which is exactly what we needed. We have now shown that if we add the rule of generalisation as an inference rule we still cannot construct a shortest proof for which DT fails, so that it must be true for FOPC as well as for $Prop_{hilbert}$ ▦

As usual, we will illustrate the inference rules of FOPC with some proofs:

(1) FOPC proof of $\forall\_xA \rightarrow \forall\_yA|_{<\_y,\_x>}$, where y does not appear free in A:

1 $\forall\_xA \vdash \forall\_xA \rightarrow A|_{<\_y,\_x>}$ (PC4)
2 $\forall\_xA \vdash \forall\_xA$
3 $\forall\_xA \vdash A|_{<\_y,\_x>}$ (MP on 1, 2)
4 $\forall\_xA \vdash \forall\_yA|_{<\_y,\_x>}$ (GEN)
5 $\vdash \forall\_xA \rightarrow \forall\_yA|_{<\_y,\_x>}$ (DT)

(2) FOPC proof of $\forall\_x\forall\_yA \rightarrow \forall\_y\forall\_xA$:

1 $\forall\_x\forall\_yA \vdash \forall\_x\forall\_yA \rightarrow \forall\_yA|_{<\_x,\_x>}$ (PC4)

But note that $A|_{<x,x>}$ is just A, so this is the same as

   2 $\forall\_x\forall\_yA \vdash \forall\_x\forall\_yA \to \forall\_yA$

By the same trick, we get

   3 $\forall\_x\forall\_yA \vdash \forall\_x\forall\_yA \to A$

Then

4 $\forall\_x\forall\_yA \vdash \forall\_x\forall\_yA$	
5 $\forall\_x\forall\_yA \vdash A$	(MP on 3, 4)
6 $\forall\_x\forall\_yA \vdash \forall\_xA$	(GEN)
7 $\forall\_x\forall\_yA \vdash \forall\_y\forall\_xA$	(GEN)
8 $\vdash \forall\_x\forall\_yA \to \forall\_y\forall\_xA$	(DT)

(3) FOPC proof of $\exists\_y\forall\_xA \to \forall\_x\exists\_yA$:

We start by translating the existential quantifiers to universals, so the goal becomes $\forall\_y\forall\_xA \to \forall\_x\forall\_yA$, and then by expanding out the 's to implications of falsity: $[(\forall\_y(\forall\_x(A) \to \dagger)) \to \dagger] \to \forall\_x([(\forall\_y(A \to \dagger)] \to \dagger)$

The proof is now as follows:

   1 $\forall\_y(\forall\_x(A) \to \dagger)) \to \dagger, A \to \dagger \vdash ((\forall\_x(A) \to \dagger)) \to \dagger$
                        (PC4 substituting _y for _y, then MP)
   2 $\forall\_y(\forall\_x(A) \to \dagger)) \to \dagger, A \to \dagger \vdash (A \to \dagger) \to \dagger$
                        (PC4 substituting _x for _x, then MP)
   3 $\forall\_y(\forall\_x(A) \to \dagger)) \to \dagger, A \to \dagger \vdash A$ (MP on 2 and PC1)
   4 $\forall\_y(\forall\_x(A) \to \dagger)) \to \dagger, A \to \dagger \vdash \dagger$ (MP on 3 and $A \to \dagger$)
   5 $\forall\_y(\forall\_x(A) \to \dagger)) \to \dagger \vdash (A \to \dagger) \to \dagger$ (DT)
   6 $\forall\_y(\forall\_x(A) \to \dagger)) \to \dagger \vdash \forall\_y[(A \to \dagger) \to \dagger]$ (GEN)
   7 $\forall\_y(\forall\_x(A) \to \dagger)) \to \dagger \vdash [\forall\_y(A \to \dagger)] \to \dagger$ (PC4, then MP)
   8 $\forall\_y(\forall\_x(A) \to \dagger)) \to \dagger \vdash \forall\_x([\forall\_y[(A \to \dagger] \to \dagger)$ (GEN)
   9 $\vdash [(\forall\_y(\forall\_x(A) \to \dagger)) \to \dagger] \to \forall\_x([(\forall\_y(A \to \dagger)] \to \dagger)$ (DT)

The proof of the soundness of FOPC also parallels the proof for Prop$_{hilbert}$ very closely. Exactly as for Prop$_{hilbert}$, the proof proceeds by showing first that all the axioms are valid, and then that any conclusion arrived at by one of the inference rules must be valid.

Theorem 3.2: Soundness of FOPC

If Γ is a set of sentences such that $<W,V> \vDash \Gamma$ and $\Gamma \vdash B$, then $<W,V> \vDash B$.

Proof:
Nothing in the statement of the axioms PC1 ... PC5, nor in the definition of a proof, rules out the possibility of derivations of formulae containing free variables. Indeed, the examples above contain several instances of such derivations. The definition of $\vDash$, however, is given only for sentences. We therefore need to consider a version of the Soundness Theorem which will cover formulae with free variables. We suggested above that formulae with free variables should be thought of as implicitly universally quantified for those variables. The obvious move, then, is to prove that it holds for the *universal closure* of each of the axioms (the universal closure A' of a formula A is the formula you get by prefixing A by $\forall\_x_i$ for each $\_x_i$ which appears free in A). Clearly, for any sentence A, A' is the same as A, so that for sentences the two are the same. However, for instances of axioms which contain free variables, we will gain something from talking about the universal closure.

Part 1: we start by showing that the universal closures of all the axioms hold in every model. This is obvious for PC1', PC2' and PC3', since these are just the axioms of Prop$_{hilbert}$. Their validity is again shown by considering the ways in which they could fail, and showing that these are all in fact impossible. The axioms PC4 and PC5 are new, and we need to show that their closures are also valid.

Validity of PC4': PC4 is $\forall\_xA \rightarrow A|_{<t,\_x>}$, where t is either a constant or is a variable which does not occur inside a sub-formula of A of the form $\forall\_xB$. If t is a constant, say a, then if $<W,V> \vDash \forall\_xA'$, then by definition $<W,V> \vDash (A|_{<a,\_x>})'$. This is exactly what we need in order to show that for any $<W,V>$, $<W,V> \vDash (\forall\_xA \rightarrow A|_{<a,\_x>})'$ so the axiom is valid where the term being substituted for the given variable is a constant. Suppose t is a variable, say $\_y$, which does not appear in a sub-formulae of the form $\forall\_xB$. We consider first the case where $\_y$ is the only free variable in $\forall\_xA$. The universal closure of the axiom instance is then $\forall\_y(\forall\_xA \rightarrow A|_{<\_y,\_x>})$. This is valid if $<W,V> \vDash (\forall\_xA \rightarrow A|_{<\_y,\_x>}|_{<b,\_y>})$ for every b in W. This holds if $<W,V> \vDash (\forall\_xA)|_{<b,\_y>} \rightarrow A|_{<\_y,\_x>}|_{<b,\_y>}$ holds for all b in W. This in turn is so if whenever $<W,V> \vDash (\forall\_xA)|_{<b,\_y>}$ holds, so does

$A|_{<y,\_x>}|_{<b,\_y>}$. This is indeed so, since if $<W,V> \vDash (\forall\_xA)|_{<b,\_y>}$ then $<W,V> \vDash$ $A|_{<b,\_y>}|_{<b,\_x>}$, which is the same as $A|_{<y,\_x>}|_{<b,\_y>}$. The proof can be adapted for cases where $\_y$ is not the only free variable by including at every step a mention of all possible substitutions for the others.

Validity of PC5': PC5 is $\forall\_x(A \to B) \to (A \to \forall\_xB)$. Again we prove it for the case where the axiom is a sentence, and then appeal to the notion that any free variables can be accounted for by referring at each step to all substitutions for free variables. The only way for $<W,V> \vDash \forall\_x(A \to B) \to (A \to \forall\_xB)$ not to hold is if $<W,V> \vDash \forall\_x(A \to B)$ holds but $<W,V> \vDash A \to \forall\_xB$ does not. This can only happen if (i) $<W\ V> \vDash (A \to B)|_{<b,\_x>}$ holds for every b in W, and (ii) $<W\ V> \vDash A$ holds, but (iii) $<W\ V> \vDash \forall\_xB$ fails. Since we have assumed the axiom is a sentence, and hence $\_x$ is not free in A, (i) means that if $<W,V> \vDash A$ then $<W,V> \vDash B|_{<b,\_x>}$ for every b. This taken with (ii) means that $<W,V> \vDash B|_{<b,\_x>}$ holds for every b in W, in which case (iii) cannot fail. There is thus no way for any $<W,V>$ to fail to be a model for a sentential instance of PC5. The proof for non-sentential forms simply entails remarking on the possible substitutions for the free variables.

Part 2: The second part of the proof shows that the inference rules do not introduce any problems. (i) If $<W,V> \vDash (A \to B)'$ and $W \vDash A'$, then $W \vDash B'$. This is justified by considering all the substitutions for all free variables in A and B, and showing that if $<W,V> \vDash (A \to B)|_{<a1,\ x1>} \dots |_{<an,\ xn>}$ and $<W,V> \vDash A|_{<a1,x1>} \dots |_{<an,xn>}$, then $<W,V> \vDash B|_{<a1,x1>} \dots |_{<an,xn>}$. (ii) If $<W,V> \vDash A'$, then $<W,V> \vDash (\forall\_xA)'$. This is obvious, since A' and $(\forall\_xA)'$ are identical apart possibly from the order of the initial quantifiers, and this cannot make any difference to whether something is a model or not.

Part 3: We now show that any proof preserves truth in a model. We prove this by induction on the length of proof, so we will assume that Γ and A are such that the proof of A from Γ is a shortest proof for which the theorem fails. Since $\Gamma \vdash A$, we know that one of the following is true - A is a member of Γ, A is an axiom, or A results from earlier formulae by MP or GEN. In the first case, if $<W,V> \vDash \Gamma$ then $<W,V> \vDash A$, since A is one of Γ. In the second case $<W,V> \vDash A$ holds for every $<W,V>$ - that's what we proved in part 1 - so clearly if $<W,V> \vDash \Gamma$ holds then so does $<W,V> \vDash A$. In the third case, we know from the induction hypothesis that $<W,V>$ is a model for the formula(e) from which the target was derived. The argument in Part 2 showed that if something is a model of the premises of an inference rule then it is a model of the conclusion, so that it must in fact be the case that $<W,V> \vDash A$ ▦.

It is evident that if A is provable from an empty set of hypotheses, then any model at all must be a model of A. We also have the following simple consequence of Theorem 3.2:

Theorem 3.3: Consistency of FOPC:

There is no proof of †.

Proof:
If there were, then by Theorem 3.2 we would have $<W,V> \vDash$ † for every model $<W, V>$. But we know, by the definition of $\vDash$, that this is not so for any model, let alone for each ▦

The Completeness Theorem for FOPC is rather harder to prove. We need some new notions, and a preliminary theorem.

Definitions: a set of sentences Γ is *consistent* if it is not the case that $\Gamma \vdash$ †, *inconsistent* otherwise. It is *complete* if for every sentence A of FOPC either A or ¬A is in Γ. It is *universal* if $\forall\_x B$ is in Γ whenever every $B|_{<b,x>}$ is in Γ.

Theorem 3.4: Extension Lemma for FOPC

If Γ is a consistent set of sentences, then there is a consistent, complete and universal set of sentences Δ such that $\Gamma \subseteq \Delta$.

Proof:
We show how to extend Γ to Δ. We first assume that we have an enumeration of the sentences of FOPC, say A_1, A_2, ... (This might appear to be rather a strong assumption. In fact we can easily write a program which will generate formulae of FOPC in a sequence and which is guaranteed to produce every formula eventually, so it is not as strong as it seems). We now define the following sequence of sets of sentences:

Step (i) Γ_0 is Γ.

Step (ii) If $\Gamma_n \cup \{A_{n+1}\}$ is consistent, then Γ_{n+1} is $\Gamma_n \cup \{A_{n+1}\}$.

Step (iii) If $\Gamma_n \cup \{A_{n+1}\}$ is inconsistent, and A_{n+1} is not of the form $\forall\_xB$, then Γ_{n+1} is $\Gamma_n \cup \{\neg A_{n+1}\}$.

Step (iv) If $\Gamma_n \cup \{A_{n+1}\}$ is inconsistent, and A_{n+1} is of the form $\forall\_xB$, then Γ_{n+1} is $\Gamma_n \cup \{\neg A_{n+1}, \neg B|_{<b,\_x>}\}$, where b is the first constant of the language which does not appear in Γ_n (we know there must be one, since Γ_n is a finite set of sentences, but the set of constants of FOPC is infinite).

We show by induction on n that each Γ_n is consistent. To do this, we look for the lowest value of n for which $\Gamma_n \vdash \dagger$, and show that there cannot be such a lowest value. We consider the routes by which Γ_{n+1} may be constructed from Γ_n one at a time.

Proof for step (i). We know that Γ_0 is consistent, since that was one of the conditions of the theorem.

Proof for step (ii). If Γ_{n+1} was obtained by step (ii), then clearly it is consistent if Γ_n was.

Proof for step (iii). If Γ_{n+1} was obtained by step (iii), then $\Gamma_n \cup \{A_{n+1}\}$ was inconsistent, i.e. $\Gamma_n, A_{n+1} \vdash \dagger$ (*). We know, since Γ_{n+1} was constructed from Γ_n by step (iii), that Γ_{n+1} is nothing but $\Gamma_n \cup \{\neg A_{n+1}\}$. Hence to say that Γ_{n+1} is inconsistent is nothing more than to say that $\Gamma_n, \neg A_{n+1} \vdash \dagger$. From this and (*) we have that $\Gamma_n \vdash \dagger$, or in other words that if Γ_{n+1} was constructed from Γ_n by step (iii) then it cannot have been the first inconsistent Γ_i.

Proof for step (iv). Finally, if Γ_{n+1} is constructed from Γ_n by step (iv) then again we have $\Gamma_n \vdash \neg A_{n+1}$ (**). Suppose $\{\Gamma_n, \neg A_{n+1}, \neg B|_{<b,\_x>}\}$ is inconsistent, i.e. that $\Gamma_n, \neg A_{n+1}, \neg B|_{<b,\_x>} \vdash \dagger$. Then by DT and MP we get $\Gamma_n \vdash B|_{<b,\_x>}$. We know that b does not appear in Γ_n, since that was part of the rule for constructing Γ_{n+1} by step (iv). Suppose we inspect a proof of $B|_{<b,\_x>}$ from Γ_n (we know there is one). There will be an infinite number of variables which do not appear anywhere in that proof. Let us choose one, say $\_y$, and substitute it for b everywhere in the proof. The result will clearly still be a proof, so we know that $\Gamma_n \vdash B|_{<y,\_x>}$, where $\_y$ appears nowhere in Γ_n. In that case we can use GEN, followed by MP and our first example proof in FOPC above, to get $\Gamma_n \vdash \forall\_xB$, i.e. $\Gamma_n \vdash A_{n+1}$. This, together with (**), means that Γ_n itself must have been inconsistent if Γ_{n+1} is to be, so step (iv) is also not a way to construct the first inconsistent Γ_i. Hence none of the routes given lead to the first inconsistent Γ_i, so all of the Γ_i must be consistent, as required.

We now take the union over all Γ_i and call it Δ. This is an infinite union, but set theory allows us to take infinite unions. Then Δ is consistent, complete and universal.

(1) Δ is consistent. If it were not, then there would be a proof of † from it. A proof is a finite sequence of formulae, and hence if there is a proof of † from Δ then there must be one from a finite subset of it. Any finite subset must be contained in one of the Γ_i, for some i, and hence there must be a proof of † from Γ_i. We have, however, just argued at length that all the Γ_i are consistent, i.e. that there is no proof of † from any of them. The fact that any inconsistent set of sentences of FOPC must have a finite inconsistent subset is known as the *compactness* of FOPC, and is crucial to all approaches to automatic theorem proving.

(2) Δ is complete. Any sentence of FOPC is A_k for some k, since the A_i were defined to be an enumeration of all the sentences of FOPC. However, we know from the way we used steps (ii), (iii) and (iv) to construct the Γ_i that either A_k is in Γ_{k-1} or $\neg A_k$ is in Γ_{k-1}, and hence either A_k or $\neg A_k$ is in Δ.

(3) Δ is universal. Suppose $\forall\_xB$ is a sentence such that $B|_{<b,\_x>}$ is in Δ for every b, but that $\forall\_xB$ is not in Δ. Since Δ is complete, it must be the case that $\neg\forall\_xB$ is in Δ. Suppose n is the number for which $\forall\_xB$ is A_{n+1}. $\{\forall\_xB\} \cup \Gamma_n$ must be inconsistent. Hence it must be the case (step (iv)) that Γ_{n+1} is $\Gamma_n \cup \{A_{n+1},$ $\neg B|_{<b,\_x>}\}$ for the first b not appearing in Γ_n. This contradicts the initial assumption that $B|_{<b,\_x>}$ is in Δ, since it would leave both $B|_{<b,\_x>}$ and $\neg B|_{<b,\_x>}$ in Δ
▓

The proof of the Extension Lemma depends on the fact that Δ is well-defined, in that each stage of the construction is clearly specified and the operation of taking an infinite union is acceptable. It should be noted, however, that routes (ii), (iii) and (iv) all depend on whether or not $\Gamma_n \cup \{A_{n+1}\}$ is consistent. This is also a perfectly clear notion, but we have not given any mechanical specification of how to show whether it is true or not. For $Prop_{hilbert}$, we had such a mechanical procedure, since we had a proof procedure which would tell us whether or not † followed from a set of sentences. We will see below that we cannot have any such procedure for FOPC. This does not invalidate the proof of Theorem 3.4, but it does show that we may not in practice know how to find an extension for a given consistent set of sentences.

We also need the following result before we can prove the completeness of FOPC. We start by defining a specific model for a set of sentences. Given a set of sentences Δ, the *canonical model* of Δ, $<W_\Delta, V_\Delta>$, is defined as follows.

W_Δ is just the set of constants appearing in Δ. W_Δ is often referred to as the *Herbrand universe* for Δ.

V_Δ maps each constant Δ to itself. For formulae of the form $P_{i,j}(a_1, ..., a_i)$, the i-tuple $<V_\Delta(a_1), ..., V_\Delta(a_i)>$ is included in $V_\Delta(P_{i,j})$ if and only if $P_{i,j}(a_1, ..., a_i)$ is in Δ.

Theorem 3.5: Herbrand Universe Lemma

If Δ is a consistent, complete, universal set of sentences then $<W_\Delta, V_\Delta> \vDash A$ holds if only if $\Delta \vdash A$ does.

Proof:
The proof is by induction on the length of A.

(i) If A is $p_{i,j}(a_1, ..., a_i)$ or † then the result follows immediately from the definition of $<W_\Delta, V_\Delta>$. If A is in Δ then it is evident that both $\Delta \vdash A$ and $<W_\Delta, V_\Delta> \vDash A$ hold. If A is not in Δ (which is a possibility if A is $p_{i,j}(a_1, ..., a_i)$ and is inevitable if it is †), then ¬A must be. In that case, no model of Δ will be a model of A, and it will not be the case that $\Delta \vdash A$.

(ii) A is B → C for some B and C. (a) We first prove that if A is not in Δ, then it is not the case that $<W_\Delta, V_\Delta> \vDash A$. By hypothesis, we can assume that $<W_\Delta, V_\Delta> \vDash B$ if and only if $\Delta \vdash B$, and that $<W_\Delta, V_\Delta> \vDash C$ if and only if $\Delta \vdash C$. If A is not in Δ, then ¬A is, i.e. ¬(B → C) is in Δ. We know that ¬(B → C) $\vdash$ B and ¬(B → C) $\vdash$ ¬C, so that $\Delta \vdash$ B and $\Delta \vdash$ ¬C, and thence by completeness and consistency of Δ both B and ¬C are in Δ. We thus have that $<W_\Delta, V_\Delta> \vDash B$ and $<W_\Delta, V_\Delta> \vDash$ ¬C both hold, which is exactly what we need in order to show that $<W_\Delta, V_\Delta> \vDash A$ does not hold. (b) For the other half of the proof, we assume that $<W_\Delta, V_\Delta> \vDash A$ does not hold. The only way this can happen is for $<W_\Delta, V_\Delta> \vDash B$ to hold but for $<W_\Delta, V_\Delta> \vDash C$ not to. In that case, the hypothesis leads us to the fact that B is in Δ but C is not. The completeness of Δ means that if C is not in it, ¬C must be. We can prove that B, ¬C $\vdash$ ¬(B → C), so that $\Delta \vdash$ ¬A, and hence by the consistency of Δ we know that A is not in Δ.

(iii) A is $\forall\_xB$. Again we split the proof into two parts. (a) Suppose $<W_\Delta, V_\Delta> \models$ A. Then for every b, $<W_\Delta, V_\Delta> \models Bl_{<b,\_x>}$. By hypothesis, we see that all the $Bl_{<b,\_x>}$ must be members of Δ. From the fact that Δ is universal, this means that $\forall\_xB$ (which is just A) must be in Δ, and hence $\Delta \vdash A$. (b) Suppose A is in Δ. Then $A \vdash Bl_{<b,\_x>}$ for every b, and hence $\Delta \vdash Bl_{<b,\_x>}$. Then $<W_\Delta, V_\Delta> \models Bl_{<b,\_x>}$ holds for every b, which is exactly what is needed for $<W_\Delta, V_\Delta> \models \forall\_xB$ to hold ▦.

Theorems 3.2, 3.4 and 3.5 are sufficient to give us the following two important results.

Theorem 3.6: Completeness of FOPC (part 1)

A set of sentences Γ is consistent if and only if it has a model.

Proof:
The fact that Γ is consistent if it has a model is simply a restatement of Theorem 3.2. The fact that it is consistent only if it has a model is a direct consequence of Theorems 3.4 and 3.5. If it is consistent we can extend it to a consistent, complete universal set Δ. Then Theorem 3.5 gives us that $<W_\Delta, V_\Delta>$ is a model of Δ, and thence of Γ, so if Γ is consistent it has at least one model ▦

Theorem 3.7: Completeness of FOPC (part 2)

A sentence A is valid if and only if $\vdash A$.

Proof:
Again, the proof that A is valid if $\vdash A$ is simply a consequence of Theorem 3.2. To prove the other half, suppose that $\vdash A$ does not hold. In that case $\{\neg A\}$ is consistent, so by Theorem 3.6 there is a model of $\neg A$, so A is not valid ▦

3.1.4 Functions, equality and arithmetic in FOPC
We have one more major theorem to prove about FOPC, but before we do that we will look at some extensions of the basic language. This will serve two purposes - to give the reader a feel for the language, and to provide some of the machinery we will need for our final major theorem.

We will start by considering a special class of predicate. The predicates we have seen so far have simply been sets of N-tuples, with no constraints placed on what sort of sets they are to be. One particular example was the relation of *parent of*, which was taken to be the set {<adam cain> <adam abel> <eve cain> <eve abel> ...}. The relation *mother of* is rather similar - {<eve cain> <eve abel> ... <mary jesus> ... <indira rajiv> ...}. There is one striking difference, however. There can be more than one element of *parent of* with the same second component, whereas no entity can appear as the second component of more than one member of *mother of*. Relations for which any two elements that share the same second components, and the same third components, and ... arid the same N-th components must also share the same initial components are called *functional relations*, or *functions*. Such relations are particularly interesting, since they can serve to pick out an individual by virtue of its interactions with other individuals.

We can supplement the language FOPC with a special notation for talking about functional relationships without changing any of its basic characteristics. Suppose P is an ordinary relation and R is a functional one. Then the sentence $\exists x(R(\_x, t_1, ..., t_n)$ & $P(t_{n+1}, ..., \_x, ... t_{n+m})$ can only be true for at most one instantiation of $\_x$. We can abbreviate this sentence to $P(t_{n+1}, ..., F_R(t_1, ..., t_n), ..., t_{n+m})$, where F_R is simply a piece of notation indicating that this sentence is an abbreviation of the first form. We have made no changes to the semantics of FOPC, beyond the requirement that we only use this notation when the relation being *functionalised* is indeed a functional relation. We will therefore use this notation freely from now on, safe in the knowledge that since it is merely a notation for abbreviating something which we could have written in the basic form it cannot make any difference to the properties of soundness and completeness that we have already established. Furthermore, any subsequent theorems we prove using it could also have been proved using the basic form. We will talk about the initial component of an element of a function as the *value* of the function for the set of entities which make up the remainder of the element, which we will call its *arguments*. The value of the function *mother of* for the argument "cain", for instance, is "eve". We call the name of the function in an functional expression its *functor*, so that the functor of $f(\_x,\_y)$ is f.

A function is constrained, by definition, to have a single value for a given set of arguments. There is, however, no reason why a given value should not correspond to different sets of arguments. Thus *mother of* can only give a single value for the argument "cain", but there is nothing to stop "eve" being the value for the arguments "cain" and "abel". We are thus in the situation where different expressions can denote the same entity. At this point it becomes useful to be able to talk about two things being equal, and to use equality as the basis for inferences. There was very little point in having equality until now, since in the basic notation only identical constants could denote identical individuals. Once we have functional notation it does become worth adding axioms for equality. These axioms are all very obvious, but they do need to be spelled out.

EQ1: $\forall\_x(\_x=\_x)$
EQ2: $\forall\_x\forall\_y(\_x=\_y \rightarrow \_y=\_x)$
EQ3: $\forall\_xy\forall\_z([\_x=\_y \,\&\, \_y=\_z] \rightarrow \_x=\_z)$

We also have the following collection of results:

$$\forall\_x_1\forall\_x_2(\_x_1=\_x_2 \rightarrow F(\_x_1) = F(\_x_2))$$
$$\forall\_x_1\forall\_x_2\forall\_x_3\forall\_x_4([\_x_1=\_x_2 \,\&\, \_x_3=\_x_4] \rightarrow F(\_x_1,\_x_3)=F(\_x_2,\_x_4))$$
...

These, however, follow from our introduction of functional notation as an abbreviation for existential quantification over function relations, and hence can be derived from the basic axioms of FOPC and EQ1, EQ2 and EQ3.

Given functional notation and the equality axioms, we can start adding axioms for dealing with simple arithmetic. For the purposes of the present chapter we will not go beyond developing axioms for addition and the linear order of the integers. We start by choosing a particular constant of our language, which we will call 0 (it could be any of the constants a_i), and a functional relation *successor of*. We will use SUCC instead of our standard notation *successor of*$_R$. The axioms we need for dealing with SUCC are the following:

SUCC1: $\exists\_x(\_x=SUCC(0))$
SUCC2: $\forall\_x(\exists\_y(\_x=SUCC(\_y)) \rightarrow \exists\_z(\_z=SUCC(\_x)))$
SUCC3: $\forall\_x\forall\_y(SUCC(\_x)=SUCC(\_y) \rightarrow \_x=\_y)$

These say, in effect, that 0 has a successor, that anything which is the successor of something else also has a successor itself, and that the only way for two things to have the same successor is if they are the same thing. This more or less characterises the basic properties of the positive natural numbers. We can extend these axioms to include the behaviour of the negative integers by adding the following axiom:

SUCC4: $\forall\_x(\exists\_y(\_y=(SUCC(\_x)) \rightarrow \exists\_z(\_x=SUCC(\_z)))$

We can include addition and the relation of numerical ordering with the following;

SUM1: $\forall\_x(\_x+0=\_x)$
SUM2: $\forall\_x\forall\_y(SUCC(\_x+\_y) = \_x+SUCC(\_y))$
ORDER: $\forall\_x\forall\_y(\_x > \_y \rightarrow [(\_x=SUCC(\_y)) \vee (\exists\_z(\_z > \_y \& \_x=SUCC(\_z))])$

With this machinery we can prove most of the basic theorems of arithmetic without stepping outside FOPC. If we add much more, we find that the language becomes incomplete. If we extend FOPC to cover all the usual properties of number theory, we find that there are formulae which are valid but for which there is no proof. This famous result, Godel's Incompleteness Theorem, sounds as though it undermines the very basis of mathematics. As with the negative result we are about to prove, the Undecidability of FOPC, its practical significance is comparatively slight. There are as yet no specific formulae of arithmetic, other than the pathological ones used in the proof of the Incompleteness Theorem, which are known to be valid but for which no proof is known. Similarly, it is far more common for theorem provers to run out of resources in the search for a proof of a theorem than for them to embark upon non-terminating searches for proofs which do not exist. Negative results of this kind are important for our general thinking about formal languages, but their practical effects are frequently insignificant. The proof of the incompleteness of arithmetic is extremely long, and is probably beside the point as far as this book is concerned. The interested reader is referred to Robbin (1969) for as clear an exposition as any. For current purposes, the negative result about FOPC in the next section is all we need. Some of the style of argument for this result is the same as in the more complex proof about arithmetic, but the details there are rather more intricate.

3.1.5 *Proof of the undecidability of FOPC*

Theorem 3.8: Undecidability of FOPC

There is no mechanical procedure which can decide whether or not there is a proof of A.

Proof:
The basic idea of the proof is very simple, though the details are very long-winded. We will describe the basic principles, and then give enough detail to enable the reader to complete it.

The proof depends on some notions from computer science. We assume that the reader is familiar with the idea of a Turing machine, and with the proof that it is not possible to construct a Turing machine which can tell whether an arbitrary Turing machine will halt when it is started in an arbitrary state. The crux of the proof of Theorem 3.8 is that we can describe Turing machines, and states of Turing machines, in FOPC. In particular, given a specific machine, we can write down a set of sentences which will be valid if and only if the machine halts. From this we see that if we had a mechanical procedure which could tell whether or not a set of sentences was valid, we would in fact have a mechanical procedure for deciding whether or not an arbitrary Turing machine halted. We know this is not possible, and hence we know that there cannot be a mechanical procedure for deciding whether or not a set of sentences is valid.

We start the proof by describing the form of Turing machine we are thinking about. We then show how to describe the states and decision tables of such machines in FOPC. This is straightforward but fairly tedious, and we shall only provide enough detail to give the general idea. The final step is to show how to construct the relevant set of sentences, and to show that these are valid if and only if the machine halts.

(1) Turing machines: the sort of machine we are thinking of has a tape which is of infinite length, and which can be moved to the left or to the right. Each square of the tape may have any of the finite set of symbols $S_1 \ldots S_k$ written on it. Initially all but a finite number of squares must have the same symbol, say S_1, written on them. The machine may be in any of the finite set of states $Q_1 \ldots Q_l$. There are three sorts of action it can perform - it can move one square to the left, denoted as ML, move one square to the right, denoted MR, or write any of the symbols $S_1 \ldots S_k$ on the current square, denoted by W_n where S_n is the symbol that gets written. There is a decision table, consisting of a finite set of rules of the form $\{S_i, Q_j => M, Q_k\}$. These rules say that if the machine is in state Q_j, and the tape square under its tape reader has the symbol S_i written on it, then it should perform the action M (which is one of ML, MR and Wn) and then put itself in state Q_k. It is well known that machines of this sort are powerful enough to compute anything which we know how to compute (Church's thesis says that they are powerful enough to compute anything which can reasonably be regarded as computable. This cannot be proved, but what can be proved is that they are at

least as powerful as anything else we know of). It is also well known that there is
no mechanical procedure for deciding whether or not one of these machines will
eventually halt (get into a state for which there is no entry in its decision table).
The proof of this for Turing machines is rather long, since they are very awkward
to write programs for. We can give a sketch of the proof by considering the
possibility of writing a LISP function which can tell whether a given piece of
LISP code will eventually halt. The proof is much easier for LISP because we
know that in LISP we can write functions which take lists of symbols and treat
them as though they were programs. The basic idea is captured by the following
very simple piece of LISP. We assume that it is possible to write a LISP function,
HALTS, which returns T if its first argument is the name of a LISP function
which will halt when applied to its second argument, and will return NIL
otherwise. From this assumption we derive a contradiction, thus showing that the
assumption itself must be wrong.

```
(DEF HALTS (FUN ARG)
   ... )
```

```
(DEF BREAK-IT (TESTPROG)
   (COND ((HALTS (CADR TESTPROG) TESTPROG)
           (BREAK-IT FUN ARG))
         (T)))
```

```
(BREAK-IT '(HALTS BREAK-IT))
```

We want to consider what happens when we call (BREAK-IT '(HALTS
BREAK-IT)). The very first thing that happens is that we get a call of HALTS
with BREAK-IT and (HALTS BREAK-IT)) as arguments. We know that
HALTS is concerned with the computation which would result from applying its
first argument to its second. In the current case, this is the same computation as
the one we are already embarked upon - a call of HALTS with BREAK-IT and
(HALTS BREAK-IT) as arguments. In other words, the computation being
considered by the call of HALTS is exactly the same as the one we set up with
our initial call of (BREAK-IT '(HALTS BREAK-IT)). This computation must
either terminate or fail to terminate. We consider the two cases. (i) If the given
computation terminated, then the call of HALTS which is considering it would
return T. In that case, there would be an immediate recursive call of BREAK-IT
with the same arguments, so we would be in a non-terminating recursive loop.
Hence if we assume that the computation terminates we can show that it in fact

must fail to terminate, so the assumption is self-contradictory. (ii) If the computation failed to terminate then the call of HALTS would return NIL, so there would be no recursive call, so the initial call of BREAK-IT would return immediately. Thus the assumption that the computation fails to terminate leads to the conclusion that it in fact terminates very rapidly - another contradiction. We thus see that there can be no such function as HALTS, since any investigation into its behaviour when called by BREAK-IT in the specified manner leads to a contradiction, and there's nothing wrong with BREAK-IT, which is a perfectly reasonable LISP function.

We can reconstruct the same argument for Turing machines. It is more awkward, since they are harder to program than LISP, but the construction of BREAK-IT (which is astonishingly simple in LISP) is essentially the same. There is very little to be gained by going into the details for Turing machines. We therefore now turn to the description of an arbitrary Turing machine in FOPC.

(2) Turing machines in FOPC: we are going to show how to construct a description of a Turing machine in FOPC. We will call the particular machine we are trying to get a description for TM. We will be using different names for the predicates and constants from the names we chose when we set up FOPC originally, but since we are only going to need a finite set of predicates and constants it is easy enough to see how to map them back on the names we originally used - just use the original names up one at a time. We start by choosing two sets of two-place predicate letters s_1 ... s_k and q_1 ... q_l (to be precise, we would use $p_{2,1}$ ... $p_{2,k}$ for the s_i and $p_{2,k+1}$ ... $p_{2,k+l}$ for the q_i. This would simply make things harder to read, without adding a great deal of precision. We will decide that we can use whatever finite set of predicate and constant names we like, in the knowledge that if we had to we could couch the argument in terms of the original set of names). We also need the machinery we developed earlier for dealing with equality, with positive and negative integers, and with numerical ordering.

We want to use the predicates s_i to make statements about what symbol is on a given square of the tape, and the predicates q_i to make statements about the state the machine TM is in. To formalise this, we define a model $<W_{TM}, V_{TM}>$ as follows:

W_{TM} consists of three sets of objects - an infinite set of instants, the set of symbols S_i and the set of states of the machine Q_i. V_{TM} assigns the set of all 2-tuples $<x,t>$ such that the symbol S_i is on square x at time t to be the valuation of s_i for each s_i. In other words, the expression $s_3(100, 40)$ would be true in the model $<W_{TM}, V_{TM}>$ if TM had the symbol S_3 written on square 100 of the tape at time 40. Similarly the valuation of q_i is the set of all 2-tuples $<x,t>$ such that at time t TM is in state Q_i scanning square x.

We now define a set of axioms involving the s_i and q_i.

(i) If the decision table of TM contains the rule $\{S_i, Q_j => MR, Q_k\}$, then we include as an axiom the formula:

$$\forall t \forall x \forall y([q_j(\_x,\_t) \ \& \ s_i(\_x,\_t)]$$
$$\rightarrow [q_k(SUCC(\_x), SUCC(\_t))$$
$$\& \ (s_1(\_y, \_t) \rightarrow s_1(\_y, SUCC(\_t)))$$
$$\& \ ...$$
$$\& \ (s_k(\_y, \_t) \rightarrow s_k(\_y, SUCC(\_t)))])$$

This sentence will be true in the model $<W_{TM}, V_{TM}>$ if any instant when the machine is in state Q_j, scanning a square with S_i, will be followed immediately by an instant when it is in state Q_k, scanning the square to the right of the one it was originally scanning, with no changes to what is written anywhere on the tape.

(ii) If the decision table contains the rule $\{S_i, Q_j => ML, Q_k\}$, then we include as an axiom the following formula:

$$\forall t \forall x \forall y([q_j(SUCC(\_x),\_t) \ \& \ s_i(SUCC(\_x),\_t)]$$
$$\rightarrow [q_k(\_x, SUCC(\_t))$$
$$\& \ (s_1(\_y, \_t) \rightarrow s_1(\_y, SUCC(\_t)))$$
$$\& \ ...$$
$$\& \ (s_k(\_y, \_t) \rightarrow s_k(\_y, SUCC(\_t)))])$$

The meaning of this sentence in the intended model is very similar to the meaning of the previous one, except that in the resulting state it is scanning the square to the left, not the one to the right.

(iii) If the decision table contains the rule $\{S_i, Q_j => W_n, Q_k\}$ we include as an axiom the following formula:

$$\forall\_t\forall\_x\forall\_y([q_j(\_x, \_t) \ \& \ s_i(\_x, \_t)]$$
$$\rightarrow [q_k(\_x, \mathrm{SUCC}(\_t))$$
$$\& \ s_n(\_x, \mathrm{SUCC}(\_t))$$
$$\& \ (\_y \neq \_x \rightarrow [(s_1(\_y, \_t) \rightarrow s_1(\_y, \mathrm{SUCC}(\_t)))$$
$$\& \ ...$$
$$\& \ (s_k(\_y, \_t) \rightarrow s_k(\_y, \mathrm{SUCC}(\_t)))])])$$

This sentence will be true in $<W_{TM}, V_{TM}>$ if immediately after any instant when TM is in state Q_j scanning a square with S_i, it is in state Q_k scanning the same square, which will now have S_n written on it, with no changes made to what is written anywhere else on the tape.

This set of axioms suffices to describe the behaviour of the machine once we have a description of its initial state, since they specify the transitions that would be brought about by the rules in its decision table. We also need an axiom which describes the initial state. This is easy enough to construct. Suppose, for instance, TM is initially in state Q_{12} scanning square 100, with the symbol S_{25} written on this square and the 14 squares to the right of it, and the symbol S_1 written everywhere else. This situation is described by the following sentence:

$$Q_{12}(100, 0)$$
$$\& \ S_{25}(100, 0) \ \& \ ... \ \& \ S_{25}(114, 0)$$
$$\& \ \forall\_y[(\_y < 100 \ \lor \_y > 114) \rightarrow S_1(\_y, 0)]$$

(3) From this description of the initial state of the machine TM and the axioms describing its transitions, we can derive the state it will be in at any time. There will be exactly one sentence whose antecedent fits the current state, and its consequent will give a precise specification of the succeeding state, so all we need to do to discover the situation at time N is to trace through the N succeeding axioms. We want to know whether TM will halt. A Turing machine halts if it gets into a situation for which it does not have a transition rule. In terms of our specification in FOPC, this means when it gets into a state where none of the antecedents of the descriptive axioms hold. The following sentence, then, will be true exactly if TM eventually halts:

$$H: \exists\_t\forall\_x[(q_{i1}(\_x, \_t) \ \& \ s_{j1}(\_x, \_t)) \ \& \ ... \ \& \ (q_{im}(\_x, \_t) \ \& \ s_{jm}(\_x, \_t))]$$

where the $q_{in}(\_x,\_t)$ & $s_{jn}(\_x,\_t)$ are the expressions appearing in the antecedents of our descriptive axioms. We now see that the following sentence is valid if and only if TM halts:

$$SENT_{TM}: (I \& D_1 \& ... \& D_t) \rightarrow H$$

where I is the sentence describing the initial situation, D_i are the sentences describing the transitions, and H is the sentence given above. $SENT_{TM}$ is certainly true in the model $<W_{TM}, V_{TM}>$ if and only if TM halts. We need to know that it is true in <u>all</u> models if and only if it halts. It is obviously true in all models only if it halts, since we have a specific model, namely $<W_{TM}, V_{TM}>$, for which it is untrue otherwise. To show that it is true in every model if TM halts is a bit more difficult. Suppose that it does halt, but that there is a model $<W_{NO}, V_{NO}>$ in which $SENT_{TM}$ is false. The only way for it to be false is for the antecedent to be true and the consequent to be false. For this to be so, there must be things in W_{NO} which correspond one-to-one with the objects in W_{TM}. Furthermore the sentences that make the antecedent of our sentence are universally quantified over the arguments of all the q_i and s_i, so the valuations V_{NO} and V_{TM} must be isomorphic. In other words, the sentence is sufficiently constrained that if it is false in one model it must be false in all. We know, however, that if the machine halts then the sentence is true in $<W_{TM}, V_{TM}>$, and hence it cannot be false in any model.

We have now shown how, given a Turing machine TM, you can mechanically construct a sentence $SENT_{TM}$ which is valid if and only if TM halts. This means that if we had a mechanical procedure which could determine whether an arbitrary sentence of FOPC was valid, we could use it to determine whether an arbitrary Turing machine halted. Since, as we argued without really proving above, we know that there is no mechanical test for whether a Turing machine halts, there can be no mechanical test for validity of sentences of FOPC ▦

Theorem 3.8 has the following obvious corollary.

Theorem 3.9:

There is no mechanical procedure for deciding whether a set of sentences of FOPC is consistent.

Proof:
The proof is obvious from Theorem 3.8, since if there were we could use it to see if the negation of an arbitrary set of sentences was valid, and from this we could work out whether the unnegated set itself was valid ▓

3.2 Problems with classical logic

We have spent a considerable amount of time proving things about the classical systems $Prop_{hilbert}$ and FOPC. We said earlier on, though, that as far as AI was concerned these languages are often seen to be inadequate. We had two reasons for spending all this effort on languages which we were going to abandon. Firstly, although we are going to find that we need more powerful languages for much of what we want to do in AI, many of the best alternatives are built directly on top of FOPC, so that a close examination of its properties will give us a good start when we come to consider the alternatives. Secondly, we needed to see what sort of results can be proved about a language, and what the proofs of these results look like, so that when we want to examine the properties of our proposed alternatives we have a good grounding in proving things about languages.

We have now covered enough material to be able to say that we have pinned FOPC down. We know what it looks like, and we know some of its formal properties. Before we pass on to particular alternatives, we end this chapter by considering in general the kinds of reasons why FOPC might be seen to be the wrong language for knowledge representation.

3.2.1 *Alternative interpretations*
The first way that we might want to change one of the languages we have seen so far is that we might say that it has the right vocabulary, but that the semantics it has been given are wrong. The most obvious version of this argument in AI is the claim that since AI systems generally work with uncertain knowledge and uncertain rules, the black and white nature of the semantics of FOPC, and indeed of the various forms of propositional calculus we have seen, is inappropriate. A considerable amount of work in knowledge representation for AI has gone into developing propositional inference schemes in which fuzzy or probabilistic values take the place of the simple two-valued truth values of classical propositional logic (Zadeh 1975, 1976). We will return to these systems in Chapter 9, but the discussion there will be very brief indeed. The problem, as we will see, is that although these languages do sometimes turn out to be very useful in practical systems, there has been very little progress in formalising their semantics, at least so far as their use in AI is concerned. As such there is very

little we can say about them as *logics*. We cannot show that the inference rules capture the intuitions they were aimed at, or that they will not permit nonsense proofs, or any of the things which we can show for the languages which are more directly based on FOPC. We will, in fact, show for at least one of these languages that the proposed semantics is very poorly behaved and that the given rules do not capture the intended intuitions correctly. Since that is just about all there is we can say about interpretations of the inference schemas of propositional and predicate calculus which are based on non-rigid truth values, they are of little interest from the point of view taken in this book, and we will relegate them to a minor topic in Chapter 9. This should not be taken as an indication that they may not be useful as the basis for practical AI systems, just that we do not yet properly understand how they work, and hence cannot say much more about them than that they sometimes seem to work.

We will also look in Chapter 9 at another alternative reading of the implication operator. This is one for which a formal semantics has been developed, and hence we can consider it abstractly to see if the inference rules and axioms do accurately capture the intended intuitions. This alternative reading arises from the so-called "paradoxes of implication". The semantics we have given for $\rightarrow$ make a number of formulae valid which at first sight seem rather odd. The axiom PH1, A $\rightarrow$ (B $\rightarrow$ A), is a good example. It says that whenever A is true then B implies A. This is clearly valid on the semantics we have given for both Prop$_{hilbert}$ and FOPC, and yet on the face of it it seems to be outright nonsense. What on earth has the truth of A got to do with whether B implies A or not? The attempts to remove these paradoxes are extremely neat, and show how careful development of the formal semantics of logical languages can illuminate difficult seeming questions. The *relevance logic* which has been developed to account for these problems has not yet had a great deal of impact on AI, and we will therefore not spend a great deal of time on it. The most accessible semantic theory for this logic, however, Lorentzen's (1959) game theoretic semantics, is coming to have some significance in the computer analysis of natural language, and we will look at it in some detail. When we do so we will also show how it deals with relevance logic.

3.2.2 *Extensions of FOPC*

The other way in which we might want to change the languages we have seen so far is that we might accept that they are alright as far as they go, but there might be things we want to say, or inference schemas that we might want to use, which we simply cannot specify in them. In the same way that we had to move from Prop$_{hilbert}$ to FOPC because we could not capture simple inferences about all entities with a given property, there might be rules and inference patterns which we simply cannot capture in FOPC. We will see in detail the forms these have taken in the rest of the book. For the moment we just leave the reader to consider how the following might be dealt with in FOPC: (i) if P must be so, and P may imply Q, then (a) is Q necessarily true, (b) is Q possibly true? (ii) if I know Alex lives with Trish, and I know Alex has a phone, why will asking Alex "What's your phone number" enable me to phone Trish? (iii) if I used to believe Q because I believe that P implies Q and I used to believe P, what should I believe if I find out that I was wrong about P? (iv) if Q is true whenever P has been performed, and R is true whenever Q is true, then for how long after I perform P will R be true? All of these are comparatively simple seeming questions. Most of the remainder of this book is concerned with showing how to extend FOPC in order to be able to deal with them. The exception is Chapter 4, which covers the topic of theorem proving, or the development of mechanical procedures for deriving proofs for formulae of FOPC.

CHAPTER FOUR

THEOREM PROVING

We suggested in Chapter 1 that the languages generally classed as *logic languages* were particularly suitable for use as knowledge representation languages for AI. We said there that the advantage of these languages was that they provided precise means for determining what conclusions followed from the facts and rules that were available. This should enable systems whose knowledge is stated in one of these languages to reason from that knowledge to conclusions that are implicit in it, and hence to discover new facts about the world. This is not going to be worthwhile if we have no way of mechanising the process of drawing conclusions from facts and rules. Before we proceed to discuss languages which are more complex than FOPC, then, we need to see how to write programs which can at least reason with facts and rules stated in FOPC.

The final theorem of Chapter 3 said that it is in fact impossible to write a program which can examine an arbitrary formula and see whether or not it is valid. This would seem to doom the current enterprise right from the start. If we have a proof that we cannot write such a program, what point is there in even trying? If we look carefully at the conclusion of Theorem 3.8, we see that it says that we cannot write a program which can tell *whether or not* an *arbitrary* formula of FOPC is valid. There are two possible escape routes. Firstly, the theorem does not rule out the possibility of writing a program which can tell you that a formula is valid, but which may never terminate if it is not. Secondly, we may be able to write a program which is guaranteed to terminate, and which can tell for some formulae whether or not they are valid, but which will be unable to decide for others. We will call the first sort of program a *complete theorem prover*, since it will prove any genuine theorem it is asked to prove, and the second sort a *safe theorem prover*, since it will prove some theorems, and it is safe to use in the sense that you know it is not going to go on trying to prove things for ever. The aim of this chapter will be to consider a number of fairly efficient theorem provers of each kind. Just to reassure the reader that it is possible to write either sort of theorem prover, given the pessimistic conclusion to Chapter 3, we will sketch very simple, and grossly inefficient, theorem provers of each sort.

The aim here is to construct a program which will eventually tell us that a formula is valid if it is, but will simply never return if it is not.

We start by dismantling the target formula into its component primitive formulae, so that if the target were $\forall\_x\ \forall\_y[p(\_x,\_y) \rightarrow [(r(a) \rightarrow q(b)) \rightarrow p(b,c)]]$ we would get $p(\_x,\_y)$, $r(a)$, $q(b)$ and $p(b,c)$. These are supplemented by taking each of them and substituting permutations of the variables that appear in the original for the constants they contain, so that the given collection is extended to $p(\_x,\_y)$, $r(a)$, $q(b)$, $p(b,c)$, $r(\_x)$, $r(\_y)$, $q(\_x)$, $q(\_y)$, $p(\_x,\_y)$, $p(\_y,\_x)$, $p(\_x,\_x)$ and $p(\_y,\_y)$. We further add the formula †. From these we can generate all possible formulae involving these predicates, variables and constants as follows. At any given point we have a list of formulae. We take the first of these and generate new formulae via the following two steps. (i) We add formulae with universal quantifiers for all combinations of variables that appear free in the chosen formula. (ii) We add all formulae of the form $A \rightarrow B$, where A is the chosen formula and B is any formula from the list generated so far. B may be the same as A. Thus if we had an initial set consisting of †, $r(\_x)$, $r(a)$ (say we were trying to prove $\forall\_x\ (r(\_x)) \rightarrow r(a))$), the sequence would grow as follows:

(1) Using †
†, $r(\_x)$, $r(a)$, † $\rightarrow$ †, † $\rightarrow$ $r(\_x)$, † $\rightarrow$ $r(a)$,

(2) Using $r(\_x)$
†, $r(\_x)$, $r(a)$, † $\rightarrow$ †, † $\rightarrow$ $r(\_x)$, † $\rightarrow$ $r(a)$,

$\forall\_x(r(\_x))$, $r(\_x) \rightarrow$ †, $r(\_x) \rightarrow r(\_x)$, $r(\_x) \rightarrow r(a)$, $r(\_x) \rightarrow$ († $\rightarrow$ †)), $r(\_x) \rightarrow$ († $\rightarrow r(\_x)$)), $r(\_x) \rightarrow$ († $\rightarrow r(a)$))

(3) Using $r(a)$
†, $r(\_x)$, $r(a)$, † $\rightarrow$ †, † $\rightarrow$ $r(\_x)$, † $\rightarrow$ $r(a)$,

$\forall\_x(r(\_x))$, $r(\_x) \rightarrow$ †, $r(\_x) \rightarrow r(\_x)$, $r(\_x) \rightarrow r(a)$, $r(\_x) \rightarrow$ († $\rightarrow$ †)), $r(\_x) \rightarrow$ († $\rightarrow r\_x)$, $r(\_x) \rightarrow$ († $\rightarrow r(a)$))

r(a) → ∀_x(r(_x)), r(a) → r(a), r(a) → († → †), r(a) → († → r(_x)), r(a) → († →
r(a)), r(a) → (r(_x) → †), r(a) → (r(_x) → r(_x)), r(a) → (r(_x) → r(a)), r(a) →
(r(_x) → († → †))), r(a) → (r(_x) → († → r_x)), r(a) → (r(_x) → († → r(a)))

(4) Using † → †

   ...

This process will eventually generate every formula involving the predicates, constants and variables appearing in our target formula. There is, of course, nothing in what we have done to give us any way of telling which of these has a proof.

To get the ones which have proofs, we have to extend the process that generates the original sequence with two further steps. (iii) The first extra step is executed immediately after the first two steps. It takes the formula currently being considered and constructs all possible instantiations of axioms involving this formula and formulae which have been considered already. This will be quite tedious, but it will eventually enumerate all instances of axioms involving the basic building blocks of the target. When, for instance, the formula † → † was added at step 1 above, formulae such as † → ([† → †] → †), [(† → †) → (r(a) → [(† → †]), ¬¬(† → †) → († → †), and so on would also be added. The axioms are marked as being valid. (iv) The second extra step is executed after the addition of each new valid formula. It starts by comparing the new valid formula with all existing ones to see if the inference rule MP can be applied to them, and if so it adds the conclusion to the list of valid formulae. It then applies the inference rule GEN to the new formula, using each variable that has been mentioned so far in turn, and then applies it again with a new variable that has not yet been mentioned. The results of all these applications of GEN are also added to the list of valid formula.

This will eventually generate all the provable formulae involving the given predicates, constants and variables (by completeness, these are all the valid formulae involving these items). Hence in order to use it as the basis of a complete theorem prover, we just run it and wait for the target formula to be generated by either step (iii) or step (iv). If the target formula has a proof, it will eventually be generated by one of these steps, at which point the theorem prover will halt.

To adapt this so that it becomes a safe theorem prover, we just put a limit on the number of formulae to be generated. If we also check the generated formulae for the negation of the target, we will have a program which may report that the target is valid (if it is generated before the cut-off point is reached), may report that it is invalid (if its negation is generated in time), but in any event is bound to terminate.

A program for generating the given sequence of provable formulae would be extremely easy to write. It would also, of course, be grossly inefficient, since the number of irrelevant formulae which would be generated would far outweigh the ones that actually contributed to generating the target. It does, nonetheless, show that the Undecidability Theorem is not as damning a result as it first seems. If we can write complete theorem provers and safe theorem provers as easily as this, then with a little more effort we may even be able to write efficient theorem provers which are either complete or safe. All the Undecidability Theorem shows is that we cannot write theorem provers which are both complete and safe, not that we cannot write ones which are useful.

4.1 Unification

We will develop several different kinds of theorem prover in the remainder of this chapter, corresponding roughly to the three presentations of propositional calculus given in Chapter 1. One thing that they all have in common is that at some point they have to substitute constants into universally quantified formulae. In order to show, for instance, that q(a) follows from p(a) and $\forall\_x(p(\_x) \rightarrow q(\_x))$, we have to decide to instantiate the second premise to p(a) $\rightarrow$ q(a). It can be difficult to work out exactly what instantiations are going to be needed, and it is a good idea to delay instantiating formulae for as long as possible. All the theorem provers we are going to look at use a technique known as *unification* for instantiation of variables. The advantage of unification is that it makes it possible to delay instantiation until the last possible moment, so that the program only commits itself to assuming values for variables when it is absolutely necessary. Unification is an important part of all standard theorem proving techniques, and is also useful in other situations where entities have to be matched against schemas. Since it will be used in all our theorem provers, we will treat it separately here and then use it as and when we need it.

The simplest way of thinking about unification is as a least commitment matching process, where we are trying to match expressions each of which may contain variables. Suppose we wanted to know whether f(a, _x, _y) matched f(_u, b, _v). These would match, so long as we bound _u to a and _x to b. _y and _v also have to match, but since they are both variables there seems no reason why they should not. What about if we wanted to match f(a, _x, _x) and f(_y, _z, c)? These again would match, so long as we bound _y to a and _x to c. This time we would also be committed to matching _x and _z, but now, since we later find that _x has to be bound to c we are also forced to bind _z to c. f(a, _x, _x) and f(_y, b, c) will not match, since we have to match _x with both b and c, which clearly is not possible. A similar, though more complicated, situation arises if we try to match f(a, _x, _x) and f(_y, _y, b). In this case we see that _y must match a, and it must also match _x, and _x must match b. We can write this down as a set of simultaneous equations _y=a, _y=_x, _x=b. These cannot all be solved together, since that would entail a=b, which is impossible.

4.1.1 *Unification as structure matching*
This style of matching, where we use variables as constraints on what can appear where, has received a great deal of attention. The simplest way to perform it is via the following algorithm:

Fig. 4.1 Basic unification algorithm

To unify X and Y:
(1) If X is a variable, see if it has previously been unified with anything.
(1.1) If so, get the item is was previously unified with and see if this unifies with Y (we call the object it was previously unified with its *value*).
(1.2) Otherwise just note that X has been unified with Y (*bind* X to Y).
(2) If Y is a variable, see if it has previously been unified with anything.
(2.1) If so, get the item that it was previously unified with and see if this unifies with X.
(2.2) Otherwise just note that Y has been unified with X.
(3) If X and Y are both complex expressions, then check that they have the same functor.
(3.1) If so, then check that their arguments unify.
(3.2) Otherwise fail.
(4) If X and Y are both constants, check that they are identical. Otherwise fail.
(5) There are no other possibilities - either they are both complex expressions, or they are both constants, or one or other of them is a variable.

This is a very simple algorithm, easily implemented in any standard programming language. The only place where there is scope for good or bad implementations is at the point in (1.1) and (2.1) where you have to see whether a variable has previously been unified with anything, and if so to retrieve whatever it was unified with. The customary way to deal with this is to represent variables as data structures which can contain pointers, and to initialise them to point to some standard object which we will call UNDEF. To bind a variable to an object, you simply make the pointer in the variable point to the object. To see whether a variable has been unified, and if so to get its value, you just see what it points to. If it points to UNDEF then it has not previously been unified, otherwise the thing it points to is its value.

We will illustrate this by going step-by-step through an attempt to unify f(a, _x, _x) and f(_y, _y, b):

Initially both _x and _y point to UNDEF. We denote this by _x = UNDEF, _y = UNDEF

(i) We examine the two expressions. They are both complex, and they have the same functor. We have to check the arguments.

(ii) The first pair of arguments are a and _y. Of these _y is a variable which has not yet been unified with anything. We go to step (2.2) of the algorithm in Fig. 3.1, and bind _y to a, so we now have _x = UNDEF, _y = a

(iii) The second pair of arguments are _x and _y. _x is a variable which has not yet been unified with anything, so we go to step (1.2) and bind it to _y. We now have _x = _y, _y = a.

(iv) The final pair is _x and b. _x is a variable which has previously been bound, so we go to step (1.1). We get the item it was previously unified with, namely _y, and see if this can be unified with b. This takes us round the loop again, but this time it is _y that is a previously unified variable, so we go to (1.1) again (note that _y is playing the role of X in the specification of the algorithm). We now have the value which _y was bound to, namely a, which we have to try to unify with b. This fails, since they are both constants but are not identical, so the entire attempted unification fails.

There is a small change which will make this algorithm more efficient. We see that at (1.1) and (2.1) the current algorithm gets the value which was previously associated with the variable, and then tries to unify this with the other argument. If, as was the case in the final step of our example, the value that was previously associated with it was in fact a variable, then we go through the whole thing again to see if this had also already been unified with anything. It is marginally more efficient to do this immediately, rather than entering a recursive call of the procedure. We can therefore rewrite this algorithm as follows:

Fig. 4.2 Improved unification algorithm

To unify X and Y:
(0) So long as X or Y is a variable which has previously been unified with something, replace it by what it was unified with.
(1) If X is a variable, it is one which has not previously been unified with anything (otherwise step (0) would have replaced it by its value). Just note that it has now been unified with Y.
(2) If Y is a variable, it is one which has not previously been unified with anything (otherwise step (0) would have replaced it by its value). Just note that it has now been unified with X.
(3) If X and Y are both complex expressions, then check that they have the same functor.
(3.1) If so, then check that their arguments unify.
(3.2) Otherwise fail.
(4) If X and Y are both constants, check that they are identical. If not, fail.
(5) There are no other possibilities - either they are both complex expressions, or they are both constants, or one or other of them is a variable.

This algorithm is fairly efficient and very simple. It will deal with most cases, including ones where the expressions being matched have complex expressions as their arguments, e.g. it would accept that f(_x, _y, g(_x, a)) and f(r(b), c, _u) matched, and would generate the bindings _x = r(b), _y = c, _u = g(_x, a). There is just one place where it does the wrong thing. Suppose we were to try to match f(_x, _x) against f(_y, g(_y)). This ought to fail, since _y and g(_y) cannot be the same thing. Our algorithm, however, goes through the following steps:

(i) The two expressions are both complex and have the same functor. We therefore check the arguments.

(ii) The first pair of arguments are both unbound variables, so we get to step (1) of the revised algorithm and bind _x to have _y as its value. The situation is now _x = _y, _y = UNDEF.

(iii) The second pair of arguments are _x and g(_y). _x is currently bound to something other than UNDEF, namely _y, so step 0 replaces it by _y, which still has UNDEF as its value. We get to step (2), and bind _y to g(_x), so the bindings are now _x = _y, _y = g(_x).

(iv) All the arguments have now been checked without encountering any problems, so the algorithm reports that it has succeeded.

The problem arises because _x has been bound, via its binding to _y, to a complex expression in which it occurs itself. Adapting our basic algorithm to include an *occurs check* would slow it down considerably, since it means that every time a variable is bound to a complex expression the complex expression has to be searched for an occurrence of the variable. This is so time consuming that many implementations of unification simply leave it out. Using a theorem prover which has a unification algorithm without an occurs check can lead to invalid formulae being derived. We therefore present an alternative view of unification which can be implemented just about as efficiently as the basic algorithm, and in which the occurs check is almost free.

4.1.2 *Unification via term equations*
There are a number of alternative unification algorithms in which the occurs check is more or less free. The one we sketch below comes from Martelli & Montanari (1982).

The basic idea goes back to the notion of unification as the task of solving a set of simultaneous equations. We suggested that the reason why f(a, _x, _x) and f(_y, _y, b) could not be unified was that the set of equations _y=a, _x=_y and _x=b could not all be solved at the same time. This indicates a different approach to unification from the recursive algorithm outlined above. Why not try to generate, and then solve, a set of equations?

We will start by looking at a simplified version of Martelli and Montanari's algorithm which is no better than the one in Fig. 4.2, and then refine it to get the occurs check. The algorithm comes in two parts, namely setting up the equations and solving them. Setting them up is very similar to the algorithm we already have, except that we do not attempt to find the values of variables:

Fig. 4.3 Setting up equations

To create a set of equations for unifying X and Y:
  (1) If X is a variable add the equation X=Y and return.
  (2) If Y is a variable add the equation Y=X and return.
  (3) If X and Y are constants, see if they are identical. If they are then return, otherwise fail.
  (4) If X and Y are complex expressions, see if they have the same functors. If so, set up the equations for each pair of arguments and then return, otherwise fail.
  (5) Fail - you can only get to here if one of them is a constant and the other is a complex expression, in which case there is a problem.

Applying this algorithm to f(a, _x, _x) and f(_y, _y, b) will lead to the required equations. Solving equations is done by *merging* them. When we merge two equations, we may find that we are committed to creating more of them. If we manage to merge all our equations without running into any trouble, the unification is successful, otherwise it fails. We will illustrate the process of merging on the example set we have derived for f(a, _x, _x) and f(_y, _y, b) before we actually develop the algorithm.

Merging the first two equations from _y = a, _x = _y, _x = b would lead us to {_y, _x} = a, _x = b. Merging these would have led to {_y, _x} = {a, b}, but at this point we would have discovered the incompatibility between a and b and therefore would have realised that the equations were not going to be solvable and that the unification must fail. The basic rules for merging equations, then, are that if you have two equations whose left-hand sides contain the same variable then you should create a new equation by joining their left-hand sides and setting up new equations for the objects that were on the right-hand sides; and that if you have an equation between two variables you should add the one on the right-hand side to any other equations with the other one on the left-hand side.

We can turn this into an algorithm:

Fig. 4.4 Processing a set of equations

To process a set of equations:
(1) For all equations of the form X = Y where both X and Y are variables, add Y to the left-hand side of any other equations with X on their left-hand sides.
(2) Merge any pair of equations which have the same variable on the left-hand side.

To merge two equations:
(1) Create a new equation whose left-hand side is the union of the two left-hand sides and whose right-hand side is the union of the two right-hand sides.
(2) Delete the original equations from the equation set.
(3) Perform the algorithm in Fig. 4.3 for each pair of items from the two right-hand sides (i.e. for the first element of the first right-hand side against each element of the second, then for the second element of the first against each element of the second, and so on).

There are several places in this algorithm where careful implementation can have a dramatic effect on its execution time. We can easily make one improvement by integrating step (2) of the algorithm for creating equations and step (1) of the one for processing them. Rather than setting up equations with variables on the right-hand side and then merging them, we do the merge at step (2) of the algorithm for creating equations. We can similarly integrate step (1) of the creation algorithm and step (2) of the one for processing, so that when we want to make a new equation with X on the left-hand side, we look to see if there is already such an equation and if so immediately merge the right-hand side of the new one with the right-hand side of the old one. If we make these two changes, there will never be more than one equation with a given variable on the left-hand side. We can further improve performance by making sure that each variable has a direct pointer to the equation on whose left-hand side it appears. The final improvement involves a change to step (3) of the algorithm for merging equations. As a side effect of the algorithm in Fig. 4.3 we can construct an expression which embodies all the information in the items from which the equations are being constructed. This is fairly intricate in detail. The basic idea is quite simple. In essence all that you have to do is build a new expression which has a constant wherever either of the originals had a constant, a complex expression wherever either of them had a complex expression, and variables everywhere else.

The resulting algorithm is just about equivalent to the recursive algorithm of Fig. 4.2. It contains a number of set operations (e.g. "delete the original equations from the equation set", make the "union of the two left-hand sides") which have to be performed as quickly as possible, but careful design of the structures for representing sets can reduce these to pointer switching operations. We have thus reproduced the performance and the effect of the standard unification algorithm with rather less straightforward code. The occurs check comes with the following refinement.

We associate a counter with every equation, preferably by reserving a location inside the structure which represents the equation. The counters are maintained as follows. (i) When an equation is created during the first phase of the algorithm, if its right-hand side is a complex expression then it is searched for occurrences of variables. If the algorithm finds any it makes sure that the counter for any equation in which they appear is incremented. This is the same work as is done by the occurs check in the standard algorithm, which we argued earlier was too expensive to be worthwhile. The difference here is that it is only done once, whereas for the earlier version it had to be done every time a variable was bound to a complex expression. (ii) Whenever two equations are merged, the resulting equation's counter is the sum of the counters of the two merged equations. (iii) Whenever a new equation is created by step (3) of the merging algorithm, the counter associated with the equation which has the left-hand side variable on its own left-hand side is decremented. These counters indicate for each variable the number of equations for which the variable occurs somewhere on the right-hand side. If, therefore, at the end of processing there are still equations whose counter is non-zero, there must be variables which occur inside complex expressions which they have been equated with. In other words, if there are any equations left with non-zero counters, there is an occurs check violation. Maintaining the counters is very cheap, since there is no search involved in deciding when to increment or decrement them.

The final check for equations with non-zero counters can be performed more or less for free by keeping a set of equations with non-zero counters, and deleting equations from this set as their counters become zero (again we need careful design of the implementation of this set to make sure that deleting items from it is just a matter of pointer switching). Furthermore, we need only process equations whose counters are zero, so we can improve things further by splitting the equations into two sets, one of equations with zero counters and one of equations with non-zero counters, with automatic transfer between the two sets as counters are decremented to zero. The resulting algorithm can be made almost as fast as the standard algorithm (of the order of 20% overhead for maintaining the pointers and merging equations) despite its much greater complexity. The occurs check can be turned on or off with virtually no overheads. We illustrate this algorithm for the task of unifying f(_x, _y) and f(_u, g(_u)).

The initial set of equations is

> _x, _u = UNDEF   counter:1
> _y = g(_u)   counter:0

These are created by the basic recursive scan which realises that _x should be bound to _u, and that _y should be bound to g(_u). Since _x and _u are both variables, the equation involving them has them both on the left-hand side and UNDEF on the right. The second equation has the variable on the left and the complex expression on the right. The counter for the first is set to 1 when the second is created because of the presence of _u inside the complex expression. Processing the second equation causes no problems, and leads to the counter for the first being decremented to 0, at which point it is ready for processing. No problems arise here either, so we have now processed all the zero-counter equations successfully. There are no non-zero ones left so the unification is successful.

If we try the algorithm with f(_x, _x) and f(_u, g(_u)) we get a single equation, namely

> _x, _u = g(_u)   counter:1

There are no zero-counter equations to process, so the algorithm has successfully done a unification without an occurs check. We can either stop here or add the occurs check by noting that there is still an equation with a non-zero counter.

The most complicated parts of this algorithm are the design of the data structures for representing sets, so that the operations of merging sets and of transferring items from one set to another can be done without doing a lot of time consuming structure copying; and the construction of a skeleton containing the information embodied in two expressions while merging them. Unification is sufficiently important in all the standard theorem proving algorithms for it to be worth putting some effort into getting it right (including the occurs check) and making sure that it is fast. Now that we have a good unification algorithm, we can turn our attention to the theorem provers themselves.

4.2 Theorem proving by backward chaining

One of the simplest techniques for theorem proving in FOPC is to rely on the single inference rule MP, supplemented by unification to instantiate universally quantified formulae when necessary. Suppose we take the view that free variables are implicitly universally quantified, so that $p(x) \rightarrow q(x)$ is the same as $\forall x(p(x) \rightarrow q(x))$. We can then perform a fairly substantial set of inferences. The following illustrate how such inferences are performed.

(1) Backward chaining proof of r(a) from p(a), p(_x) $\rightarrow$ q(_x), q(_y) $\rightarrow$ r(_y).

  (i) To prove r(a), find a rule of the form A $\rightarrow$ B where B unifies with r(a).
  (ii) q(_y) $\rightarrow$ r(_y) is such a rule. If we do the unification, _y gets bound to a. So to apply MP to this in order to get the desired conclusion, we need to prove q(a). For this we need a rule A $\rightarrow$ B where B unifies with q(a).
  (iii) p(_x) $\rightarrow$ q(_x) is a suitable rule. Doing the unification shows that we can apply MP if we can prove p(a).
  (iv) But p(a) is one of our basic facts, so we can use it as the basis of the required proof. We have now shown that we have everything we need for deriving q(a). We could go back through the various steps to actually construct the proof p(a), p(a) $\rightarrow$ q(a), q(a), q(a) $\rightarrow$ r(a), r(a), but normally we would simply recognise that we could construct a proof, and that therefore the conclusion must follow from the premises, without actually bothering to fill in the steps.

(2) Backward chaining proof of r(a, b) from p(a) & q(b), (p(_x) & q(_y)) $\rightarrow$ r(_x, _y).

  (i) We look for a rule A $\rightarrow$ B where B unifies with r(a, b). We find (p(_x) & q(_y)) $\rightarrow$ r(_x, _y), with _x bound to a and _y to b.
  (ii) We now need to show that p(a) & q(b) holds. We have this as a basic fact, so we have derived all we need for the proof to be constructed.

(3) Failed attempt to prove r(a) from p(a, b) & q(c), (p(_x, _y) & q(_y)) $\rightarrow$ r(_x).

  (i) The rule we need is (p(_x, _y) & q(_y)) $\rightarrow$ r(_x). Doing the unification leaves us needing to prove p(a, _y) & q(_y).
  (ii) We have a basic fact, p(a, b) & q(c). The first part of this unifies with the first part of p(a, _y) & q(_y), so the first step is successful. In

succeeding, however, it binds _y to b, so that the second goal becomes q(b). q(_y) would have succeeded, but that is not what we now have. q(b) fails, since the only fact we have which involves q is q(c).

We have assumed that free variables in the premises should be regarded as having implicit universal quantifiers. If we make the opposite assumption for free variables in the goal, namely that free variables have implicit existential quantifiers, we can deal with partially specified goals.

(4) Proof of lives-near(Allan, _x) from works-in(_u, _v) → lives-near(_u, _v) and works-in(Allan, Brighton).

(i) Find a rule whose consequent unifies with lives-near(Allan, _x). This is works-in(_u, _v) → lives-near(_u, _v), with _u bound to Allan and _x bound to _v.

(ii) Find something which corresponds to works-in(Allan, _v). This is the fact works-in(Allan, Brighton), with _v bound to Brighton.

(iii) We now have all we need for the proof to go through. Furthermore we have unified the _x in the goal with _v, and _v with Brighton, so that not only do we have a proof of lives-near(Allan, _x), we actually have one of lives-near(Allan, Brighton).

Backward chaining is not a bad theorem proving technique. It is very easy to implement, it is nearly safe, and it will deal with quite a useful set of proofs. In particular it will deal with proofs of partially specified goals, and will often instantiate the specifications as well as deriving the proof. As we have described it, however, it is not much good for proving negations. We can supplement it by assuming *negation as failure*.

4.2.1 *Negation as failure*

The assumption of negation as failure is simply, as its name suggests, the assumption that if you cannot prove something it is safe to assume that it is false. If you had a complete theorem prover, this would be perfectly acceptable and would lead to no confusion. If we can derive some formula from a set of premises then the negation of the formula must be inconsistent with the premises. If we had a complete theorem prover, the converse would be true, namely that if we cannot derive the formula from the premises then the negation must be consistent with them, and we would therefore be quite safe to add it to them. Note that even this would not mean that we had proved it, merely that adding it would not lead to any problems. With an incomplete theorem prover, such as one based on backward chaining applications of MP, even this conclusion is not really justified. The fact that we cannot prove that something follows from a set of premises no longer means that it is not entailed by them, and therefore no longer justifies the belief that its negation is consistent with them. Use of negation of failure with an incomplete theorem prover does not necessarily lead to the derivation of inconsistent sets of formulae, but it can lead to confusing situations. Suppose, for instance, our set of assumptions simply contained the formulae ¬p and ¬r → p. We can clearly derive ¬p from this set, since it is one of the premises. We can, however, also derive p from it, as follows:

(5) Proof by backward chaining with negation as failure of p from ¬p and ¬r → p.

   (i) To prove p, we need a rule of the form A → B where B unifies with p. Clearly ¬r → p will do. We need to prove ¬r.
   (ii) We can prove this either by finding an appropriate rule of the form A → B, or by failing to prove r. There is no suitable rule, so we try to prove r.
   (iii) This fails, since there is no rule which implies r and r is not a basic fact. So we have a proof of ¬r, via negation as failure.
   (iv) We now have what we needed to apply MP to ¬r → p, so we have a proof of p.

We have now derived what seems to be an inconsistent set of sentences from a consistent set. It can be argued that what has really happened is that we have derived an inconsistent set from an inconsistent set, since the addition of negation as failure alters the semantics of FOPC in such a way as to mean that the original set was already inconsistent. Alternatively, we can protect ourselves by saying that if we have negation as failure we cannot permit concrete statements of negated formulae, nor can we permit rules of the form A → ¬B. Either way we end up with a language which is a logic, in the sense that it has a clearly specified syntax, semantics and set of inference rules, which we can use as a knowledge representation language. This language, however, is not FOPC, and should not be confused with it.

   The language we end up with if we use backward chaining and negation as failure, with a ban on premises of either of the forms ¬A or A → ¬B, is the so-called "logic programming language" PROLOG. This is a perfectly coherent language which looks a bit like FOPC, but it should not be confused with it.

4.2.2 *Non-termination with backward chaining*

We remarked above that theorem provers based purely on backward chaining are not only incomplete with respect to negation, they are also not entirely safe. There are simple problems for which a proof clearly is not available, but for which they will fail to terminate. The following example is typical:

(6) Attempted proof of married-to(janet, russ) from married-to(pat, mike) and married-to(_x, _y) → married-to(_y, _x).

> (i) Find a rule whose consequent matches married-to(janet, russ). married-to(_x, _y) → married-to(_y, _x), with _y bound to janet and _x bound to russ, will do. Now try to prove its antecedent, married-to(russ, janet).
>
> (ii) The rule which will help with this is married-to(_x, _y) → married-to(_y, _x), for which this time we will want to bind _y to russ and _x to janet. The next move is to try to prove the antecedent, married-to(janet, russ).
>
> (iii) For this we want the rule married-to(_x, _y) → married-to(_y, _x), with _y bound to janet and _x bound to russ. The required antecedent is now married-to(russ, janet).
>
> (iv) ...

We can block this sort of loop by comparing each sub-goal with the outstanding goals which depend on it. If it unifies with one without binding any variables to constants or complex terms, then we are in a loop of this kind, and we should give up and try to find another proof. The constraint that the unification must not bind a variable to a constant or complex term is needed if we want to use rules of this kind with partially specified goals, such as trying to deal with married-to(mike, _u).

(7) Proof of married-to(mike, _u) from married-to(pat, mike), married-to(_x, _y) → married-to(_y, _x).

> (i) Try to find a rule whose consequent matches married-to(mike, _u). This is married-to(_x, _y) → married-to(_y, _x), with _y bound to mike and _u bound to _x.
>
> (ii) Find something which matches married-to(_u, mike). This goal does unify with an outstanding goal, namely married-to(mike, _u), but it binds _u to a constant and therefore should not be taken as grounds for supposing

we are in a loop. What it matches is married-to(pat, mike), so the original goal is proved with _u bound to pat.

The check for loops is normally omitted from backward chaining when it is used as the basis of PROLOG, on the grounds that it is quite an expensive check, and that such loops only arise from bad programming. This is perhaps acceptable if we are using it as the basis of a programming language, which is to be used by programmers who can be held accountable for the behaviour of their programs. It is not acceptable if we are using this kind of theorem prover with FOPC as a basis for knowledge representation in an AI system, since in this context the rules may be things which the system has inferred for itself, and which may well lead to looping behaviour of the kind illustrated above.

4.3 Theorem proving by resolution

The technique we have been considering is a special case of a more general theorem proving technique called *resolution*. Resolution uses the CUT rule of $Prop_{gentzen}$, suitably adapted to use unification for applying universal quantification, as its only rule of inference. It depends on the fact that for any formula of FOPC we can construct an equivalent formula of the form P_1 & ... & $P_n \rightarrow Q_1$ V... V Q_m, where all the P_i and Q_j are primitive formulae, with the whole thing implicitly preceded by universal quantifiers for all the free variables that appear anywhere in it. Formulae of this sort are said to be in *clausal form*. A clausal formula such as P_1 & ... & $P_n \rightarrow Q_1$ V ... V Q_m will frequently be written as $\overline{P_1}$ V ... V $\overline{P_n}$ V Q_1 V ... V Q_m This comes from translating P_1 & ... & $P_n \rightarrow Q_1$ V ... V Q_m to the equivalent disjunctive form $\neg P_1$ V ... V $\neg P_n$ V Q_1 V ... V Q_m and then denoting negated formulae by writing a line above them rather than a $\neg$ before them.

For formulae of this form, the only inference rule which can possibly apply is CUT. CUT says that from $(P_1$ & ... & $P_{n1}) \rightarrow (Q_1$ V ... V Q_{m1} V R) and $(R'$ & P'_1 & ... & $P'_{n2}) \rightarrow (Q'_1$ V ... V $Q'_{m2})$ you can derive $(P''_1$ & ... & P''_{n1} & P'''_1 & ... & $P'''_{n2}) \rightarrow (Q''_1$ V ... V Q''_{m1} V Q'_1 V ... V $Q'''_{m2})$, so long as R and R' unify. P''_i and P'''_i are derived from P_i and P'_i by substituting the values variables were given by the unification of R and R' for the variables themselves, and similarly for Q''_i and Q'''_i. This version of CUT is also known as resolution. The clause that results from performing resolution on two clauses is called the *resolvent*. It may be that a resolvent contains two identical literals of the same sign. If this happens, we need to delete the copies. If a resolvent contains two unifiable literals, we also need to include the clauses that can obtained by doing the required unification, applying the derived substitution throughout the clause, and deleting identical literals. This process is known as generating the *factors* of the clause. The clause $\{\overline{p(\_x,\_y)}\ \overline{p(a,\_x)}\ q(\_y,\_z)\}$, for instance, contains the unifiable literals $\overline{p(\_x,\_y)}$ and $\overline{p(a,\_x)}$. The unification leads to the binding $\_y = \_x$, $\_x = a$, so that the factor obtained by this unification is $\{\overline{p(a,\_x)}\ q(\_x,\_z)\}$.

Resolution will prove to be the basis of a powerful theorem proving technique, so long as clausal form is rich enough for us to express what we want in it. To show that this is indeed the case, we need the following result.

Theorem 4.1: Normal Form Theorem

Any formula of FOPC is equivalent to a conjunction of formulae each of which is in clausal form.

Proof:
The proof consists of showing how to convert a formula to clausal form. This is very nearly trivial. The trivial part depends on the following easily checked equivalences - (i) $A \rightarrow B \equiv \neg A \vee B$, (ii) $\neg(A \vee B) \equiv \neg A \& \neg B$, (iii) $\neg(A \& B) \equiv \neg A \vee \neg B$, (iv) $\exists\_xA \equiv A|_{<\_x,sk>}$ for some constant sk which has not been used before, (va) $A \vee (B \& C) \equiv (A \vee B) \& (A \vee C)$ and (vb) $(B \& C) \vee A \equiv (B \vee A) \& (C \vee A)$. Systematic application of (i) to (iv) will get rid of $\rightarrow$'s, redistribute $\neg$'s until they are attached to primitive formulae, and get rid of $\exists$'s. The next move is to replace all universally quantified expressions by expressions which are identical except that some unique variable has been substituted for the variable of quantification. We thus convert, say, $\forall\_x(p(\_x) \rightarrow q(\_x))$ to $\forall\_x_1(p(\_x_1) \rightarrow q(\_x_1))$, where $\_x_1$ is some variable that we have not used previously. The formulae produced by this process of *naming apart* will be equivalent to the originals, but the use of different variables for different instances of quantification means that we cannot get into confusions about variable scope if we subsequently decide to move the $\forall$'s around. Once we have got rid of the $\exists$'s, we can in fact move all the $\forall$'s to the front of the formula, and then delete them and agree to treat free variables as though they were universally quantified. We can do this safely because we have already introduced new variables for different instances of quantification, and hence cannot get confused about the scope of variable bindings. At this point repeated application of (va) and (vb) will reorganise things so that the resulting formula is of the form $(A_i \vee \ldots \vee A_n) \& (A_{n+1} \vee \ldots \vee A_m) \& \ldots \& (A_k \vee \ldots \vee A_l)$, where each A_i is either a primitive formula or a primitive formula preceded by $\neg$ (a formula which is either a primitive formula or a primitive formula preceded by $\neg$ is called a *literal*). This final form is what

we are looking for, since any disjunction of literals can be converted into a formula $B_1 \,\&\, ... \,\&\, B_m \rightarrow A_1 \lor ... \lor A_n$, where the Bi are what you get by stripping off the ¬ from the negated elements of the disjunction and the A_i are the elements that were not negated in the first place.

The only difficulty concerns the application of $\exists\_xA \equiv A|_{<x,sk>}$. In cases where the $\exists$ is the only quantifier, it is easy to see that $\exists\_xA$ will have a model if and only if $A|_{<x,sk>}$ has a model, where sk is some constant which does not appear in A. We will ignore the case where _x is not actually free in A, since in that case the quantifier and the substitution are both irrelevant. If $A|_{<x,sk>}$ has a model then clearly $\exists\_xA$ also has one, since the semantics of $\exists$, as derived from the semantics of $\forall$, simply requires us to find a constant which we can substitute in for _x and get a true sentence. Similarly, for $\exists\_xA$ to be true, it must be the case that $\neg\forall\_x\neg A$ is true, and the definition of the semantics of $\forall$ means that this will be the case just so long as we can find a constant which we can substitute in for _x to obtain a true sentence. Since we know that there is such a constant, we can pretend we know what it is, and call it sk. This is fine for formulae where the $\exists$ is the only quantifier, so long as each time we do it we choose a new name, so we in fact need sk_1, sk_2, ... The constants that we use for replacing $\exists$'s are called *Skolem constants*.

This approach will lead to trouble if we try to use it when there are further quantifiers. The formula $\forall\_x\exists\_y(mother(\_y, \_x))$ has a perfectly reasonable interpretation as saying that everyone has a mother. If we try to get rid of the $\exists\_y$ by substituting in a Skolem constant we will end up with something like $\forall\_x$ $(mother(sk_7, \_x))$, which says that sk_7 is a constant which names someone who is everyone's mother, a very different state of affairs. What we need to realise is that when an existential quantifier appears inside the scope of a universal quantifier, the constant that is to be substituted for it may be different for different instantiations of the universally quantified variable. The same sort of argument that we used for the basic case indicates that substituting a Skolem function, rather than a Skolem constant, will give us a formula which has a model exactly when the original has one. Thus $\forall\_x(mother(sk_7(\_x), \_x))$ is what we are looking for. $\forall\_x\exists\_y(mother(\_y, \_x,))$ would be true if no matter what constant c we substituted for _x, the formula $\exists\_y(mother(\_y, c))$ was true. For this to be the case, we have to be able to find for each c a constant sk_c to substitute for _y such that $mother(sk_c, c)$ is true. If there is always such a constant, we can make up the set $\{<sk_1, c_1>, <sk_2, c_2>, ...\}$. This is a function, and is indeed the function we want. Clearly if there were more universal quantifiers outside the existential one, the relevant Skolem function would need more arguments, so that $\forall\_n\forall\_m\exists\_z(\_z = \_m+\_n)$ would have to be turned into $\forall\_n\forall\_m(sk(\_m,\_n) = \_m+\_n)$.

The above argument shows that we can replace formulae with ∃'s in them by ones with Skolem constants and functions, in such a way that the resulting formulae have models if and only if the originals did. This is exactly what we need when using resolution to derive proofs by contradiction. We can derive a proof by contradiction exactly when the negation of the goal has no models. We have now shown that this holds exactly when the corresponding Skolemised clause set has no models, so that all we need for our proof is to show that this clause set is inconsistent. This completes our proof that any formula of FOPC is equivalent to a formula in clausal form ▦

The standard way of using resolution as an inference rule is to try to use it for proofs by contradiction. We add the negation of our real goal to our set of premises, and from this we try to derive a contradiction. If we get one then it cannot be the case that the negation of the goal holds at the same time as the premises, in other words whenever all the premises are true so is the goal itself. We detect the presence of a contradiction when we derive an empty clause, which we will denote as ∅. The only way to get to an empty clause via resolution is to resolve two clauses of the form A → and → A. The first of these says that A is false, the second says that A is true, so they cannot both be satisfied at the same time. We will generally restrict the term *resolution theorem prover* to apply to theorem provers which use resolution in order to derive proofs by contradiction.

Before we prove the completeness of resolution, we will provide a couple of proofs to illustrate it in practice. We will be using the first of these, a problem due to Bob Moore, to illustrate several points about resolution. On this first occasion we are simply using it as an illustration of how to construct a resolution proof by hand.

(1) Resolution proof of Moore's three blocks problem:
The problem concerns a simple blocks world situation. We have three blocks, A, B and C, with A on top of B and B on top of C. A is green, C is not green, and we do not know anything about the colour of B. The task is to show that there is a green block on top of one which is not green. Informally the argument is that B is either green or it is not. If it is then it is a green block on top of one which is not, namely C, and if it isn't then it is one which is not green which has a green one, A, on top of it. The clausal form of the problem is as follows:

(i) {on(A,B)}

(ii) {on(B,C)}

(iii) {green(A)}

(iv) {$\overline{\text{green(C)}}$}

(v) {$\overline{\text{green(\_x)}}$ $\overline{\text{on(\_x,\_y)}}$ green(_y)}.

Resolution proof:

(vi)	{$\overline{\text{on(A,\_y)}}$ green(_y)}	(from (iii) and (v))
(vii)	{green(B)}	(from (i) and (vi))
(viii)	{$\overline{\text{on(B,\_y)}}$ green(_y)}	(from (v) and (vii))
(ix)	{green(C)}	(from (ii) and (ix))
(x)	∅	(from (iv) and (ix))

There are three important things to note about this proof. The first is that we used clause (v) twice during it, once with on(B,C) and once with green(B). There is no reason, in general resolution theorem proving, for a clause not to be used more than once. The second point is that although the proof does show that there is a green block on top of one that is not green, it does not show which block it is. This is fair enough, since there is not enough information in the problem statement for us to work out which it is - it might be A or it might be B. The third point is that the proof required us to make choices about which clauses to resolve. Resolution theorem proving is partly a mechanical process of working out which clauses will resolve and what the resolvent will be, and partly a search task of selecting which of the potential resolutions should actually be performed. We will return to the matter of search strategies for resolution in the next section.

(2) Resolution proof of A → A.

We want to prove A → A for arbitrary A. We know from Theorem 4.1 that for any formula A there is an equivalent set of clauses. Suppose that for A these are $\{P_1^1 P_2^1 \ldots P_{n1}^1\}$, $\{P_1^2 P_2^2 \ldots P_{n2}^2\}$, ... The resolution proof of A → A proceeds by assuming ¬(A → A) and trying to derive a contradiction. ¬(A → A) is the same as A & ¬A, so we need the clausal form of A & ¬A. The clausal form for this is found by taking the union of the sets of clauses for A and ¬A. If the set of clauses for A is as given, the set for ¬A is the set of all $\{\neg P_i^1 \neg P_j^2 \neg P_k^3 \ldots \neg P_1^n\}$ for all combinations of choices of literals from the clauses for A itself, with repetitions deleted. In particular, taking the clauses for the negation of A will give us $\{\neg P_1^1 \neg P_1^2 \neg P_1^3 \ldots\}$, $\{\neg P_2^1 \neg P_2^2 \neg P_2^3 \ldots\}$, $\{\neg P_3^1 \neg P_3^2 \neg P_3^3 \ldots\}$ ..., where if P_j^i was in fact a negative literal then $\neg P_j^i$ is taken to be the positive version.

Resolving the first of these with the clause $\{P_1^1 \ P_2^1 \ P_3^1 \ ...\}$ (which is one of the clauses for A itself) will produce the clause $\{\neg P_1^2 \ \neg P_1^3 \ \neg P_1^4 \ ... \ P_2^1 \ P_3^1 \ P_4^1 \ ...\}$. Resolving this with $\{\neg P_2^1 \ \neg P_2^2 \ \neg P_2^3 \ ...\}$ will produce $\{P_3^1 \ P_4^1 \ P_5^1 \ ... \ \neg P_1^2 \ \neg P_1^3 \ \neg P_1^4 \ ... \ \neg P_2^2 \ \neg P_2^3 \ \neg P_2^4 \ ...\}$. Resolving this in turn with $\{\neg P_3^1 \ \neg P_3^2 \ \neg P_3^3 \ ...\}$ produces $\{P_4^1 \ P_5^1 \ ... \ \neg P_1^2 \ \neg P_1^3 \ \neg P_1^4 \ ... \ \neg P_2^2 \ \neg P_2^3 \ \neg P_2^4 \ ... \ \neg P_3^2 \ \neg P_3^3 \ ...\}$. Eventually, by repeatedly resolving against the positive clauses we get rid of all the P_j^1, to get a clause of the form $\{\neg P_1^2 \ \neg P_1^3 \ \neg P_1^4 \ ... \ \neg P_2^2 \ \neg P_2^3 \ \neg P_2^4 \ ... \ \neg P_3^2 \ \neg P_3^3 \ \neg P_3^4 \ ...\}$. If we resolve this with $\{ P_1^2 \ P_2^2 \ P_3^2 \ ...\}$ and delete all literals which appear in both positive and negative forms in the result, we get $\{\neg P_1^3 \ \neg P_1^4 \ \neg P_1^5 \ ... \ \neg P_2^3 \ \neg P_2^4 \ \neg P_2^5 \ ... \ \neg P_3^3 \ \neg P_3^4 \ \neg P_3^5 \ ...\}$, in other words a clause where all formulae P_i^2 and $\neg P_i^2$ have been deleted. Resolving this with $\{P_1^3 \ P_2^3 \ P_3^3 \ ...\}$ gets rid of all the P_i^3 and $\neg P_i^3$, and so on. Eventually we will remove everything, ending up with the empty clause $\varnothing$ which denotes the presence of a contradiction in the initial set.

Resolution has until very recently been the basis of nearly all work on theorem proving. We look at a recent competitor later on in this chapter, but resolution has had so much attention that we should try to see what its potential shortcomings are and what might be done about them before moving on to any alternatives. The following theorem shows that resolution will enable us to prove anything we want to prove.

Theorem 4.2: Completeness of resolution

If $\Phi_1, ..., \Phi_n$ is an unsatisfiable set of clauses, then $\varnothing$ can be derived from $\Phi_1, ..., \Phi_n$ by repeated applications of resolution.

Proof:
The proof depends on the fact, which we established in Chapter 3, that any unsatisfiable set of formulae of FOPC has a finite unsatisfiable subset. In particular, if $\Phi_1, ..., \Phi_n$ are unsatisfiable then there is a finite set of ground instances of the Φ_i which is unsatisfiable (a *ground instance* of a formula is obtained by consistently substituting constants for all the universally quantified variables appearing in it, so that, for instance, p(a, b) → q(b) is a ground instance of ∀_x∀_y(p(_x, _y) → q(_y))). This result follows fairly directly from Theorem 3.6. Suppose that $\Phi_1, ..., \Phi_n$ are unsatisfiable. Then Theorem 3.6 tells us that they are inconsistent, in other words that $\Phi_1, ..., \Phi_n \vdash \dagger$. If there is such a proof, it must by definition be finite, and hence must be based on at most a finite subset of $\Phi_1, ..., \Phi_n$. No such finite set of formulae can contain more than a finite number of constants. We can therefore replace all formulae containing universal quantifiers by conjunctions over this finite set of constants without affecting the

validity of the proof. We now have a finite set of ground instances of the formulae Φ_i from which we can derive †, and hence (using Theorem 3.6 in the other direction) we have an unsatisfiable set of ground instances of the Φ_i.

Problems involving finite sets of ground formulae can be regarded as problems of propositional calculus. Any proof involving such a set can be written according to the rules of propositional calculus. We can therefore prove meta-theorems *about* such proofs using the proof theory and semantics of propositional calculus. This technique of proving properties of predicate calculus by showing how to reduce them to properties of finite sets of ground formulae is often referred to as *lifting*. In the current case, we are going to show that if we have an unsatisfiable finite set of ground clauses then we can reduce them to ∅ using resolution. The demonstration of this point will make use of the fact that such sets can be discussed using the semantic theory associated with propositional calculus. The fact that any unsatisfiable set of clauses can be replaced by a finite set of ground clauses will then enable us to lift the result to the general case of arbitrary sets of clauses.

We start, then, by considering a finite unsatisfiable set of propositional formulae $F_1, ..., F_n$. These will contain a finite set of proposition letters. Suppose there are three of them, say p_1, p_2, p_3. We can construct the following *semantic tree* (not to be confused with semantic tableaux) to represent all possible valuations of these:

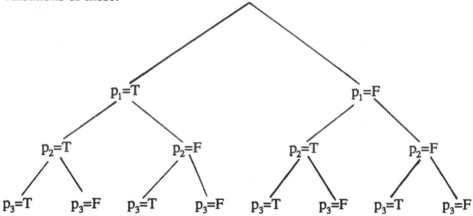

Each branch of this tree represents a family of valuations. The leftmost branch, for instance, represents the set of all valuations which assign T to each of p_1, p_2, p_3. Clearly if $F_1, ..., F_n$ had any models at all they would have been represented by branches of this tree. We can work out whether a set of formulae of propositional calculus has a model by setting up a semantic tree for its proposition letters, and inspecting it to see whether it contains any branches which represent models for it. In particular, if a set of clauses is unsatisfiable, each branch of its associated semantic tree will contradict one of the clauses. Suppose for instance we had the following set of clauses, derived from $p \rightarrow (q \rightarrow r)$, $p \rightarrow q$ and $\neg(p \rightarrow r)$: (i) $\{\bar{p}\ \bar{q}\ r\}$, (ii) $\{\bar{p}\ q\}$, (iii) $\{p\}$ and (iv) $\{\bar{r}\}$. The following fragment of the semantic tree for this set of clauses contains enough information to rule out each of them in turn:

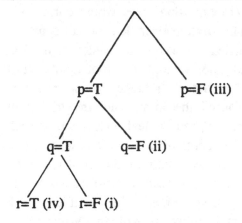

This tree has been annotated to show which branches rule out which clauses, with the leftmost branch ruling out clause (iv) and so on. The interesting thing about it for present purposes is that it contains a node each of whose children provides the information required for cancelling out some family of valuations. Adding r=T cancels one family by showing that they are not models of clause (iv), adding r=F cancels another by showing that they are not models of clause (i). In other words, once we have decided to give both p and q the value T, the value assigned to r becomes irrelevant, since the clause that we would get by resolving between (i) and (iv) on the literal r is already contradicted. If we remove the leaves of the tree which assign values to r, we obtain the following tree:

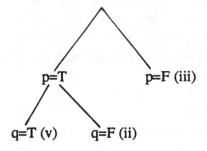

The annotation of q=T with (v) marks the fact that the values p=T, q=T rule out the resolvent $\{\bar{p}\ \bar{q}\}$ of (iv) and (i) with respect to r (we will call this resolvent (v)). We are clearly in just the same situation as we were before, with a tree with two terminal nodes which between them rule out two clauses and in so doing show that it is irrelevant whether a specific proposition letter is given the value T or F. In the present case it is the letter q which is irrelevant, and which can be eliminated by resolving (ii) and (v).

This example shows how, given a closed semantic tree, we can gradually eliminate nodes until the tree becomes empty, using steps which correspond exactly to resolutions between clauses. An illustrative example is not, of course, a proof that the procedure can always be carried out. The main results we need in order to convert our example into a general proof are that any unsatisfiable set of clauses has a finite closed semantic tree; that each branch of such a tree constitutes a contradiction of one of the clauses; that in any such tree there will always be at least one node both of whose children are leaf nodes, and as such each embody the information to complete the contradiction of a clause; and that the act of removing these two nodes corresponds exactly to the act of resolving on the clauses which are defeated by the leaf nodes. Each of these results can be obtained straightforwardly by generalising from our specific example, a task which we leave to our more zealous readers. For now we will simply recap how the arguments above prove that resolution is a complete inference rule for FOPC.

The first step is to show that any unsatisfiable set of clauses corresponds to an unsatisfiable finite set of ground clauses. We then argue that finite sets of ground clauses can be interpreted as sets of clauses of propositional calculus. Unsatisfiable sets of propositional clauses have finite closed semantic trees. $\emptyset$ can be derived from any set of clauses with a finite closed semantic tree by resolution. Hence $\emptyset$ can be derived from any unsatisfiable set of clauses of FOPC by finding a suitable set of ground instances and then finding an appropriate reduction order ▦.

It must be recognised, however, that the proof that there is a way of deriving $\emptyset$ from such a set gives very little indication of how to actually find it. Both finding a suitable set of ground instances and finding an appropriate reduction order are extremely open tasks. The next few sections of this chapter show how to perform the process reasonably efficiently.

4.3.1 *Search strategies in standard resolution*

A very substantial proportion of the work on resolution theorem provers has been concerned with devising good search strategies. There is no universal agreement as to which are the best strategies - almost certainly, as with most such problems, the choice will depend on characteristics of the kind of problem being solved as much as on the general properties of resolution.

The proposed strategies fall into two groups. Some of them, *restriction strategies*, put restrictions on the clauses that may be considered for resolutions - at least one of the inputs to a resolution must be from the initial set, for instance, or at least one must be descended from the negation of the goal. These restrictions are intended to improve performance by cutting down the number of possibilities that need to be considered, and hence actually pruning the search space of possible resolutions. The other group of strategies, *order strategies*, constrains the order in which the possibilities are considered - try resolutions whose input clauses have fewer literals first, for instance. Many strategies of each kind have been proposed. Rather than attempt a complete survey here, we will simply consider one example of each type to give the reader a feel for what is going on, and leave pointers to the literature for anyone who wants to follow the matter further. We will follow the two particular search strategies with a general change of representation which should improve the effectivenesss of almost any search strategy.

4.3.2 *Set of support*
Set of support is an example of a strategy which cuts the search space by putting constraints on the clauses that are allowed to be used in resolutions. If the negation of the goal is inconsistent with the premises, any proof should involve at least some of the clauses that are derived from the negation of the goal (if it does not, it means that the premises themselves were inconsistent). It turns out that we can insist that every step of the proof involves either a clause from the negation of the goal or one which was the result of an earlier resolution. The proof we gave earlier for Moore's three blocks problem was a set of support proof. The first step involved the sole clause which resulted from the negation of the goal, and all further steps used the resolvent of some previous step. Set of support puts a limit on the combinations of clauses which we need to search to see if they combine resolvable literals, so that it cuts down the number of possibilities to be considered if we are using something like breadth-first search to explore the space of possible moves.

We can show that using set of support preserves the completeness of resolution, so that we can use it without worrying that something which is valid is unprovable.

Theorem 4.3: Completeness of set of support resolution

Proof:
We assume that the premises without the addition of the goal are consistent. It is therefore the addition of the negation of the goal that makes the entire set of clauses inconsistent. In this case, there is at least one step in the derivation of $\emptyset$ which involves resolving something with one of the clauses in the set of support, i.e. the set of clauses derived from the negated goal. Suppose $C_{support}$ is a clause from the set of support which is involved in the derivation of $\emptyset$. Consider the clause which is resolved with $C_{support}$, and in particular consider the literal in this clause on which the resolution is performed. This literal must be a descendant of some literal in a clause in the original set corresponding to the negated goal and the premises. We know, then, that there is a literal in a clause somewhere in the original set of clauses which resolves with $C_{support}$, since the way that literals descend from earlier literals guarantees that if the descendant resolves with something then the ancestor must also, since the descendant is either identical to the ancestor or is more specialised than it.

We therefore take the clause which contains something which resolves with a literal in $C_{support}$, and start our proof by resolving these two clauses. If this produces the empty clause, then we have clearly generated a set of support proof. If not we can inspect the clauses from which the one which we are resolving with $C_{support}$ was originally derived. We pick the one which contains a literal that was resolved with something in $C_{support}$. If this was a member of the original set we resolve immediately against $C_{support}$, otherwise we trace back through its ancestors until we find something from the original set which will resolve with $C_{support}$ and use that. We can work our way like this through all the ancestors of clauses that appear in the given proof, making sure that we always resolve on some ancestor which is from the original set. The result will be a set of support proof ▦

To see how this works out in practice, consider the derivation of b & d from a, a $\rightarrow$ b, c, c $\rightarrow$ d. The clausal form of this is $\{a\}$, $\{\overline{a}\ b\}$, $\{c\}$, $\{\overline{c}\ d\}$, $\{\overline{b}\ \overline{d}\}$. There are several derivations of $\emptyset$ from this. We consider one which does not satisfy the set of support conditions:

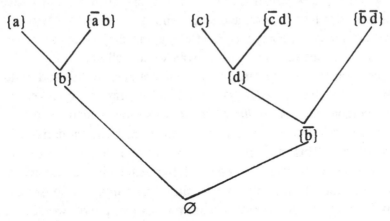

We can convert this to a set of support proof as follows. We see that the derivation of $\{\bar{b}\}$ is the only step which directly involves a member of the set of support (which just consists of $\{\bar{b}\ \bar{d}\}$). We consider the other parent of this, namely $\{d\}$ and see that it inherits, from $\{\bar{c}\ d\}$, the literal which will later be resolved with something from $\{\bar{b}\ \bar{d}\}$. We therefore start by resolving this directly against the clause from the set of support, deriving $\{\bar{c}\ \bar{b}\}$. We now resolve this with $\{c\}$ to get $\{\bar{b}\}$, then this against $\{\bar{a}\ b\}$ to get $\{\bar{a}\}$, and this with $\{a\}$ to get $\varnothing$.

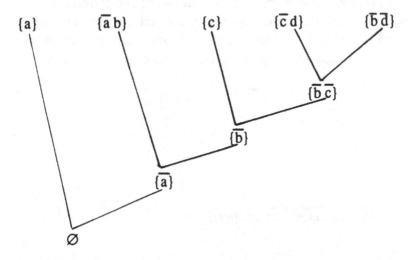

Set of support roughly corresponds to backward chaining. It is reasonable to think of a resolution as a step on the way to proving the inconsistency of the base clauses invoked to date. Using set of support, then, amounts to starting with clauses derived from the negation of the goal and concentrating on proving that they are inconsistent with some relevant subset of the clauses derived from the premises. In the example just given, the natural way to try to prove $\{\bar{b}\ \bar{d}\}$ is to start by finding some clause which resolves with it, and then finding a clause which resolves with this latter clause, and so on until you get to ∅. There are in this case a number of ways of applying this strategy, but they all lead directly to proofs, so it does not matter very much which way we actually go.

There have been proposals for a large number of strategies of this sort, putting constraints on the conditions under which a clause may be involved in a resolution. One notable example is *linear input* resolution, which requires that every resolution has as one of its inputs a clause from the basic set derived from the problem statement. This strategy has the advantage that it is safe when supplemented by a check to ensure that no resolution results in a clause which is one of its own ancestors. In fact resolution using linear input to constrain the search space is nothing but the backward chaining theorem prover we described in the previous section, and which, as we noted there, forms the basis of the programming language PROLOG. The main problem with linear input is that it is incomplete. This is inevitable, given that no theorem prover for FOPC can be both safe and complete, and we have already noted that linear input resolution is safe. To see that it is incomplete, we consider all the possible moves in an attempt to solve the three blocks problem using linear input as the restriction strategy. We will demonstrate the various options by starting with the five basic clauses as shown below, and showing what resolutions can be performed.

The following diagram shows the clauses that are derived when the statement of the three blocks problem is converted to clausal form. Laying them out in this way makes it easier to trace what is going on during the course of a proof.

{on(a,b)}   {on(b,c)}

{$\overline{\text{on}(\_x,\_y)}$ $\overline{\text{green}(\_x)}$ green(y)}

{green(a)}   {$\overline{\text{green(c)}}$}

We will investigate all the possible resolutions that can be arrived at under the restriction to linear input. There are four possible starting points, corresponding to the resolutions between on(b,c) and $\overline{on(\_x,\_y)}$, between on(a,b) and $\overline{on(\_x,\_y)}$, between green(a) and $\overline{green(\_x)}$, and between green(c) and green(_y). We will see that each of these leads to the construction of clauses containing literals which can in turn be resolved with literals in input clauses, but that none of these starts a chain of resolutions which ends with ∅.

(1) The first attempt starts by resolving on {on(b,c)} and the first literal of {$\overline{on(\_x,\_y)}$ $\overline{green(\_x)}$ green(y)}. This produces {$\overline{green(b)}$ green(c)} as its resolvent, which in turn resolves with {$\overline{green(c)}$} to produce {$\overline{green(b)}$}. This fails to resolve with any base clause, so the attempt starting with {$\overline{on(\_x,\_y)}$ $\overline{green(\_x)}$ green(_y)} comes to a dead end. Note that once we chose to start with this clause we had no choices about how to proceed, so this really is a dead end.

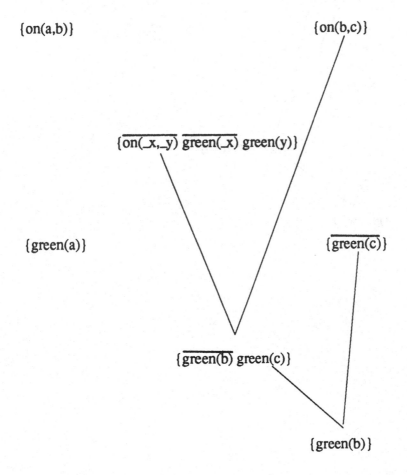

{on(a,b)}   {on(b,c)}

{$\overline{on(\_x,\_y)}$ $\overline{green(\_x)}$ green(y)}

{green(a)}   {$\overline{green(c)}$}

{$\overline{green(b)}$ green(c)}

{green(b)}

(2) Starting with {on(a,b)} and the first literal of {$\overline{\text{on}(\_x,\_y)}$ $\overline{\text{green}(\_x)}$ green($\_y$)}, we construct {$\overline{\text{green}(a)}$ green(b)} and then {green(b)}. {green(b)} fails to resolve with anything, so again we are at a dead end.

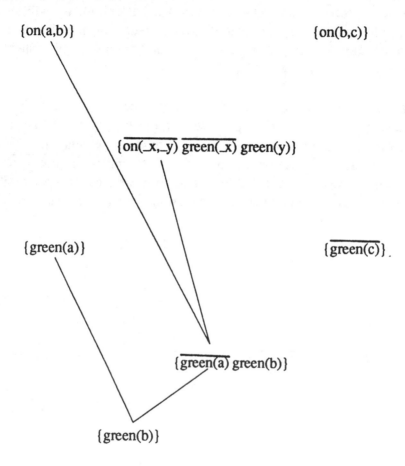

(3) From {green(a)} and the second literal of {$\overline{on(\_x,\_y)}$ $\overline{green(\_x)}$ green(_y)} we get {$\overline{green(a,\_y)}$ green(_y)}, followed by {green(b)}. This is the same dead end as last time.

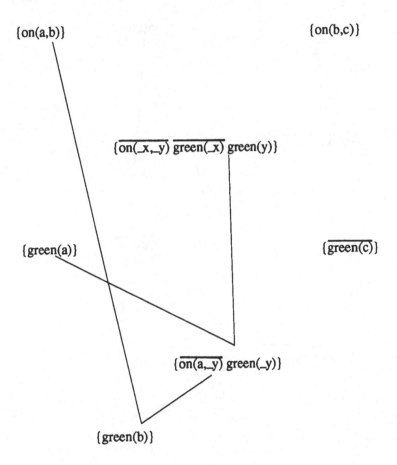

(4) Starting with {$\overline{\text{green(c)}}$} and the third literal of {$\overline{\text{on(\_x,\_y)}}$ $\overline{\text{green(\_x)}}$ green(_y)} we get {$\overline{\text{on(\_x,c)}}$ $\overline{\text{green(\_x)}}$}, and then on to {$\overline{\text{green(b)}}$}. Yet another dead end.

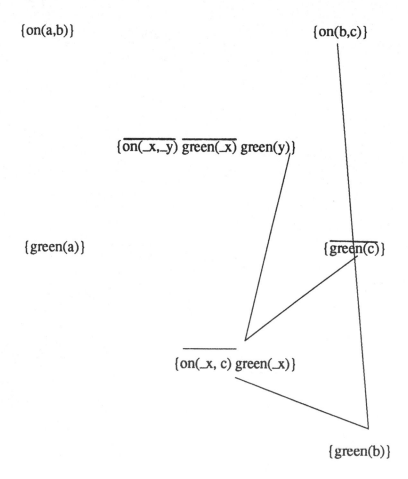

{on(a,b)}   {on(b,c)}

{$\overline{\text{on(\_x,\_y)}}$ $\overline{\text{green(\_x)}}$ green(y)}

{green(a)}   {$\overline{\text{green(c)}}$}

{$\overline{\text{on(\_x, c)}}$ green(_x)}

{green(b)}

We have now considered all the possible starting points, and all possible ways of continuing them according to the linear input restriction, and have come to a dead end every time. Yet we know that there is a derivation of $\emptyset$ from this set of clauses, so we have provided a fairly simple example illustrating the incompleteness of resolution with the linear input restriction strategy. Loveland (1978) gives a very detailed survey of restriction strategies for resolution, including proofs concerning their completeness or otherwise. For our purposes it is sufficient to be aware of what such strategies look like, to realise that we generally have a choice between completeness and safety, and that it sometimes happens that if we combine two strategies each of which was complete we may end up with a strategy which is incomplete.

4.3.3 *Unit preference*

The restriction strategies cut down the number of resolutions which need to be considered at any one time. There will still, however, generally be more than one possibility to consider, and hence some way of choosing which to try first is required. The two simplest choices are just to proceed breadth-first or depth-first. As usual, breadth-first search guarantees that a proof will be found if one exists, but may take a long time to find it, whereas depth-first search will sometimes find a proof quickly and sometimes go off down blind alleys from which it never returns. These ordering strategies are generally used with one or more restriction strategies of the type considered above. Breadth-first search, then, is only guaranteed to find a proof if one exists under the chosen restriction strategy - you cannot use breadth-first search with, say, linear input as a restriction strategy, and hope to find a solution to the three blocks problem.

It does not seem possible to use a heuristic search algorithm such as A* to improve the efficiency of a resolution theorem prover because there is no reasonable way of estimating how far some partial solution is from being complete. Furthermore, it is important when trying to include a heuristic component into a search problem to make sure that the costs of ordering choices according to the heuristic do not outweigh its potential benefits. The most widely used ordering principle for resolution theorem provers is the principle of *unit preference*. By and large, the result of a resolution step is a clause whose length is the sum of the lengths of the contributing clauses minus two. It may be possible to delete some literals from the resolvent if there are any exact repeats, in which case the length of the resolvent will be less than this, but in general it will be this long. If one of the input clauses contains exactly one literal, then, the resolvent will be shorter than the other one. If they both contain exactly one literal then the resolvent will in fact be $\varnothing$, but at any rate it will be nearer to $\varnothing$ than the longer of the input clauses is. This is a very simple measure to obtain, and hence to use as a guide when choosing which clause to resolve on. Furthermore, if we make sure that we never resolve on a clause which is identical to one of its own ancestors then this strategy will not harm the completeness of our system if the restriction strategy we employ is itself complete. Any resolution involving a unit clause can only have a finite number of distinct unit descendants, and hence delaying a breadth-first search of non-unit descendants cannot delay them for an indefinitely long period. We therefore see that unit preference is intuitively likely to provide an improvement over basic breadth-first search, without losing the benefits of completeness relative to the chosen restriction strategy.

4.3.4 *Connection graph resolution theorem proving*

We have seen that we can improve the performance of breadth-first resolution
theorem provers by using a restriction strategy to cut down the search space, and
then possibly by using an ordering strategy to improve the success rate of
searching through the remaining set of options. To get any further improvements
in performance we can continue to try to get better restriction and ordering
strategies, or we can try to improve the basic mechanisms. The most obvious
implementation technique to improve performance involves constructing an
index of potentially resolvable literals. In the discussion so far we have talked of
choosing from among all the potential resolutions, but we have not said anything
about how to work out what the potential resolutions are. The obvious first step
is to construct a table of positive and negative literals involving particular
predicates, with pointers back to the clauses those literals appear in and their
positions within them. Thus for the three blocks problem we might initially have
the following table:

Name/arity	Positive literals	Negative literals
on/2:	on(a,b) (ii, 1),	on(_x,_y) (v, 1)
	on(b,c) (iii, 1)	
green/1:	green(a) (i, 1),	green(c) (iv, 1)
	green(_y) (v, 3)	green(_x) (v, 2)

This table can easily be constructed by simply inspecting each literal in each
clause and seeing where to add it. There is no search involved, just a single pass
through all the clauses. If the problem is in fact set in terms of formulae of FOPC
which are converted to clausal form as described in the proof of Theorem 4.1,
then the index can be constructed as part of the process of conversion. Once we
have such a table, it is a trivial matter to find potential resolutions - we just go
along the rows of positive and negative literals for each predicate. In the current
case we see that we have potential resolutions between the first literal of clause
(ii) and the first literal of clause (v), between the first literal of clause (iii) and the
first of clause (v), the first of clause (i) and the first of clause (iv), and so on. As it
happens this last resolution will not in fact work, since it would entail unifying
green(a) and green(c), but at least we have a very straightforward way of finding
things which have a good chance of resolving with each other.

The table is maintained as new clauses are generated by applications of
resolution. As soon as a new clause is created, its positive and negative literals
are compared with the corresponding negative and positive entries in the table to
see what resolutions it might possibly contribute to, and then entries for its own

literals are added to the table. It is important to do it in this order to avoid making the same suggestion more than once.

Using this kind of table can improve the performance of a resolution theorem prover by ensuring that time is not wasted in searching for potential resolutions. More importantly, though, it leads naturally to a radically different representation of the whole problem. Kowalski (1975) pointed out that representing the set of clauses as a graph, where the nodes are clauses and the connections are links between resolvable literals, can lead to quite dramatic improvements. Representing a set of clauses as a *connection graph* leads to two different kinds of benefit. Firstly, it gives you a view of the problem space as a whole, so that you can easily see parts of the space which can be pruned without further exploration, and so that you can sometimes tell in advance that some problem is going to be insoluble without going through all the steps of trying to find a solution. Secondly, the use of the graph makes it possible to avoid ever doing any work twice. Given that resolution theorem proving is inherently a search task in which the steps that lead to a dead end may easily be repeated on a later branch of the search, the chance of avoiding repeated work is very tempting.

We will start by considering the connection graph just as a way of representing the clause set in a standard resolution theorem prover, and work our way gradually to the refinements. The very first thing is to look at an example proof.

Connection graph proof for the three blocks problem.

The initial graph for the three blocks problem is as follows:

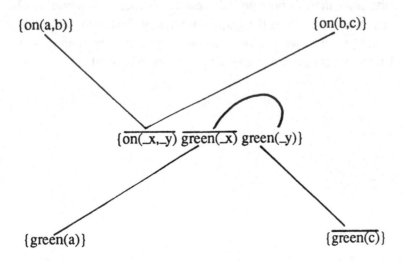

We can create this graph in just the same way that we created the index described above - the links are little more than an alternative, slightly more concrete, way of thinking about the table entries. Processing is now just a matter of resolving on the links shown and adding the resolvent to the graph. The resolvent inherits all the links connecting its literals to other clauses, so that after resolving on, say, the link between on($\_$x,$\_$y) and on(a,b) the graph would look as follows:

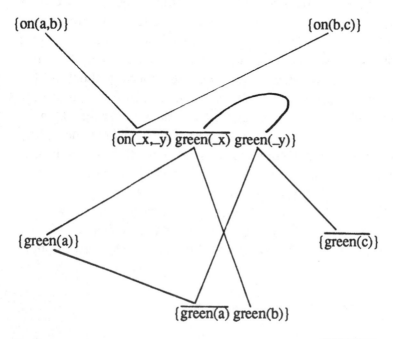

Having resolved on the link between on(a,b) and on($\_$x,$\_$y) we delete this link from the graph, and since there is now no link between on(a,b) and anything else we can in fact delete this clause from the graph completely. Resolving on the link between green(a) and green(a), we get the following graph (where clauses which have literals which are not connected to anything have been deleted).

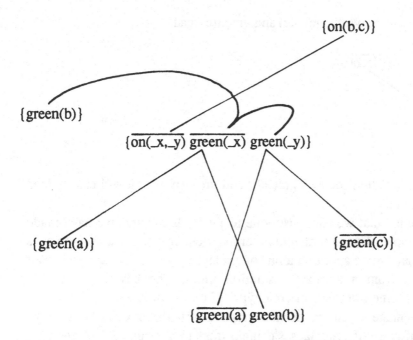

Resolving on the link between on(b,c) and $\overline{\text{on}(\_x,\_y)}$, and then deleting clauses with literals which are not connected to anything, leads to

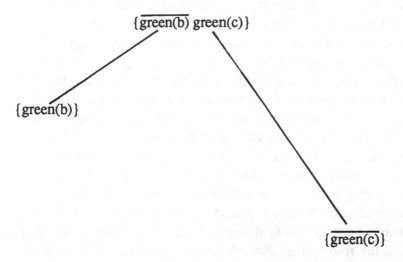

Notice how the graph has collapsed after the removal of the last link to $\overline{\text{on}(\_x,\_y)}$. Once the last link to this literal is removed, the clause in the centre of the graph can be removed, at which point literals in several other clauses also lose their last links so that the clauses containing them can be removed.

Resolving on the link between green(c) and $\overline{\text{green(c)}}$ leads to

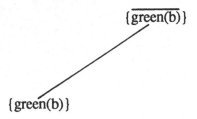

$\{\overline{\text{green(b)}}\}$

$\{\text{green(b)}\}$

This contains a single link between green(b) and $\overline{\text{green(b)}}$ which will clearly lead to the derivation of $\varnothing$.

There is little in what we have just done to justify the claims we have made for connection graphs. The presentation in terms of changes to the arcs and nodes of a graph may have some appeal in terms of readability, but essentially the proof was no different from a standard resolution proof. The advantages of the connection graph come from two different types of observation.

The first advantage of the connection graph is that the inheritance of links guarantees that if two different clauses contain links to the same literal, then the effects of any resolutions involving that literal will be inherited by both the parents (all the parents if there are more than two).

The second advantage of using connection graphs is that if there are methods for detecting clauses that can never be involved in successful derivations of $\varnothing$, we may be able to propagate their application throughout the graph. Two specific cases concern *tautologies* and *pure literals*. A tautology is a clause with the same literal appearing both positively and negatively. It is clear that if there is a derivation of $\varnothing$ which involves resolving with a clause containing a tautology, then there must also be one which does not involve this clause. Suppose the literal that appears both negatively and positively is p. To arrive at $\varnothing$, we have to get rid of each occurrence. To do this, we will have to perform resolutions on clauses which involve p and $\overline{\text{p}}$. Any extra literals which are introduced as a result of the resolutions which get rid of p and $\overline{\text{p}}$ from the tautology will have to be removed by further resolutions. We could instead arrive at $\varnothing$ by simply resolving the clauses that were used to get rid of the occurrences of p directly with each other, and reducing the resolvent of this resolution as we did in the original derivation. Consider, for example, the following proof, involving resolution with a tautology:

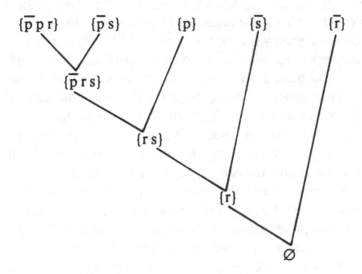

This can be replaced by a proof which ignores the tautology as follows:

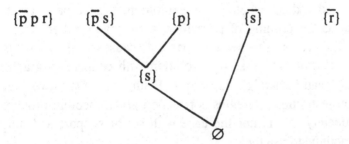

Since any proof involving a tautology can be replaced by one not involving it, we can delete any tautologies from the graph. More sensibly, in fact, we can simply not add them when we are building it.

Pure literals are ones with no links to them. If a literal has no links, then it can never be removed from the clause in which it appears, nor from any descendant of that clause. There is therefore no point in ever doing a resolution on a clause which contains a pure literal, since it is never going to be possible to get rid of the literal, and hence never going to be possible to get to Ø. We can therefore delete any clause containing a pure literal from the graph. Deleting a clause from the graph, however, entails deleting any links connected to its literals. This can quite easily make a literal in some other clause become pure, so that this clause can be deleted in turn, with possible further knock-on effects. This sort of gangrene, which is very reminiscent of the constraint propagation in Waltz'

(1975) filtering algorithm for interpreting line drawings, can have drastic effects on the graph. It is this effect that led to the dramatic simplification of the graph in the three blocks problem at the point when the literal $\overline{on(\_x,\_y)}$ became pure.

It is possible to make up examples in which enormous portions of the graph are deleted after a single resolution. In most practical problems, the benefits are certainly noticeable, without generally being on quite the scale that can be obtained with carefully chosen examples. There are further advantages to be gained by using a connection graph representation. If, for instance, we impose a direction on the links in the graph, by working outwards from the set of support and making links point in the direction leading away from it, we can often make definitive statements about termination of the proof procedure before we actually embark on it. If the graph is directed in this way then we know, for instance, that if it is acyclic the search for a proof is bound to terminate. Note that this is not a way of making the proof procedure both safe and complete, since as we know already it cannot be, but it does work for quite a large number of cases. The existence of this test for termination depends on the fact that the connection graph makes the entire search space visible. The improvements in performance stem from the fact that, with the search space visible, it is possible to make decisions about when, and indeed whether, to explore particular parts of it. Deletion strategies such as the pruning of pure literals are really rather drastic steps, since they act directly on the search space. Because of this, proofs concerning the completeness or otherwise of resolution with connection graphs are much harder to obtain than for straight resolution. Eisinger (1987) shows that for some of the common restriction strategies connection graph theorem provers are not complete. Fortunately this is not the case with set of support and unit preference, so we can continue to use them.

4.3.5 *Problems with resolution*

Connection graphs seem in some sense to be the last word in resolution based theorem proving. Once we have pared the process down to choice of a link, resolution on that link, and creation of a resolvent with all its links already in place, there seems to be very little scope for improvement. There are, however, still some aspects of theorem proving with this kind of system which are unattractive. Since the connection graph provides the best currently available approach to resolution, and since it is hard to see where any further improvements are to come from, the only hope of circumventing the remaining problems is to try something other than resolution. Before we can see what alternatives we might consider, we will have to see what the problems are.

The first irritating thing about resolution, and particularly about connection graph resolution, is that it is unnatural. You get fairly used to it, of course, just as you do to working with any formal system. Nonetheless it never comes to feel like the way that you would solve the problem yourself, and it never becomes easy to read through a resolution proof. If a resolution theorem prover is to form part of a system which needs to explain its reasoning to its users, it will almost certainly be necessary to post-process its proofs to get them into a shape which is comprehensible even to an experienced user. Traces of connection graph theorem provers at work are almost impossible to follow, even for their designers. It would be much better, then, if we could find some form of inference engine which worked in a way that was closer to our introspections on how we ourselves work, not least because its proofs would be that much easier for us to follow.

The second point at which there seems to be something wrong with resolution is the conversion to clausal form. This is quite a lot of work, a lot of which is often unnecessary, and it leads to the destruction of any structure the original problem statement may have had. It might even be true to say that it is the conversion to clausal form that makes resolution proofs so hard to follow, since the relation of particular clauses to the original statement can often be quite hard to unravel. The following very simple example illustrates both the unintuitive nature of resolution and the inefficiency introduced by conversion to clausal form:

Resolution proof of r from s, s → p ∨ q, p ∨ q → r:

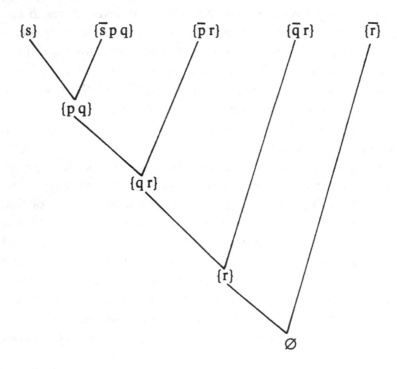

This is far less straightforward than simply applying MP twice, to get p ∨ q from s and s → p ∨ q and then r from p ∨ q and p ∨ q → r. The reason is that the conversion of p ∨ q → r to clausal form breaks it into two clauses ({p̄ r} and {q̄ r}), which each have to be resolved to reduce the occurrence of {p q} which results from applying resolution to s and {s̄ p q}. Furthermore, the normal result of resolving {q̄ r} and {q r} would be {r r}. We have chosen to use a factor of this, namely {r}, instead, since the full result would not have led to ∅. The alternative to resolution that we are looking for, then, should probably avoid reduction to a normal form in which the original problem structure is destroyed. The best current candidate is Bibel's (1982) *connection method*. The similarity of the names of the two approaches is unfortunate, but it reflects the fact that they both make use of graphical representations to make the problem structure more visible and accessible.

4.4 Connection method theorem proving

The connection method is an intricate encoding of the sort of reasoning embodied in tableau proofs. The aim is to demonstrate the validity or inconsistency of a set of formulae by considering the constraints that they put on the world, and thence showing that in every world in which the constraints are obeyed some other formula is constrained to be true or false. Some of the work that is done by connection method theorem provers is similar to work done by resolution based theorem provers. The essential difference is that resolution theorem provers have to keep constructing new clauses in their attempt to derive $\emptyset$, whereas connection method theorem provers work very largely with the original set of formulae, but need to build structures to keep track of their view of the world.

Many of the original papers on the connection method are very opaque. We will try to lead up to the more difficult aspects of the technique fairly gently, in the hope that when we do get to the difficult parts they will at least be in a reasonable context. We will start by considering a very simple problem, just to illustrate the general idea. The problem is to show that r follows from p, $p \rightarrow q$ and $q \rightarrow r$. We deal with this, as with resolution, by showing that the set $\{p\}$, $\{\bar{r}\}$, $\{\bar{p}\ q\}$, $\{\bar{q}\ r\}$ is inconsistent. We start by writing the set of formulae as a matrix, where columns represent disjunctions:

$$
\begin{array}{cccc}
\overline{} & \overline{} & \overline{} & \overline{} \\
p & p & q & r \\
\\
\\
 & q & r &
\end{array}
$$

Clearly the original set of formulae can only be consistent if it is possible to find a consistent set of formulae by taking one entry from each column. The aim, then, is to show that there is no such set. We show this by showing that all attempts to construct one are doomed. Suppose we work across the matrix from left to right. We have to pick p from the first column. In the second column we have a choice between $\bar{p}$ and q. We clearly cannot choose $\bar{p}$, since this would give us both p and $\bar{p}$. We therefore choose q, so we have now constructed a partial path $\{p\ q\}$ through the matrix. In the third column we have a choice between $\bar{q}$ and r. Again we cannot choose $\bar{q}$, so the only possibility for extending the path is to add r. In the fourth column, the only option is $\bar{r}$. The only path which gets as far as the fourth column, then, cannot be consistently extended to include an entry from it, so there are no consistent paths, and hence the original set was inconsistent.

This illustrates the basic idea of the connection method. We represent the problem as a matrix where horizontal movement denotes conjunction and vertical movement denotes disjunction, and try to show that every *path* through this matrix contains a *connection*, i.e. a pair of formulae one of which is the negation of the other. The method has to be extended in three ways. (i) It has to be extended to cover non-clausal formulae. (ii) It has to be extended to deal with quantified formulae. (iii) Simplifications similar to the pruning strategies of connection graph resolution have to be developed. We will take these one at a time.

4.4.1 *Connection matrices for non-clausal formulae*

In the original example, the entries in the matrix were all literals. To allow for non-clausal formulae, we permit matrices to have other matrices as entries. The notion of a path extends easily to matrices whose entries are themselves matrices - if you want to extend a path by adding a matrix to it, you have to find a path through the matrix. We examine this extended version in the context of a problem which would lead to considerable redundancy with pure resolution. The problem is to show that t follows from (p & q) V (r & s) and (p V r) → t). We show embedded matrices inside boxes

$$
\boxed{\begin{array}{c} p\,q \\ \\ r\,s \end{array}} \qquad \boxed{\begin{array}{c} \overline{p}\,\overline{r} \\ \\ t \end{array}} \qquad \overline{t}
$$

If we examine the possible paths through this, we see that they all contain connections:

(i) Path is p q $\overline{p}$ $\overline{r}$. Connection is between p and $\overline{p}$.

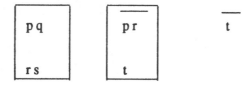

(ii) Path is p q t t̄. Connection is between t and t̄.

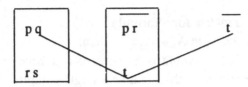

(iii) Path is r s p̄ r̄. Connection is between r and r̄.

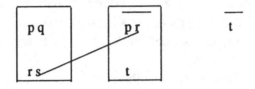

(iv) r s t t̄. Connection is between t and t̄.

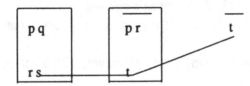

We can make the connection method for propositional calculus more concrete by providing the algorithms for constructing a matrix and searching it for connection-free paths. The algorithm for constructing a matrix makes use of the notion of the *sign* of a formula. The sign of a formula is one of the letters T and F, indicating whether the formula is expected to be true or false. To construct a matrix for seeing whether some set of formulae is inconsistent, we convert the set to a single conjunction, assign it the sign T and then go through the following procedure.

Fig. 4.5 Algorithm for constructing matrices

To build a connection method matrix for a formula F:
  (1) If the formula is of the form A_1 & A_2 & ... then:
      (1.1) If the sign of the formula is F, construct matrices for A_1,
      A_2, ... with sign F and write them out as a single column.
      (1.2) Otherwise construct matrices for A_1, A_2, ... with sign T and
      write them out as a row.
  (2) If the formula is of the form A_1 ∨ A_2 ∨ ... then:
      (2.1) If the sign of the formula is F, construct matrices for A_1,
      A_2, ... with sign F and write them out as a single row.
      (2.2) Otherwise construct matrices for A_1, A_2, ... with sign T and
      write them out as a column.
  (3) If the formula is of the form B → C, then:
      (3.1) If the sign of the formula is F, construct a matrix for B with
      sign F and one for C with sign T and write them out as a row.
      (3.2) Otherwise construct a matrix for B with sign F and one for
      C with sign T and write them out as a column.
  (4) If the formula is ¬A with one of the signs, construct a matrix for
  A with the other sign.
  (5) If the formula is atomic, simply write it down, with a bar over the
  top if its sign is F.

Applying this algorithm to the problem given above would lead to the following
sequence of steps:

(i)   [(p & q) ∨ (r & s)] & [(p ∨ r) → t] : T   t : F

(ii)   p & q : T   p ∨ r : F   t : F
         r & s : T   t : T

(iii)   p : T, q : T   p : F, q : F   t : F
         r : T, r : T   t : T

Having constructed the matrix, we have to check that each path through it
contains a connection.

Fig. 4.6 Basic connection method algorithm

To check that every path through a matrix contains a connection:
(1) Construct an initial empty path.
(2) If the matrix is non-empty, pick a column from it. Delete it from
the matrix, and for each element of the column do the following.
    (2.1) Add the element to the path. If the path now contains a
    connection, move on to the next element (a path contains a
    connection if it contains the same formula twice, once with a bar
    on top and once without).
    (2.2) Try to show that all paths extending the given path through
    the matrix with the current column deleted contain connections.
(3) If the matrix is empty, report that there is a path with no
connections.

This basic algorithm is as simple as you could ask for. The main complexities are both hidden at the start of step (2). The first is an implementation point. The algorithm contains two matrix operations, namely deleting a column and inspecting each element of a column. In any standard representation of a matrix, deleting a column would entail making a copy of the matrix with the given column missing. It is perfectly possible to construct a representation for matrices in which deletion of columns can be done without copying, but it does need to be considered carefully. Without appropriate care at this point, Bibel's (1982) claim that the connection method is far less wasteful of space than the connection graph is simply not true. The second point concerns the choice of which column to work through next. The order the columns are considered in makes no difference in the long run, so long as some sort of 'fair' strategy is followed to ensure that no column gets ignored forever. Nonetheless, it can have quite an impact on the speed with which a proof is found, as can be seen by considering the following matrix.

t	p	a	d	$\bar{t}$
	q	b	e	
	r	c	f	

If we work through this matrix from left to right, we will have to consider 27 different paths, each of which contains the same connection between t and $\bar{t}$. If we simply start with the first column, and then choose the last column for the next stage, we only need to consider one path, since all of them will be extensions of the same partial path, which is known to contain a connection. We see, therefore, that it is essential to make sensible decisions about the order in which we are going to try the columns of the matrix. We need many of the same mechanisms that we used in the connection graph approach to resolution theorem proving - indexes of complementary literals, pruning strategies, and so on. To develop an effective theorem prover using the connection method, then, we need to do very much the same sort of pre-processing that was required when we reduced our problem to clausal form for resolution. The advantage of the connection method over more orthodox methods is not that it requires less pre-processing, but that the result of the pre-processing contains fewer redundancies.

4.4.2 *Extending the connection method to quantified formulae*

We have developed the connection method so far only for propositional logic. For it to be of serious interest, we need to extend it to deal with predicate calculus as well. To see how this is done, we will first consider the three blocks problem as an example. We will start by doing a bit of cheating to make it work. The basic statement of the three blocks problem is the same as before (as usual we are negating the goal, with the hope of deriving a contradiction):

on(a,b), on(b,c), green(a), ¬green(c),
∀_x∀_y(¬on(_x,_y) ∨ ¬green(_x) ∨ green(_y))

We know, from the definition of ∀, that we can instantiate _x and _y in the last of these formulae to be anything we like, and in particular we can choose to instantiate _x to a and _y to b, or _x to b and _y to c. We will therefore add the formulae which result from these instantiations to the problem statement. The connection matrix for the resulting problem is as follows (green and on are abbreviated to g and o respectively to save space):

o(a,b)	o(b,c)		o(a,b)	o(b,c)	g(a)	g(c)		o(_x,_y)
g(a)	g(b)							g(_x)
g(b)	g(c)							g(_y)

Suppose we start investigating paths that start with entries in the left-hand column. It is clear that any path starting on(a,b) must eventually go through on(a,b), so that all such paths contain connections. Similarly, any path starting with $\overline{\text{green(a)}}$ will eventually go through green(a), so all paths that start here also contain connections. The only slightly problematic case is that of paths starting with green(b). There are three possible continuations. If we continue the path with $\overline{\text{on(b,c)}}$ we see that it must eventually go through on(b,c), and hence will contain a connection. If we continue it with $\overline{\text{green(b)}}$ then we have a connection immediately. If we continue it with green(c), we will get a connection when we come to $\overline{\text{green(c)}}$. Hence all paths through this matrix contain connections, so the original clause set is inconsistent, as required.

This is a perfectly good connection method proof. The only problem with it is that we have not said how we decided to include the results of instantiating _x to a and _y to b, and _x to b and _y to c. It is not difficult to see what we did. With the original graph (before the addition of any instantiations of the quantified statement), we needed to find a connection between on(a,b) and something else. There was nothing explicitly available, but it was possible to create something by unifying on(a,b) and on(_x,_y). We thus saw that instantiating _x to a and _y to b was a useful move, and were led to include the first column of the final matrix. Trying to check all paths through entries in this column, we found that green(b) had no explicit match in the matrix but that again there was a substitution which would create one for us. This led to the creation of a matrix as shown below, where the second column was very much as in the target matrix above except that _y has not yet been bound to anything:

$\overline{o(a,b)}$	$\overline{o(b,\_y)}$	o(a,b)	o(b,c)	g(a)	g(c)	$\overline{o(\_x,\_y)}$
$\overline{g(a)}$	$\overline{g(b)}$					g(_x)
g(b)	g(_y)					g(_y)

As soon as we start extending paths starting with green(b) so that they go through this new second column, we find that the obvious connection to follow $\overline{\text{on(b,\_y)}}$ is with on(b,c), thus binding _y to c, and leading to the matrix which we constructed by magic earlier on.

We thus see that we can extend the connection method by allowing connections with formulae containing variables, so long as we ensure that any disjuncts of the connected formula are considered with the same set of bindings. We do not actually need to include explicit new columns with the bindings instantiated. It will be sufficient for us just to record that we have made a connection with such a formula, with a specific set of bindings, so that we realise that we must also consider all its disjuncts with the same set of bindings. The following sequence of diagrams illustrates the investigation of a set of paths through the basic matrix for the three blocks problem. The difference between this proof and the one above is that in the proof below we do not have to explicitly copy and instantiate the final column of the matrix, but we do have to keep careful track of the bindings we have committed ourselves to.

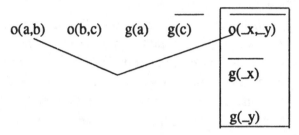

We start by choosing the connection between on(a,b) and $\overline{on(\_x,\_y)}$, committing ourselves to investigating the final column with _x bound to a and _y to b.

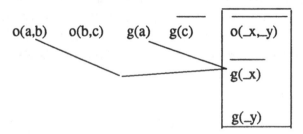

With this binding we see that any path through the second entry in the right-hand column will contain a connection to green(a).

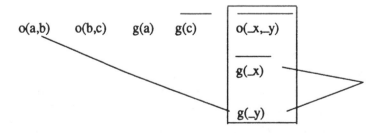

When we try to extend the partial path starting with on(a,b) through the third row of the final column, we find that the only useful place we can go is to the second row of the same column. This now commits us to investigating paths through this final column which have _x bound to b (the value that we were previously committed to for _y). It is important to note that since we are now concerned with a second pass through the final column, we start constructing a new set of bindings. We now need to consider the continuations of the path {on(a,b), green(_y)} through the other rows of the final column:

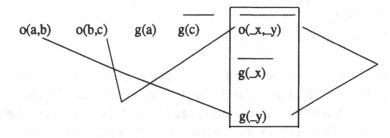

The first of these goes through $\overline{\text{on(\_x,\_y)}}$, which connects to on(b,c). This connection only works if we bind _x to b, in addition to the extant binding of _y to c. This leads us to consider the final case, where the path goes from on(a,b) to green(_y) with _y bound to b, then back to green(_y) with _y now bound to c. This again has a connection (to $\overline{\text{green(c)}}$), so the proof is complete.

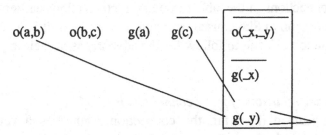

We have now seen most of what is required for an efficient implementation of a connection method theorem prover for predicate calculus. We need to build the matrix, constructing a table of possible connections as we go. We then explore the matrix to see whether every path through it contains a connection. To do this, we may need to make connections to entries with variables in them, in which case we need to commit ourselves to exploring all the alternatives to the given entry using the bindings that were produced when the connection was first made.

We have not, however, seen how to deal with existentially quantified statements. The simplest thing to do is to follow Andrew (1981) and get rid of them by Skolemisation. We noted at the beginning of the discussion of the connection method that one of the chief arguments for it is that it prevents the construction of redundant copies of the same literal that occurs in conversion to clausal form. There are, however, other normalisations that can be performed without this side-effect. In particular, we can always push negations inwards, to get a *negation normal form*, using the following equivalences:

$$\neg(A \ \& \ B) \equiv \neg A \ V \ \neg B$$
$$\neg(A \ V \ B) \equiv \neg A \ \& \ \neg B$$
$$\neg \forall\_xP \equiv \exists\_x\neg P$$
$$\neg \exists\_xP \equiv \forall\_x\neg P$$

Having done this, we can get rid of existential quantifiers as usual by replacing their bound variables by suitable Skolem constants and functions. This will enable us to follow exactly the procedure outlined above as a theorem prover for full FOPC. Bibel (1982) and Wallen (1987) argue that it is possible, and desirable, to avoid conversion to normal form at all, and that Skolemisation can be avoided by construction of appropriately descriptive indices for the entries in the matrix. Their discussion is very dense, and their notation almost entirely impenetrable. It seems likely that the construction and use of their indices involves very much the same work as is involved in conversion to negation normal form and Skolemisation. It may be that they manage to detect instances of unresolvable connections in the table of potential connections earlier than can be done using conversion to Skolemised negation normal form. It is a pity that their presentations are too difficult to follow for the advantages of their approach to be clear.

4.4.3 *Search space reductions for the connection method*
As we have presented it so far, the connection method is a competitor to resolution. Resolution is a very broad term, covering a variety of implementation and representation techniques and a large set of search strategies and search space reductions. The connection method is very similar. Any sensible implementation of the connection method will construct a table of possible connections as it constructs the matrix itself, just as any sensible implementation of resolution will construct a table of possible resolutions during conversion to clausal form. Furthermore, there will at any time be a range of possible connections to choose from, some of which will help show that all paths through the matrix are closed and some of which will be irrelevant. Again the strategies for choosing which connections to try first will be very similar to those used in resolution, and we will not discuss them further.

The critical difference between the connection method and resolution, apart from the avoidance of repeated literals, concerns the use of search space reductions. It seems that the most effective implementation of resolution is via the connection graph, which enables us to avoid doing repeated work and which also makes it possible to identify sections of the search space which are irrelevant to the search for a proof. It is possible to identify the same kinds of dead ends in connection matrices - tautologies, pure literals, and so on. However, whereas connection graph theorem provers react dynamically to the presence of dead end clauses by physically removing them from the graph as they go, implementations of the connection method try to reorganise the graph before starting to explore possible paths. This has an effect on a property of search strategy called *confluence*. In essence, a search strategy is confluent under the following conditions. Given any two points, P_1 and P_2, in the search space, each of which can be reached from the starting point under the rules of the strategy, then any other point P_3 which can be reached from P_1 must also be reachable from P_2 (again subject to the rules of the strategy). Search strategies which are not confluent can lead to failure to explore the space properly, in that although there may be a solution in it the strategy may fail to find it.

Eisinger (1987) argues that a number of obvious search strategies for connection graph resolution fail to satisfy the conditions for confluence, so that although resolution itself is complete, connection graph resolution may not be. This stems from the fact that some moves in a connection graph proof make permanent cuts in the search space, so that the moves that would have got you from P_2 to P_3 will no longer be available after you have have explored the consequences of P_1. Bibel (1982) shows that the connection method is confluent for his chosen search strategies, even when the reductions for pruning dead ends are included. The essential difference is that the connection graph is permanently altered by the deletions, whereas the connection matrix is not. The exact details of conditions under which the two approaches are and are not confluent are intricate, and it is hard to tell whether the comparison is fair. We can certainly restrict the application of pruning strategies in the connection graph so that it no longer runs the theoretical risk of non-confluence (for instance by only applying them before we start trying our resolutions), but this clearly costs us some of the claimed benefits. It remains unclear which approach is to be preferred, and to what extent the risk of non-confluence leads to undesirable behaviour in practice.

4.5 Prospects for automatic theorem proving

The connection graph and connection method seem to approach optimal performance of the basic operation required for theorem proving, namely the analysis of sets of formulae to see whether they are consistent. There is very little work which could easily be avoided being done under either approach. Experience with search strategies and heuristics also seems to indicate that there is not much to be done that will obviously improve the performance of either of these techniques - you simply cannot get a reliable way of seeing which is the best choice to explore next. The best current hope for improvement seems to lie with the discovery of techniques for pruning the search space, or even for transforming it so that what looked like a full FOPC problem is reduced to something simpler. The pruning strategies discussed in Section 3.3.1 are instances of ways of deleting sections of the search space. Bibel (1987) introduces a number of further strategies which seem at first sight to be of roughly the same kind. He observes first that if a clause in a connection graph contains a literal which is connected to just a single complementary literal (an *isolated* literal), it is worth resolving on that literal before considering any other moves. The point here is that resolving on a link of this kind cannot increase the complexity of the graph, and may well make it possible to apply pruning operations (since at the very least the literal which was chosen will have become pure, so that we can apply pure literal deletion). His second observation concerns the presence of ground unit clauses, i.e. simple statements of facts about individuals. The point here is that if all the positive literals containing some predicate are in fact ground unit clauses (or if all the negative ones are - it makes little difference), we can treat the predicate as defining an implicit class. If, for instance, we had a collection of statements of the form

        human(socrates)
        human(plato)
        human(boadicea)
        human(bessie smith)

and no other statements from which it was possible to infer that someone was a human, we could replace them by a reference to a finite class. We would thereby be in a position to use more straightforward algorithms, for instance refinements of unification or techniques from relational database theory, to deal with occurrences of the predicate human. Bibel argues that this *database reduction* can lead to the collapse of sets of clauses to single clauses containing isolated literals, and hence can transform problems which were previously intractable to rather simple ones. This is illustrated with a hand proof of Schubert's "Steamroller problem", one of a well-known set of challenges for automatic theorem provers (Pelletier 1982). It seems, however, that the combination of bottom-up processing of isolated literals with database reduction is just an example of a much broader notion. The reason why database reduction is so useful is that it provides a way of recognising that some problem which was couched in terms of FOPC does not in fact draw on the full power of the language, so that simpler reasoning processes can be applied to it. Furthermore, database reduction can be used even when it is only part of the main problem that can be dealt with by the simpler techniques, and when it was not at all obvious in the original presentation of the problem that these techniques were likely to be relevant. The Steamroller is like this - we do need to employ the full power of FOPC after we have done the reductions, and some of the places where database reductions are possible are extremely hard to spot in the original problem specification.

Manthey and Bry's (1988) *model generation* approach similarly exploits the fact that one of the theorem proving techniques we have considered (the backward chaining approach of Section 4.2) is extremely well-suited to a subset of FOPC. Backward chaining works excellently if your problem can be expressed entirely in terms of clauses with no more than one negative literal (*Horn clauses*). Manthey and Bry argue that quite a lot of problems contain a substantial part which can be expressed as Horn clauses, with a much smaller part which requires full FOPC. They show that if you separate the two parts of the problem, you can use the non-Horn clause part to generate goals to be proved, by backward chaining, using the Horn clause part. If the original set of sentences is inconsistent, then the compactness of FOPC shows that they can be proved to be inconsistent after consideration of some finite set of goals generated from the non-Horn clause part of the problem. Manthey and Bry provide an elegant PROLOG program implementing this idea, and show that its performance compares very favourably with that of other mechanisms.

The lesson from these recent developments is that the next advances in automatic theorem proving seem likely to come from the discovery of other restricted reasoning systems which can be incorporated as pre-processing filters to simplify the search space before we try to apply the standard rules of FOPC. To improve the performance of your FOPC theorem prover, find parts of your problem which do not require the whole of FOPC, and deal with them using special purpose algorithms.

CHAPTER FIVE

MODAL LOGIC

The theories we have seen so far (propositional calculus and FOPC) suffice for certain sorts of reasoning, mainly about facts and rules which happen to be true in the world as it is. Most of the rest of this book will be concerned with extensions of these theories to cover reasoning in contexts where the basic theories just don't work properly. The first such extension, the theory of *modal* logic, was originally developed to capture the distinction between facts and rules which just happen to be true, and ones which could not have been otherwise. The theory has had most impact in AI when interpreted as being about the difference between things which happen to be true and ones which are known to be true, but we will start by considering it in its original form.

We have an intuitive feel for the distinction between things that happen to be true (*contingent truths*) and things which could not be false (*necessary truths*). Most people would agree that the fact that 1+1 is 2 is necessarily true, that it is so much a part of what 1, 2 and + actually are that for it to be false would be to change the meaning of the terms appearing in it. In contrast, the fact that I have a cup of coffee on the desk as I am writing this seems to be something which could just as easily not have been the case. Furthermore we have some intuitions about the relations between necessary and contingent truths - that if A is necessarily true it is also contingently true, that if A & B is necessarily true then both A and B are necessarily true, and so on. The aim of modal logic is to sharpen and make more precise those intuitions.

The first thing to do is to consider some putative examples of necessary truths:

(i) if all humans are immortal and Socrates is a human then Socrates is immortal.

(ii) nothing can travel faster than light.

(iia) nothing can travel faster than 187000 miles/sec.

(iii) God exists.

(iv) for any collection of sets, there is a function which will pick out exactly one member of each set.

(v) once someone is dead, they will never be alive again.

(vi) only physical objects are coloured.

What is it about these that makes you able to decide whether you regard them as necessary or contingent? The test seems to be whether you are prepared to regard worlds in which they are false as possibilities. Can you imagine a world in which (i) is false? It would have to be a world in which humans were immortal, Socrates was a human, and yet he was not immortal. It seems difficult to see how this could be, even if you were to change the meanings of the words *human* and *mortal*, so that *human* denoted what we normally denote by *dog*, and *immortal* denoted what we normally denote by *green*. It seems as though we would have to change the meanings of the words *if*, *all*, *is* and *then* to make (i) false, and this does so much violence to our feelings about our language that we are unwilling to do it. We would have to make similarly violent changes to our conceptions of what a physical object is, and what it means to be coloured, to see how (vi) could be false. The other examples seem to be less convincing. Many people, for instance, would say that (iii) was not even a contingent truth, let alone a necessary one, despite Descartes' claim to have a proof of it from first principles. (iv) is a statement from the foundations of mathematics (the *Axiom of Choice*) whose status caused mathematicians considerable confusion until some relatively recent work by Cohen (1966). The relation between (ii) and (iia) is particularly illuminating. It seems that current theories about the physical structure of the universe lead physicists to say that in any universe of basically the same kind as the one we inhabit, (ii) will be true. If matter is the sort of thing it is in our universe, then the speed of light will be a limit on the speed with which physical objects can travel. So for any contemporary physicist, (ii) appears to be a necessary truth - it is true of any worlds which are sufficiently similar to our own for words like *light* and *travel* to retain their existing meanings. Science fiction writers, however, have long regarded (ii) as a contingent truth, one which can be discarded without any complaints from their readers that their stories no longer made sense, as they would if an author were to base a story on the premise that either (i) or (vi) were untrue in their fictional world. (ii), then, appears to be a necessary truth in some contexts and a contingent one in others. (iia), on the other hand, appears to say the same thing as (ii) but does not have any feeling of necessity about it. It looks as though the way the universe is constituted requires that the speed of light must be a constant and that nothing can go faster than it, but not that the value of that constant has to be 187,000 miles/second.

The moral of this is that whereas the question of whether something is true or not should be decided by inspecting the world as it is, the question of whether it is necessarily true can only be settled after we have described the worlds that we are prepared to regard as possible. The statement *nothing can travel faster than light* is necessarily true if we are considering necessity relative to worlds in which matter is the same as it is in the real world, contingently true if we can conceive of matter as being essentially different from the way it is in the real world. The behaviour of the inference rules governing necessity varies according to the general characteristics of the set of worlds which we are prepared to countenance.

The most important characteristic of this set of worlds is the *accessibility relationship* between them. Suppose, for instance, that we decided that a world, W_1, was a possibility as far as we in the real world, W_0, were concerned if W_0 could be changed into W_1 by an action which was physically possible in W_0. This restriction on which worlds are to be viewed as possible would induce an accessibility relationship between worlds, since if W_1 could be produced from W_0 by some physically possible action in W_0, and W_2 could be produced from W_1 by some physically possible action in W_1, we would want anyone in W_0 to regard W_2 as a possible world. We might find, with this example, that there were significant restrictions on the accessibility relationship. If in W_0 I have an apple in one hand and a sharp knife in the other, then the set of possible worlds clearly contains one, W_1, where I have cut the apple in half, and another, W_2, where I have cut it in three. But note that W_0 is not accessible from W_1 or W_2, and neither W_1 nor W_2 is accessible from the other. Properties such as whether or not the accessibility relationship will always enable you to get back to where you started from have a major influence on the set of axioms and inference rules that hold for necessity. The freedom to choose the constraints on what we regard as possible worlds means that we can fit the rules of modal logic to a variety of topics, and simply pick the correct axiomatisation by checking properties of the accessibility relationship. We will therefore accompany the introduction of particular axioms with the associated properties of the accessibility relation.

5.1 Formal details of possible worlds semantics

To get a rigorous treatment of necessity, we need to extend the vocabulary of the language so we can talk about necessary and contingent truth, and then simultaneously provide a set of axioms and inference rules and a precise semantics that matches them. The first step is easy. We just add two new operators, $\Box$ and $\diamond$, whose intended interpretations are 'necessarily' and 'possibly' respectively. To simplify the proofs of meta-theorems about these operators, we choose to assume that $\diamond(P)$ is just a shorthand for $\neg\Box(\neg P)$. This seems to be a reasonable move - something is possible just so long as its negation fails in some world, which is exactly what saying its negation is not a necessary truth ought to mean.

The rest of the task is rather more complicated. We start by setting out a general framework for the semantics of $\Box$ in terms of possible worlds.

The language of modal logic is intended to be a superset of FOPC. We want to be able to say anything we could say in FOPC, and to have it mean as nearly as possible the same as it always did. We will find that the interpretation of constants and quantifiers in possible worlds semantics is rather problematic, so we start by considering modal logic as an extension of the propositional part of FOPC, i.e. the part where only 0-ary predicate letters are allowed. We will later want to allow the rest of FOPC as well, so we start with the propositional part of FOPC rather than with propositional calculus itself. This means that we can base our semantics on the semantics we already have for FOPC, but deferring the problems about constants and variables until later.

Since FOPC is used for talking about the facts and rules that are true in a single world, it seems natural to use the models that appear in the semantics of FOPC as the worlds of our possible worlds semantics for modal logic. From here on, therefore, when we use the term *world* in any technical context, we mean a model of the sort used in the semantics of FOPC. The semantics of modal logic is then defined in terms of a set of such worlds $\{W_0, W_1, ...\}$ and an accessibility relation R between worlds. A pair consisting of a set of worlds and an accessibility relationship is called a *modal frame*, or often just a *frame*. The accessibility relationship is initially just an arbitrary relation. Specifying an interpretation for it, or specifying constraints on it, will particularise the language to an intended domain, but initially we just take it to be a completely arbitrary relationship.

Given such a relation and set of worlds, the semantics of modal logic is defined as follows:

(i) A formula of the form $\Box(P)$ is true at W_i in the frame $<\{W_0, W_1, ...\}$ $R>$ iff. P is true in all worlds W_j in this frame such that W_j is accessible from W_i (we will generally write this as $R(W_i, W_j)$).

(ii) Any other formula is true at W_i in the frame $<\{W_0, W_1, ...\}$ $R>$ iff. W_i is a model for it in the sense defined for FOPC. Note that this means that a formula such $\Box(P)$ & $\Box(Q)$ will be true at W_i if and only if $\Box(P)$ and $\Box(Q)$ are both true at W_i, and hence if P and Q are each individually true at all worlds accessible from W_i.

(iii) A formula is true in a frame if it is true at every world within that frame.

The extension of the notion of validity to modal logic is slightly tricky. We do not want to use it simply to mean that a formula P is true in all the worlds within a specific frame, since that is simply to say that P is true in the frame. We cannot afford to say that a formula is valid if it is true throughout all frames, since different properties of the accessibility relationship can affect the truth of a formula in a world. Validity has to be defined relative to the characteristics of the accessibility relationship, for instance some formula might be true in all frames whose accessibility relationship was transitive. As we introduce possible axioms for modal logic, we will investigate properties of the accessibility relationship which make them valid. The stronger the axiom, the stronger the constraints on the accessibility relationship.

5.2 Axioms for modal logic

The first result we have is that all the axioms of FOPC are modally valid no matter what accessibility relationship is chosen. The worlds which go to make up a frame are all assumed to be first-order models, so that the axioms of FOPC are all true in each of them. From this it follows that given any world W_i, any axiom A of FOPC is true in all worlds accessible from W_i, since it is valid in all worlds, accessible or not. This holds for the whole of FOPC, not just the propositional part, since by definition every world in a frame is just a model of standard FOPC. This condition is exactly what is needed for $\Box(A)$ to be true in W_i. We used no special properties of W_i or of the accessibility relationship to show that $\Box(A)$

must be true in it, so it must be true in all worlds no matter what accessibility relationship they have to other worlds, in other words it must be valid.

This result means that we can carry over the entire machinery of FOPC (not just the propositional part) to any version of modal logic, since the semantics for modal logics are defined in terms of sets of worlds and accessibility relationships, and the details of the accessibility relationship have no bearing on the validity of the axioms of FOPC. We would be in trouble if we could not do so, but since we can there is little more to be said about it. The next few axioms are each valid subject to constraints on this relationship. The names of the axioms are often used as the names of the theories arrived at by accumulating them on top of FOPC, so that the logic K is what you get by adding the axiom K to FOPC, the logic T is what you get by adding the axiom T to the logic K. The origins of the names are not particularly illuminating.

The first axiom we will consider is the following:

K: $\Box(P \rightarrow Q) \rightarrow (\Box(P) \rightarrow \Box(Q))$

For the moment, we will assume that the predicates appearing expressions in these axioms are drawn from the propositional part of FOPC. K is the weakest axiom commonly included in modal logics, apart from the basic axioms of FOPC. To investigate the constraints on the accessibility relationship for which it is valid, we will consider the circumstances under which it could be false. The ordinary first-order semantics of $\rightarrow$ shows that the only way for it to be false would be for $\Box(P \rightarrow Q)$ and $\Box(P)$ both to be true in some world W_i, and for $\Box(Q)$ to be false in that world. This could only be true if $P \rightarrow Q$ and P were both true in all worlds W_j which were accessible from W_i, but Q was false in some such world. In other words, there must be a world which is accessible from W_i in which P and $P \rightarrow Q$ are both true and Q is false. Since all worlds are taken to be proper models of FOPC, this clearly cannot be the case, so K cannot have been false in W_i.

We see that K is also valid with respect to absolutely any accessibility relationship, so that for any version of modal logic which has the semantics we have given to $\Box$, K will be valid. We refer to a modal logic which has K as an axiom as a *normal modal logic*, and assume from now on that all the logics we will consider in this chapter are normal in this sense.

The next axiom says that any formula which is necessarily true is indeed true:

T: $\Box(P) \rightarrow P$

It might seem unnecessary to include this. Surely necessary truth must include truth? There are two responses to this observation. The first is that the whole point of logic is to make absolutely precise which axioms are actually required, and that this one is indeed required since it does not follow from anything else we have established so far (the only axiom we have so far that refers to □ is K, and the only thing K can be used to do is to confirm that some formula □(Q) follows from the current set of assumptions). The second point is to recall that although □ and ◇ were introduced to deal with necessity and possibility, their relevance for AI lies more in the fact that they can be given alternative interpretations. In particular, it is sometimes useful to interpret □(P) as saying "P is believed", from which there is no reason to suppose that it is in fact true.

To investigate the range of accessibility relationships with respect to which T is valid, we again consider what it would take to make it false. As before, the only way for it to be false at a world W_i is for □(P) to be true in W_i but for P itself to be false there. From the definition of the semantics for □ this means that P must be true in all worlds that are accessible from W_i but false in W_i itself. This is perfectly possible, so long as W_i is not accessible from itself. To see how this could happen, consider taking the accessibility relationship to be "later than". This gives us an interpretation of □ as "will become true and stay true". The axiom K holds for this axiom, but T does not. The sentence *it will become true and stay true that I am dead* is indeed true in the world as it is now, but *I am dead* is not.

T, then, is valid for all frames in which the accessibility relationship is reflexive (i.e. where any world is accessible from itself). There are, however, non-pathological frames with irreflexive accessibility relationships; the relationship of being "later than" is an example.

The next axiom says that anything which is necessarily true is necessarily necessarily true:

S4: □(P) → □(□(P))

To see how this one could fail, we have to consider a world W_i in which □(P) is true but □(□(P)) is false. This can only happen if there is a world W_j which is accessible from W_i but where □(P) is false. This is possible so long as there is a further world, W_k, which is accessible from W_j in which P is false. We now have the following arrangement of worlds:

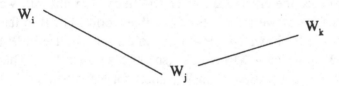

Suppose that W_k were also accessible from W_i, as in:

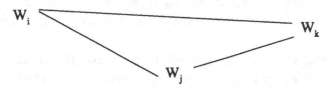

We would then be in an awkward situation where P was not true in W_k, since that is how we chose W_k; but that □(P) was true in a world, W_i, from which W_k was accessible. This, of course, would be an untenable situation. What we therefore need is to accept that it is possible for W_k to be inaccessible from W_i, despite the fact that it is accessible from W_j which is in turn accessible from W_i. In other words, for S4 to fail, the accessibility relationship must not be transitive. It must not be possible to infer that if $R(W_i, W_j)$ and $R(W_j, W_k)$ both hold then so must $R(W_i, W_k)$.

To make this more concrete, we will consider the relationship between worlds as being "is within 24 hours of". This relationship is clearly reflexive, but is not transitive. For if W_j is the state of the world 23 hours after W_i, and W_k is the state of the world 23 hours after W_j, then W_k is more than 24 hours after W_i and is therefore not accessible from it according to the relationship we have chosen. This accessibility relationship would support an interpretation of □ as "will be true from now for at least 24 hours". It is clear that anything that will be true from now for the next 24 hours is indeed true now, so under this relationship the axiom T holds. This is as it should be, since the relationship is symmetric. It is equally clear that, supposing the date today is 14 October, the statement □(*the date is either 14 or 15 October*) is currently true, but □(□(*the date is either 14 or 15 October*)) does not hold, so we have a counter-example to S4.

The final axiom we will consider is:

B: ¬P → □(¬□(P))

In terms of necessity and possibility, this is intended to say that if P is false then it must be the case that it is not a necessary truth, in other words that it is possible for it to be false. Trying to see the circumstances under which B might fail, we again consider the relationships between the sets of possible worlds. For B to fail there must be an initial world W_i in which $\neg P$ is true (so P itself is false in W_i) and an accessible world W_j in which $\neg\Box(P)$ is false (so $\Box(P)$ is true in W_j). This can only be the case if W_i is not accessible from W_j, since if it were then the fact that $\Box(P)$ is true in W_j would mean that P must be true in W_i, which we already know is not so.

Thus for B to fail there must be a pair of worlds W_i and W_j such that $R(W_i, W_j)$ holds, but $R(W_j, W_i)$ does not, in other words the accessibility relationship must not be symmetric.

We complete the axiomatisation of modal logic by including the inference rule of necessitation (NEC): if we have already proved A, then we can infer $\Box(A)$.

Theorem 5.1: Soundness of modal logic

Suppose F is a modal frame for some collection of modal axioms, i.e. a set $\{W_0, W_1, ...\}$ of models of FOPC and a relationship R between the W_i which satisfies the constraints required by the chosen set of axioms. If we have a proof of A from the axioms of FOPC and the chosen modal axioms, using the rules MP and NEC, then A will be true throughout F.

Proof:
The proof proceeds by induction on the length of the proof of A, deriving a contradiction from the assumption that there is a shortest proof for which the theorem fails. We will suppose that A is a theorem whose shortest proof is as short as any proof for which the theorem fails. There are three cases to consider - that A is an axiom, that it follows via MP from formulae which have already been proved, or that it follows by NEC from a formula which has already been proved.

(i) We have already checked the correspondence between the axioms and the accessibility relationship. Indeed the very statement of the theorem assumes that the accessibility relationship satisfies the constraints required by the chosen axioms, so this part must be true - any axiom is true in any appropriate frame.

(ii) Suppose the proof proceeded by deriving A from B and B $\rightarrow$ A, using MP. Then we must have already constructed shorter proofs of B and B $\rightarrow$ A, so that by the inductive hypothesis both B and B $\rightarrow$ A will be true throughout F. But then, since every world in F is itself a model of FOPC, A must be true in all of them, in contradiction to the assumption that the theorem failed for it.

(iii) Suppose A is in fact $\Box(B)$, so that the proof proceeded by deriving A from B, using NEC. Then we must have already had a proof of B. By the inductive hypothesis B must have been true throughout F. If the theorem is to fail for A, there must be a world W_i in F such that A is not true in W_i, in other words $\Box(B)$ is not true in W_i. For this to be the case, there must be a world W_j which is accessible from W_i and in which B itself is false. This contradicts the inductive hypothesis that B is true throughout F ▦

There are a number of other possible axioms for $\Box$, each of which imposes its own constraints on the accessibility relationship. Lewis (1973) shows that there are exactly 42 different configurations of such constraints, e.g. reflexive and symmetric but not transitive, reflexive and transitive but not symmetric, and so on. Note that some configurations are simply not possible: you could not have a relationship which was symmetric and transitive but not reflexive, unless there were isolated worlds. Suppose you had such a relationship, and consider a pair of worlds W_i and W_j such that W_j was accessible from W_i. Then by symmetry W_i would be accessible from W_j, and hence by transitivity W_i would be accessible from itself via W_j. It is also clear that the three constraints we have considered so far - symmetry, transitivity and reflexivity - are not sufficient to generate 42 different combinations, especially when some possibilities must be ruled out in advance. The extra properties are presented in Lewis (1973) and also in Wallen (1987).

Lewis shows that the various configurations each correspond exactly to some particular choice of axioms (in other words that the axiom set and inference rules are complete with respect to the classes of frame as well as sound. We proved the soundness above. For proofs of completeness, see Hughes & Cresswell (1968, 1984)). Rather than trying to cover all the options in detail here, we will simply note that there is no possibility of discovering new sets of axioms for which the possible worlds semantics still works but which are not equivalent to some combination that Lewis has already considered. Any set of axioms we could come up with must correspond to some set of constraints on the accessibility relationship, but Lewis has already done an exhaustive analysis of all the possible sets of constraints and found axiom sets corresponding to each of them.

Our aim in using modal logic in AI is not to derive new modal logics, i.e. new sets of axioms governing the behaviour of the operator □. It is rather to discover new accessibility relationships, which we can use to give new interpretations of □. We can then investigate the properties of our chosen accessibility relationships to see which of the existing varieties of modal logic describes the inferences that can be made with the new interpretation of □. We will consider a couple more simple examples, to re-emphasise the range of applications of modal logic, before moving on to the most significant AI application to date.

The first of these examples is one we have already seen, namely taking R to be "later than". When we introduced it earlier on, it was simply as an illustration of a relation which was not reflexive and hence for which T did not hold. We can now see that it also fails to be symmetric, but that it is transitive, so that for the interpretation which it gives to □, namely "will happen", the axioms K and S4 hold but T and B do not.

The next example concerns the well known 'blocks world'. This is a simple model of a world containing a collection of building blocks, and a robot which is capable of picking up blocks, moving them around, and putting them down. It has been widely used in AI as a testbed for planning programs, and for experimenting with other programs which need background knowledge about some small, well-behaved domain. The actions the robot is capable of carrying out are all reversible - if it picks a block up it can put it down again, if it moves either a block or itself from A to B then it can move them back from B to A. Indeed by reversing any sequence of actions it has carried out it can reinstate the world state from which it started. Within this framework we can introduce a new notion of accessibility between worlds, namely that W_j is accessible from W_i if there is some sequence of actions the robot could carry out which would turn W_i into W_j. Consider a world W_1 containing three blocks A, B and C such that A was on B and B was on C. W_1 could be transformed into another world W_2 in which C was on B and B was on A by a suitable sequence of actions by the robot. It could not, however, be transformed by any actions of the robot into a world which contained an additional block D, or one in which C no longer existed.

This example shows the importance of staying within the framework given by the chosen accessibility relationship. If $R(W_i, W_j)$ means that W_i could be changed into W_j by actions the robot could perform, then R is symmetric, reflexive and transitive. All the axioms we have seen so far - K, T, S4 and B - will therefore hold for the induced interpretation of □, and we can use all of these for reasoning about states of the world that could be achieved within this context. We cannot, however, assume that they will continue to hold if we permit a wider range of actions - chopping blocks in half, for instance, or allowing a second robot to provide temporary support while we build metastable structures. The simple blocks world is an example of a domain which can be correctly characterised by the full set of axioms introduced above, a fact which Chapman's (1987) planner TWEAK takes advantage of. Making the blocks world richer and more realistic may mean that we have to retract one or more of the axioms, as the accessibility relationship between worlds loses one or more of the required properties.

5.2.1 *First-order modal logic*

We have seen so far that we can add axioms to account for different interpretations of the operator □, and that the possible worlds semantics gives us a straightforward way of seeing which axioms are valid for a given interpretation. Most of the rest of this chapter will be concerned with a specific interpretation which has received a good deal of attention within AI, namely as a characterisation of knowledge. Before we move on to that, however, we must consider some potential problems associated with the first-order version of modal logic.

The first point concerns the identity of individuals across possible worlds. In a restricted context, such as the blocks world, it is not too difficult to see whether the individuals mentioned in two different worlds are the same or not. If A, B and C are blocks in both W_i and W_j, then they are presumably the same in each world. There is nothing in the operations that the robot can perform that could transform them into different blocks, so, at least if W_i and W_j are accessible from each other, there seems to be no problem. In more general situations, some people have difficulty with the notion. Suppose, for instance, we consider a world where Albert Einstein was born with a twin brother, Rudolf, and where Albert discovered the general theory of relativity but Rudolf discovered the quantum theory. At least in terms of imaginative reconstructions of history this seems to be a possible world. It is very hard, however, to see how we would decide which, if either, of the Einstein twins in this imaginary world was the same individual as the Albert Einstein who was born in the real world.

We, fortunately, do not need to settle this question in general here (see (Kripke 1972) and (Lewis 1973) for various different viewpoints on it). All we need is to be able to settle it for any particular interpretation of □ that we choose to apply in our systems. If we are happy with it for the blocks world, we can use modal logic for the blocks world. If we are happy with it for reasoning about knowledge, we can use modal logic for reasoning about knowledge.

In cases where we are sure we know what it means for something to be the same object in different worlds, we still need a way of referring to objects which is reliable across worlds. In ordinary FOPC, we had a set of names (constants) each of which was given a value when we constructed a model for the language. There was no question of worrying about whether the name was intimately bound up with the object that it named, so that nothing else could have had that name. We were even able to use functions, such as mother-of, in order to refer to individuals, since we had a guarantee that any function picked out just one individual for each set of arguments. Once we start considering possible worlds, we have to make decisions about which names are to count as reliable *rigid designators* (r.d.'s) across worlds. If we are prepared to consider a possible world in which Bette Davis is my mother, then mother-of is not available to us as an r.d. If, on the other hand, we take the view that being the child of specific parents is one of the properties that determines whether or not someone in one world is the same as someone in another world, then mother-of would act as a rigid function.

We therefore see that the specification of the set of r.d.'s and rigid functions is a further component of the definition of the accessibility relationship. If mother-of is a rigid function then only worlds in which the person picked out as my mother is in fact the particular person who is my mother in the real world are accessible. If it is not, then various other worlds, for instance ones where Bette Davis is my mother, are accessible. This leads us on to consider the *Barcan formulae*:

B1: $\Box(\forall\_xP(\_x)) \equiv \forall\_x(\Box P(\_x))$
B2: $\exists\_x(\Box P(\_x)) \equiv \Box(\exists\_xP(\_x))$

B1 says that saying it is necessarily the case that P(_x) holds for every _x is the same as saying that for every _x it is necessarily the case that P(_x) holds. Taking this in terms of possible worlds, $\Box(\forall\_xP(\_x))$ means that in every world that is accessible from the current world, P holds for every individual in that world. $\forall\_x(\Box P(\_x))$ means that for every individual in the current world, P is true of that individual in all accessible worlds. These do seem to be equivalent, at least so long as all worlds accessible from the current one contain exactly the same set of individuals, even if none of them have reliable names.

B2 says that saying it is necessarily the case that P(_x) holds for some _x is the same as saying that for some _x it is necessarily the case that P(_x) holds. Taking this in terms of possible worlds, $\exists\_x(\Box P(\_x))$ says that there is an individual in the current world for which P holds in all accessible worlds. This constrasts with □(∃_xP(_x)), which says that in any accessible world there is an individual for which P holds. Suppose we take P(_x) to be mother-of(_x, Julian). We might well take the view that □(∃_x mother-of(_x, Julian)) - that as far as we are concerned the only worlds which we are prepared to regard as accessible from the real one are ones in which Julian has a mother. Only if we regard mother-of as a rigid function, however, will we want to accept ∃_x(□ mother-of(_x, Julian)) - that there is someone who, in every possible world, is Julian's mother.

Accepting or rejecting B1 and B2, then, has further consequences for the accessibility relationship. In particular, B1 seems to be valid if and only if accessible worlds are constrained to have exactly the same sets of individuals in them. B2 is valid for rigid properties, so long as what we substitute in for the variable _x is an r.d. and not just some name whose value varies from world to world. The choice of which properties are rigid and which are not, however, is a major facet of the accessibility relationship. This will have considerable significance when we come to consider the application of modal logic to reasoning about knowledge. Before we look at particular AI applications, however, we should make sure that we can produce theorem proving systems which can deal adequately with the formalism. There will be no point in showing that modal logic is exceptionally well-suited as a representation language for some domain if we cannot actually use it.

5.3 Theorem proving techniques for modal logic

We saw two major types of theorem prover in Chapter 4, namely resolution based systems (including connection graph systems) and connection method systems. The presentations in Chapter 4 are not directly applicable to any form of modal logic. We will consider what has to be done to adapt them for modal logic in general, and hence for the knowledge oriented version in particular, in the next two sections. For both major proof techniques we will work our way up gradually, starting out by demonstrating them for propositional modal logics and then lifting them to the first-order cases. The basic idea behind all of them, however, is the same. We are going to treat a formula like □P as meaning something like ∀_wP(_w), i.e. we are going to include an extra argument in the formula denoting worlds in which it is true, and we are going to take □ to indicate universal quantification over worlds. Of course □ does not really mean universal quantification over worlds, it means quantification over worlds which we regard as possible. We will therefore need to include some restrictions on the way quantification works. The details of exactly how we do this will be different in the two approaches, but both of them will draw on this basic notion.

5.3.1 *Modal propositional connection method proofs*

We will start by considering a tableau proof system for the simplest normal modal propositional logic, namely the logic K which contains no special modal axioms apart from K. We take tableaux to be attempts to provide valuations for sets of formulae. For the straightforward case of classical propositional calculus we did not need to make explicit mention of anything about valuations. When we move to modal logic, we do need to keep track of the worlds represented by particular valuations in order to be able to examine the accessibility of one from another. The way we will do this is by attaching an *index* to each formula. This index is intended to provide constraints on the set of worlds in which the formula is known to be true. The details of this system are as follows:

Basic definitions:
An index may be a variable, a constant, or a term of the form $succ(I_1, I_2)$, where I_1 is a variable or a constant and I_2 is an index. We will use I_1, I_2, I_3 ... for talking about indices in general, $\_W_0$, $\_W_1$, $\_W_2$ ... for variables which are being used as indices and w_0, w_1, w_2, ... for constants which are being used as indices. The intended interpretation is that an index represents what we know about some world. A variable denotes any world whatsoever, whereas a constant denotes some specific world. A term of the form $succ(I_1, I_2)$ denotes a path, where I_1 represents what we know about the last world in the path and I_2 represents the earlier part of the path. We will call I_1 the *destination* of the index $succ(I_1, I_2)$ - it is the world you get to by following the path represented by the index. If I_1 is a variable, then $succ(I_1, I_2)$ denotes any world which you can get to by continuing the path represented by I_2. If it is a constant it denotes some specific continuation of I_2.

An *indexed formula* is a 2-tuple consisting of a formula of propositional modal logic and an index. We will write such an indexed formula as F:I, where F is the formula of modal logic and I is the index. F is the *content* of F:I, I is its index. Two indexed formulae $F_1:I_1$ and $F_2:I_2$ are complementary if (i) F_1 is $\neg F_2$ or F_2 is $\neg F_1$, and (ii) I_1 and I_2 can be unified. The point here is that I_1 and I_2 are the most general possible descriptions of the worlds in which F_1 and F_2 are known to be true. If they can be unified then any world which you could get to by the steps permitted by I_1 could be reached by steps which were permitted by I_2, and vice versa, so that F_2 would be true in any world in which F_1 was, and F_1 would be true in any world in which F_2 was.

A *modal tableau* is a tree of indexed formulae. A branch of such a tableau is *closed* if it contains a pair of complementary formulae. A modal tableau as a whole is closed if every branch can be made closed by a consistent set of unifications. To see why we need a consistent set of unifications, we need to recall how tableau proofs work. The aim of a tableau proof is to show that the original set of formulae is inconsistent, by showing that it requires some formula to be both true and false at the same time. Once we move to modal logic, the phrase "at the same time" clearly comes to mean "in the same world". We therefore have to check that the indices associated with the putative contradiction are compatible, so that we can be sure that the two contradictory formulae are indeed required to be true at the same time.

Non-modal rules:

(i) If $\Phi \cup \{(P \& Q):I\}$ is a branch of a modal tableau, it can be extended to $\Phi \cup \{(P \& Q):I, P:I, Q:I\}$. The original tableau is closed if the extended version is. This has exactly the same effect as the standard tableau rule for &, which simply adds the conjuncts to the end of the given tableau. The only change is that we include an index, I, which is unchanged by this rule.

The other rules for compound formulae whose major connectives are from the set $\{V, \neg, \rightarrow\}$ are also exactly as for the non-modal case, apart from the fact that they include an index, which is unchanged in the extended tableaux. In particular, rules which split a tableau, such as the rule for V, construct two new tableaux with the same index.

(ii) If $\Phi \cup \{(P \ V \ Q):I\}$ is a branch of a modal tableau, the tableau can be extended by replacing this branch by the two branches $\Phi \cup \{(P \ V \ Q):I, P:I\}$ and $\Phi \cup \{(P \ V \ Q):I, Q:I\}$. The original tableau is closed if the extended version is.

(iii) If $\Phi \cup \{(P \rightarrow Q):I\}$ is a branch of a modal tableau, the tableau can be extended by replacing this branch by the two branches $\Phi \cup \{(P \rightarrow Q):I, \neg P:I\}$ and $\Phi \cup \{(P \rightarrow Q):I, Q:I\}$. The original tableau is closed if the extended version is.

(iv) Suppose $\Phi \cup \{\neg P:I\}$ is a modal tableau, where P is itself a complex formula. The correct way to extend the given tableau depends on the form of P. If P is $P_1 \& P_2$, we need to extend it with both of $\Phi \cup \{\neg P:I, \neg P_1:I\}$ and $\Phi \cup \{\neg P:I, \neg P_2:I\}$. If P is $P_1 \ V \ P_2$, we need $\Phi \cup \{\neg P:I, \neg P_1:I, \neg P_2:I\}$.

If it is $P_1 \rightarrow P_2$, we need $\Phi \cup \{\neg P{:}I, P_1{:}I, \neg P_2{:}I\}$. Finally, if P is $\neg P_1$ the required extension is $\Phi \cup \{\neg P{:}I, P_1{:}I\}$.

Modal rules:
All we need to do now is to provide rules for dealing with $\Box(P)$. We need two rules, one to be used if $\Box(P)$ originally appeared inside a negation, the other to be used in all other cases.

(v) If $\Phi \cup \{\neg(\Box(P)){:}I\}$ is a modal tableau, it should be extended to $\Phi \cup \{\neg(\Box(P)){:}I, \neg P{:} \text{succ}(I', I)\}$ where I' is a new constant. This rule supplements rule (iv) by introducing a term describing a new world which is accessible from the worlds denoted by I. This is just what we want - a formula is not necessarily true in one world if there is an accessible world in which it is actually false.

(vi) If $\Phi \cup \{\Box(P){:}I\}$ is a modal tableau, it should be extended to $\Phi \cup \{\Box(P){:}I, P{:}\text{succ}(I', I)\}$ where I' is a new variable. In other words, if P is necessarily true in all worlds denoted by I then it ought to be true in any worlds accessible from any of these.

We will demonstrate these rules with some simple proofs.

(1) Tableau proof of $\Box(P \& Q) \rightarrow \Box(P)$:

The tableau starts with an indexed formula whose content is the negation of the goal, and whose index is some arbitrary constant w_0. The subsequent extensions are all sanctioned by the rules given above.

$$\neg(\Box(P \& Q) \rightarrow \Box(P)) : w_0$$
$$\Box(P \& Q) : w_0$$
$$\neg\Box(P) : w_0$$
$$P \& Q : \text{succ}(\_W_0, w_0)$$
$$P : \text{succ}(\_W_0, w_0)$$
$$Q : \text{succ}(\_W_0, w_0)$$
$$\neg P : \text{succ}(w_1, w_0)$$
$$\text{CLOSED}$$

The tableau is now closed, since its sole branch contains two indexed formulae whose contents contradict each other and whose indices unify. What this proof shows is that if we assume that $\neg(\square(P \& Q) \rightarrow \square(P))$ is true in some world w_0, there must be another world w_1 in which both P and $\neg$P hold. P holds in w_1 because it holds in any world which is accessible from w_0, $\neg$P holds there because we chose w_1 that way. In other words, if any world whatsoever satisfies the negation of our goal, we can show how to find a world which is not in fact a model of FOPC.

(2) Tableau proof of $(\square(P) \vee \square(Q)) \rightarrow \square(P \vee Q)$:

Again we start with an indexed version of the negation of the goal, and expand the tableau according to the given rules.

$$\neg(\square(P) \vee \square(Q)) \rightarrow \square(P \vee Q)) : w_0$$
$$\square(P) \vee \square(Q) : w_0$$
$$\neg\square(P \vee Q) : w_0$$
$$\neg(P \vee Q) : \text{succ}(w_1, w_0)$$
$$\neg P : \text{succ}(w_1, w_0)$$
$$\neg Q : \text{succ}(w_1, w_0)$$

$\square(P) : w_0$	$\square(Q) : w_0$
P : succ($\_W_0, w_0$)	Q : succ($\_W_1, w_0$)
CLOSED	CLOSED

The proof is complete, since each branch of the tableau can be closed by a consistent set of unifications (by binding both the variables $\_W_0$ and $\_W_1$ to w_1).

We finish the discussion of tableau proofs for the logic K by considering two attempted proofs which fail when we come to check the unification of indices.

(3) Non-proof of $\square(P) \rightarrow P$:

$$\neg(\square(P) \rightarrow P) : w_0$$
$$\square(P) : w_0$$
$$\neg P : w_0$$
$$P : \text{succ}(\_W_0, w_0)$$

We have complementary formulae P and $\neg$P, but their indices w_0 and succ($\_W_0$, w_0) fail to unify, so this attempted proof is not acceptable. Furthermore, no other extensions to the tableau are sanctioned by the rules, so there is no proof within this system of axiom T. This is as it should be, since the proof system is only aimed at K.

(4) Non-proof of $\Box(P \lor Q) \rightarrow (\Box(P) \lor \Box(Q))$:

$$\neg(\Box(P \lor Q) \rightarrow (\Box(P) \lor \Box(Q))) : w_0$$
$$\Box(P \lor Q) : w_0$$
$$\neg(\Box(P) \lor \Box(Q)) : w_0$$
$$\neg\Box(P) : w_0$$
$$\neg\Box(Q) : w_0$$
$$\neg P : succ(w_1, w_0)$$
$$\neg Q : succ(w_2, w_0)$$
$$P \lor Q : succ(\_W_0, w_0)$$

$P : succ(\_W_0, w_0)$	$Q : succ(\_W_0, w_0)$
CLOSED	CLOSED

Each branch of the tableau seems to close satisfactorily. The unification required to close the left-hand branch, however, binds $\_W_0$ to w_1, whereas the unification for the right-hand branch binds it to w_2. These bindings are incompatible, so the proof fails, as it ought. $\Box(P \lor \neg P)$ holds, by NEC, for any P, but we would not want to conclude that $\Box(P) \lor \Box(\neg P)$ also held for any P.

The proof system defined by the given tableau rules provides a decision procedure for the modal logic K. To see whether a formula F is a theorem of K, just apply the given rules until no more apply. If all branches of the tableau are closed with a consistent unification for all the indices of the complementary formulae then F is a theorem, otherwise it is not. It is easy to see that this algorithm must terminate, since each application of a rule produces shorter formulae, and we cannot go on producing shorter formulae for ever.

To extend it to deal with other propositional modal logics, we have to alter the rules governing the indices of potential contradictions. The index associated with a formula reflects the moves that we took while demonstrating the existence of a world in which it was true. When we wanted to show for K that we had in fact been forced to accept the existence of a world in which two contradictory formulae were true, we simply attempted to unify the indices. If they unified satisfactorily, then each move on one path that led us to a specific world was matched either by a move on the other which led us to the same world, or by one which was unconstrained about which of the accessible worlds it led us to. In the first case we already knew that the two worlds we were considering were the same, in the second we could immediately see that the less constrained path could have been taken to be identical to the constrained one.

For T and S4, we have to be prepared to delete moves from paths. If we consider T, for example, it is clear that if we had a path containing a move which took us to an arbitrary successor world, we ought to be prepared to consider matching this with a path which did not have any move at that point. Suppose we had two indexed formulae $P:succ(\_W_1, succ(\_W_0, w_0))$ and $\neg P:succ(\_W_2, w_0)$. The first of these says that P is true in any world $\_W_1$ which is a successor to any world $\_W_0$ which is a successor to w_0. It is clear that if the accessibility relationship is reflexive, $\_W_0$ is a successor to $\_W_0$. We therefore need to define R_T in such a way as to permit steps which introduce variable indices to be ignored.

In fact, if the accessibility relationship is reflexive, no step that introduces a variable can be crucial to the demonstration that a world containing a contradiction must exist. Suppose that some contradictory pair of statements, say P and $\neg P$, holds in every world which is accessible by the path denoted by the index $succ(\_W, I)$. Take any world W' which was accessible by the path denoted by I. Then clearly W' is one of its own successors, and therefore P and $\neg P$ were already both true in W'. But W' was an arbitrary representative of the worlds accessible by the path denoted by I, so there was no need to include the step out to $succ(\_W, I)$ in the first place. This justifies us in removing all variables from our indices. We do this recursively. If I is an index of the form $succ(J, J')$, we first remove all variables from J' to get J''. Then if J is a variable we replace I by J'', otherwise we replace it by $succ(I, J'')$. In the case where J is a variable, we have to unify J with the last entry in J'. If J' is of the form $succ(K, K')$ then this last entry is K, otherwise it is J' itself.

The unification is needed if the logic is first-order. We will find that existential quantification has to be dealt with by Skolem functions which refer to the index of the worlds in which they are known to be true. We keep track of the variables in these Skolem functions by unifying variables as we delete them from indices. $R_T(I, I')$ holds if the paths you get by applying the above process to I and I' are identical.

This way of dealing with R_T is slightly long-winded. We start by constructing paths containing variables which will eventually turn out to be irrelevant, and then delete them. As we delete them, we have to use unification in order to show where they have come from. If we were simply dealing with T, it would probably be more efficient not to add them in the first place, in other words to replace the rule that deals with formulae of the form $\Box(P):I$ by the following:

(vii) If $\Phi \cup \{\Box(P):I\}$ is a modal tableau, it should be extended to $\Phi \cup$

{□(P):I, P:I} if the destination of I is a variable, and to $\Phi \cup$ {□(P):I, P:succ(V, I)}, where V is a new variable, if the destination of I is a constant.

With this version of the rule, we would not introduce any unnecessary variables into indices, so there would be no need to delete them when comparing paths. We will use the more complex version in the remainder of the chapter, partly to demonstrate the common pattern for the various forms of modal logic that we are considering and partly because it is more easily integrated with the constraints that we will apply to deal with S4.

The argument for S4 is similar. Suppose we have two indexed formulae, P:succ(w_2, succ(w_1, w_0)) and ¬P:succ($\_W_0$, w_0). The first of these indicates that we have been forced to concede that there is path from w_0 through w_1 to w_2, and that P holds in w_2. The second indicates that we have also been forced to accept that ¬P holds in any successor of w_0. If the accessibility relationship is transitive, however, chains of succession can be collapsed. Since w_2 is a successor of w_1 and w_1 is a successor of w_0, w_2 is directly accessible from w_0. In other words we also have the indexed formula P:succ(w_2, w_0). From this and ¬P:succ($\_W_0$, w_0) we can see that we have been forced to accept the existence of a contradiction.

In this case the move to a canonical form involves replacing all instances of three successive constant indices by the outer pair, e.g. succ(w_3, succ(w_2, succ(w_2, w_0))) would be reduced successively to succ(w_3, succ(w_1, w_0)) and then to succ(w_3, w_0). We do not include any unifications in this process. If the contradictions we find mention anything about particular worlds whose existence we have been forced to concede then the proof will fail. R_{S4}(I, I') holds if the results of applying this process to I and I' can be unified. As with R_T, it could be argued that we are doing more work than we need, since we could simply decline to add any more specific worlds to an index if it already terminates with two of them.

R_T and R_{S4} are slightly more complex than straight unification, but they can both be computed fairly quickly. We can therefore use them as the bases for theorem provers for T and S4. This should not be surprising, since R_T simply captures the requirement that the accessibility relationship between worlds should be reflexive, and R_{S4} captures the requirement that it should be transitive. We can show that the axiom T can be proved within the tableau system if we use R_T for checking that the proof is acceptable, and that S4 can be proved if we use R_{S4}.

(5) Proof of T ($\Box(P) \to P$):

$$\neg(\Box(P) \to P) : w_0$$
$$\Box(P) : w_0$$
$$\neg P : w_0$$
$$P : \text{succ}(\_W_0, w_0)$$
$$\text{CLOSED}$$

This is an acceptable proof subject to the relation R_T so long as $R_T(w_0, \text{succ}(\_W_0, w_0))$ holds. This is clearly so, since removing the variables from w_0 just leaves us with w_0 itself, and removing them from $\text{succ}(\_W_0, w_0)$ also leaves us with w_0, with the side effect that $\_W_0$ has been unified with w_0.

(6) Proof of S4 ($\Box(P) \to \Box(\Box(P))$):

$$\neg(\Box(P) \to \Box(\Box(P))) : w_0$$
$$\Box(P) : w_0$$
$$\neg\Box(\Box(P)) : w_0$$
$$\neg\Box(P) : \text{succ}(w_1, w_0)$$
$$\neg P : \text{succ}(w_2, \text{succ}(w_1, w_0))$$
$$P : \text{succ}(\_W_0, w_0)$$
$$\text{CLOSED}$$

This is acceptable so long as $R_{S4}(\text{succ}(w_2, \text{succ}(w_1, w_0)), \text{succ}(\_W_0, w_0))$ holds. Applying the relevant reduction to $\text{succ}(w_2, \text{succ}(w_1, w_0))$ and $\text{succ}(\_W_0, w_0)$ leaves us with $\text{succ}(w_2, w_0)$ and $\text{succ}(\_W_0, w_0)$, which unify.

The essence of the tableau method is the same as it was for classical propositional logic, save that each formula has an index associated with it so that putative contradictions can be checked to make sure that they are both true in the same worlds. Bibel's connection method for classical logic was shown in Chapter 4 to be nothing more than a concise encoding of tableau theorem proving techniques, so we ought to be able to adapt it to deal with tableaux containing indexed formulae. We do this by annotating the sub-matrices with indices, using the rules given above to tell us exactly what indices are required. These rules would generate the following matrix for the negation of axiom K:

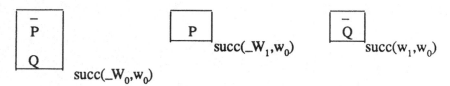

To use this matrix as a basis for a proof of K, we investigate the paths that start
with entries in the first column. The first entry is $\bar{P}$. Any path through this will
also have to go through the single entry P in the second column, so that there will
be a connection so long as succ($\_W_1$, w_0) and succ($\_W_0$, w_0) can be unified. This
can be done, leaving us with $\_W_1$ bound to $\_W_0$.

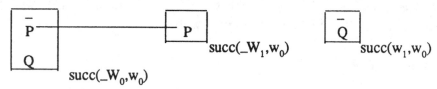

We then consider the other entry in the first column, i.e. Q. Any path through this
must also pass through the single entry Q in the rightmost column. This will
constitute a connection if we can unify succ($\_W_0$, w_0) and succ(w_1, w_0), which is
possible since the only binding we have established so far, between the two
variables $\_W_0$ and $\_W_1$, is compatible with binding $\_W_0$ to the constant w_1.

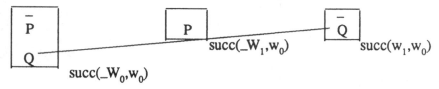

We can adapt the connection method so that the relations R_K and R_{S4} are used
instead of simple unification to check that paths are acceptable. The next move is
to extend the method to cope with proofs of first-order modal theorems.

5.3.2 Modal first-order connection method proofs

We start by reconsidering the significance of the indices introduced in the last
section. The function of these indices was to identify the worlds which have to be
considered in order to check the validity or otherwise of modal propositions. In
effect we are saying that $\square(P)$ is equivalent to $\forall\_w(R(\_w, w_0) \rightarrow P)$. In other
words, $\square(P)$ is true in the real world, w_0, if P is true in all worlds which are
suitably related to w_0. Different constraints on R give us the various different
modal logics. The tableau method described above takes advantage of the fact
that the R's corresponding to most of the standard modal axiom sets can be dealt

with without calling on the whole of FOPC, so that we can deal with this part of the problem by calling on special purpose routines for dealing with the clauses that arise from the presence of R. For the logic K, for instance, all we need for dealing with R is unification. The clauses that arise from R are implicit in the indices, and the theorem proving to deal with them is embodied in the conditions on the acceptability of connections.

To adapt this for first-order modal logic, we need to adapt the construction of indices so that they capture the relevant facts about variable scopes and scope of the operator □. We will illustrate this by constructing a tableau proof of ∃_x□(P) → □(∃_yP), and by then showing that we cannot construct a proof of □(∃_yP) → ∃_x□(P). We need new rules for extending indexed tableaux using quantified formulae. The first of these extends the rule for negation so that it pushes the negation inside any quantifier and switches the quantifier:

> (viii) If Φ ∪ {¬∀_xP:I} is an indexed tableau it should be extended to Φ ∪ {¬∀_xP:I, ∃_x¬P:I}. If Φ ∪ {¬∃_xP:I} is an indexed tableau it should be extended to Φ ∪ {¬∃_xP:I, ∀_x¬P:I}.

The next two rules eliminate quantifiers by introducing specific terms to replace the quantified variables. Just as for FOPC, the tableau rule for existential quantification replaces the quantified variable by a new constant, and the one for universal quantification replaces it by any constant that has been seen already. In the current case, however, the constant introduced when expanding an existential quantifier must be a function, one of whose arguments is the destination of the index of the given formula. If the constant introduced for a universal quantifier is in fact a function with an argument which is a destination, and this destination is a variable, then this argument must be unified with the destination of the current index. What we are trying to capture here is the idea that if we have an existentially quantified statement which is true in a specific world, then we should be able to pick a specific constant for which the statement is true in the world. If we have an existentially quantified statement which is true in all successors of some world, we need to realise that the instantiations may differ for each successor world. We therefore leave a trace of the destination of the index, so that when we subsequently decide to check a potential contradiction we can clamp any references to objects which were not fully specified when we introduced them.

> (ix) If Φ ∪ {∃_xP:I} is an indexed tableau, it should be extended to Φ ∪ {∃_xP:I, P|_{<_x,sk(D)>}:I}, where sk is a new Skolem function and D is the

destination of I.

(x) If $\Phi \cup \{\forall\_xP{:}I\}$ is an indexed tableau, it can be extended by to $\Phi \cup \{\forall\_xP{:}I,\ P|_{<\_x,a>}{:}I\}$, where a is any constant that already appears in some formula in the tableau. If the chosen constant is a Skolem function one of whose arguments is a destination which is a variable, this variable must be unified with the destination of I.

Proof of $\exists\_x\square(P) \rightarrow \square(\exists\_yP)$:

We start with an indexed tableau consisting of just the antecedent of the goal and the negation of its consequent in an arbitrary constant world w_0:

$$\exists\_x\square P(\_x) : w_0$$
$$\neg\square(\exists\_xP(\_x)) : w_0$$
$$\neg\exists\_xP(\_x) : succ(w_1, w_0)$$
$$\forall\_x\neg P(\_x) : succ(w_1, w_0)$$
$$\square P(sk0(w_0)) : w_0$$
$$P(sk_0(w_0)) : succ(\_W_0, w_0)$$
$$\neg P(sk_0(w_0)) : succ(w_1, w_0)$$

$sk_0(w_0)$ is some constant for which P necessarily holds in w_0. It is marked as a constant which was chosen relative to the specific world w_0. We then see that since $\forall\_x\neg P(\_x)$ is true in some world reached by the index $succ(w_1, w_0)$, we must be able to substitute the constant which we chose in w_0 into this formula in this world. The proof now closes on the contradiction between $P(sk_0(w_0))$ and $\neg P(sk_0(w_0))$. These formulae have indices $succ(w_1, w_0)$ and $succ(\_W_0, w_0)$, which unify, so the proof is valid for any normal logic.

This proof corresponds to a connection method proof based on the following matrix, where the relation R has been taken care of in the indices on the columns.

$$\boxed{P(sk(w_0))}\ _{succ(\_W,w_0)} \qquad \overline{\boxed{P(sk(w_0))}}\ _{succ(w_1,w_0)}$$

We thus see that we can derive the first half of the existential Barcan formula, $\exists\_x\square(P) \rightarrow \square(\exists\_xP)$. We can also show that the right-hand half, $\square(\exists\_xP) \rightarrow \exists\_x\square(P)$, does not have a proof via the tableau method. As usual the first two entries in the tableau arise directly from the supposition that there is some world w_0 in which the formula is untrue, and the remainder of the tableau is constructed in an attempt to derive a contradiction.

$$\neg\exists\_x\Box P(\_x) : w_0$$
$$\Box\exists\_xP(X): w_0$$
$$\exists\_xP(X) : succ(\_W, w_0)$$
$$P(sk(\_W)) : succ(\_W, w_0)$$
$$\forall\_x\neg\Box P(\_x) : w_0$$
$$\neg\Box P(sk(w_0)) : w_0$$
$$\neg P(sk(w_0)) : succ(w_1, w_0)$$

The line that introduces $sk(\_W)$ says that for any world you get to that could be reached by a path matching $succ(\_W, w_0)$, there is a constant for which P holds in that world. When we subsequently use sk to supply a specific constant in w_0, we have to fix it to be $sk(w_0)$. As a consequence, when we come to try to close the tableau on the contradiction between $P(sk(\_W))$ and $\neg P(sk(w_0))$, we find that we are blocked by the constraint that $sk(\_W)$ and $sk(w_0)$ have to unify but so too do $succ(\_W, w_0)$ and $succ(w_1, w_0)$. The reason the attempted proof fails is that we have been forced to commit ourselves to a particular choice of constant in w_0 for the negated instance of P, and that we know nothing about the properties of this constant in w_1, which is where the potential contradiction shows up. We had no other possible ways of extending the tableau, so there cannot be a proof of the second part of the Barcan formula in a normal modal logic. Furthermore, the changes to the way that indices are compared when we use R_T and R_{S4} would make no difference. The only thing that would make a difference is if we required all constants to be rigid designators, in which case we would not have to include the destination as an argument of the Skolem function. We would not then fall foul of the fact that we introduced sk in one world, instantiated it in that world, and then found a contradiction in another.

5.3.3 *Reified propositional modal proofs*
To adapt the connection method so it would work for modal logic, we added indices to entries in the graph to correspond to the relations between worlds which are implicit in the possible worlds semantics for modal logic. The objects that appear in the connection matrix are now more complex than the ones that occurred when we just had matrices without indices, so that the actual moves of the proof process have to be made more complex. Instead of just checking that a path can be extended to include a given entry without contradicting any variable values established by earlier moves, we now have to check that the indices are well-behaved as well. Modal connection method theorem provers have to be

made a bit more complicated than non-modal ones.

An alternative approach is to try to use some existing first-order theorem prover unchanged. To do this, we might convert the target formula to some more complex form which refers explicitly to possible worlds. The *reified* approach to proving theorems of modal logic does just this (Moore 1984). In this approach, a specific model <W, V> for FOPC is assumed. The universe W of this model is the set of formulae of the relevant modal logic, together with an infinite set of worlds. Two new predicates, R and TRUE, are introduced. R is intended to be interpreted as a relation between worlds, just as in the previous section. TRUE is intended to be interpreted as a relationship between formulae and worlds, namely TRUE(W, P) is supposed to hold if P is a formula which is true in the world W.

A proof of a theorem of modal logic in this context would consist of a standard FOPC proof of $\forall\_w(\text{TRUE}(\_w, f))$, where f is some constant of FOPC such that V(f) is the required formula. The problem with this approach is that we have no systematic relationship between constants of FOPC and formulae of modal logic. If f_1 and f_2, for instance, are constants of FOPC, then $V(f_1)$ and $V(f_2)$ should both be formulae of modal logic. We know that in that case $V(f_1) \rightarrow V(f_2)$, for instance, is also a formula of modal logic, and hence that there ought to be some constant f_3 of FOPC such that $V(f_1) \rightarrow V(f_2)$ is $V(f_3)$. Unfortunately we have no way of getting f_3 just from f_1 and f_2.

To deal with this problem we proceed as follows. We start by assuming the constants of the modal language, say f_1, f_2, ..., are a subset of the constants of FOPC, and that $V(f_i)$ is f_i for every constant of modal logic. We then need to introduce a collection of functions, $F_\&$, $F_\lor$, $F_\rightarrow$, $F_\square$, and so on. These functions are taken to map their inputs onto appropriate formulae, so that F(p, q), for instance, would have as its value the formula V(p) & V(q). These are perfectly well-defined functions, since for any N-place operator Φ and any N-tuple of input formulae p_1, ..., p_N there will be exactly one formula Γ such that Γ is $\Phi(p_1, p_2, ..., p_N)$. We simply define F_Φ to be that function such that $V(F_\Phi(P_1, ..., P_N))$ is just $\Phi(V(P_1), ..., V(P_N))$ for all combinations of $P_1 ... P_N$. Once we have these functions we can refer in FOPC (which we will call the *meta-language*) to any formula of modal logic (which we will call the *object language*). Proofs of object language formulae will be derived from meta-language proofs about terms referring to them. To prove $\square(P) \rightarrow P$, for instance, we would have to prove $\forall\_W(\text{TRUE}(\_W, F_\rightarrow(F_\square(P), P)))$. We can only do this if we have axioms describing the behaviour of the functions F_Φ, and axioms describing the behaviour of the relation R. The following set of axioms suffices for propositional modal logic.

Translation axioms:

L_{AND}: $\forall$_W (TRUE(_W, $F_\&$(A, B)) ≡ (TRUE(_W, A) & TRUE(_W, B)))

L_{OR}: $\forall$_W (TRUE(_W, $F_\lor$(A, B)) ≡ (TRUE(_W, A) ∨ TRUE(_W, B)))

$L_{IMPLIES}$: $\forall$_W (TRUE(_W, $F_\to$(A, B)) ≡ (TRUE(_W, A) → TRUE(_W, B)))

L_{NOT}: $\forall$_W (TRUE(_W, $F_\neg$(A) ≡ ¬TRUE(_W, A))

L_{NEC}: $\forall$_W_1 (TRUE(_W_1, $F_\Box$(P)) ≡ $\forall$_W_2(R(_W_2, _W_1) → TRUE(_W_2, P)))

The first of these, L_{AND}, captures the fact that the intended model of FOPC is the relation between worlds and formulae, and that any pair of formulae A and B will be true together in a world exactly when their conjunction is. $F_\&$(A, B) is a term denoting the formula you would get by conjoining A and B. L_{OR}, $L_{IMPLIES}$ and L_{NOT} are similar.

L_{NEC} captures the possible worlds interpretation of □, namely that □(P) should be true in a world if and only if P itself is true in all accessible worlds, where R denotes the relationship of accessibility between worlds. With these axioms we can prove K (□(P → Q) → (□(P) → □(Q))) as follows:

We assume ¬K and try to derive a contradiction. The first move is simply to write out the negation of the goal. To make this and subsequent proofs legible, we will replace the functions $F_\Box$, $F_\&$, $F_\lor$, $F_\neg$ and $F_\Box$ by IMPLIES, AND, OR, NOT and NEC respectively, and we will write IMPLIES, AND and OR as infix operators. These names are just an alternative notation for the originals, so that p AND q, for instance, is still just a term denoting a specific formula (namely p & q in this case).

$\qquad$ ¬$\forall$_W_0(TRUE(_W_0, (NEC(P IMPLIES Q)
$\qquad\qquad\qquad$ IMPLIES (NEC(P) IMPLIES NEC(Q))))))

We can push the outermost ¬ inwards to get

$\qquad$ ∃_W_0(¬TRUE(_W_0, NEC(P IMPLIES Q)
$\qquad\qquad\qquad$ IMPLIES (NEC(P) IMPLIES NEC(Q)))))

We can now substitute a new constant w_0 for the existentially quantified variable _W_0:

¬TRUE(w_0, NEC(P IMPLIES Q)
                    IMPLIES (NEC(P) IMPLIES NEC(Q)))

From this we can use the axiom $L_{IMPLIES}$:

¬[TRUE(w_0, NEC(P IMPLIES Q))
                    → TRUE(W_0, NEC(P) IMPLIES NEC(Q))]

In other words, there is a world w_0 in which it is not the case that TRUE(w_0, NEC(P IMPLIES Q)) implies TRUE(w_0, NEC(P) → NEC(Q)). The standard rules for → then lead to

TRUE(w_0, NEC(P IMPLIES Q))
                    & ¬TRUE(w_0, NEC(P) IMPLIES NEC(Q))

The same two steps applied to ¬TRUE(w_0, NEC(P) IMPLIES NEC(Q)) take us to

TRUE(w_0, NEC(P IMPLIES Q))
                    & TRUE(w_0, NEC(P)) & ¬TRUE(w_0, NEC(Q))

We can apply L_{NEC} three times to this to get

∀$_{-}W_1$(R($_{-}W_1$, w_0) → TRUE($_{-}W_1$, P IMPLIES Q))
                    & ∀$_{-}W_2$(R($_{-}W_2$, $_{-}W_1$) → TRUE($_{-}W_2$, P))
                    & ∃$_{-}W_3$(R($_{-}W_3$, $_{-}W_1$) & ¬TRUE($_{-}W_3$, Q))

The rule governing IMPLIES then leads us to

∀$_{-}W_1$(R($_{-}W_1$, w_0) → [TRUE($_{-}W_1$, P) → TRUE($_{-}W_1$, Q)])
                    & ∀$_{-}W_2$(R($_{-}W_2$, $_{-}W_1$) → TRUE($_{-}W_2$, P))
                    & ∃$_{-}W_3$(R($_{-}W_3$, $_{-}W_1$) & ¬TRUE($_{-}W_3$, Q))

Suppose w_0 and w_3 are constants which could be inserted in this formula without changing its truth value (remember that an existentially quantified statement is true in a model exactly if we can substitute constants for the existentially quantified variables). We can substitute w_3 for $_{-}W_1$ and $_{-}W_2$ as well, since these are universally quantified, to get

$$[R(w_3, w_0) \rightarrow TRUE(w_3, P \rightarrow Q)]$$
$$\& [R(w_3, w_0) \rightarrow TRUE(w_3, P)]$$
$$\& [R(w_3, w_0) \& \neg TRUE(w_3, Q)]$$

From this we can infer $TRUE(w_3, P \rightarrow Q) \& TRUE(w_3, P) \& \neg TRUE(w_3, Q)$. The axiom $L_{IMPLIES}$ then gives us $TRUE(w_3, P) \rightarrow TRUE(w_3, Q)$ from $TRUE(w_3, P \rightarrow Q)$, and from this and $TRUE(w_3, P) \& \neg TRUE(w_3, Q)$ we can derive a contradiction ▓

This is quite a long proof, but it was in fact rather simple. All we did was to apply the translation axioms whenever we could, and only turn to other rules when there weren't any applicable translation rules. If you do this you normally get quite rapidly to a standard first-order formula, to be proved by whatever means are at your disposal. To get the logics T and S4, we just add axioms concerning the relation R:

RT: $\forall\_W_0(R(\_W_0, \_W_0))$
RS4: $\forall\_W_0\forall\_W_1\forall\_W_2(R(\_W_1, \_W_0)$
$$\rightarrow [R(\_W_2, \_W_1) \rightarrow R(\_W_2, \_W_0)])$$

With these axioms we have first-order theories capable of proving theorems about formulae of the three propositional modal logics we have been considering. These first-order theories treat the formulae of modal logic themselves as objects, with properties such as being true in particular worlds. The name *reified modal logic* reflects this attitude to formulae of the object language as being mere things to be discussed and analysed within the meta-language.

5.3.4 Reified first-order modal proofs
To extend this approach to first-order modal logics, we need to add axioms for talking about first-order object language formulae. We take much the same approach as before. We set up a universe W consisting of all the constants, variables, predicate letters and connectives of the object language (which is now first-order modal logic), and define some valuation V which will enable us to refer to each of these objects using some constant of the meta-language. We again assume that this valuation can be set up in such a way that we refer to the object language formula P(a,b,c) with a meta-language term P(a,b,c)', with the prime denoting the fact that this is a term rather than a formula. In particular, the meta-language term P(a,b)' IMPLIES Q(a)' has as its valuation the object language formula $P(a,b) \rightarrow Q(a)$. We supplement the functions IMPLIES, AND,

OR, NOT and NEC with ALL and SOME, corresponding to ∀ and ∃ respectively.

The axioms governing the relationship between the predicate TRUE and the functions IMPLIES, AND, OR, NOT and NEC are exactly as before, but we also need axioms for ALL and SOME as well. The axiom for ALL should reflect the fact that ALL(_x', P) should denote the object language formula ∀_x(P), which will be true in a world if and only if all substitutions of constants for _x in P produce formulae which are true in that world. We need therefore to be able to talk about substitutions of object language constants into meta-language terms. Worse than that, since the translation axioms are themselves expressed as universal quantifications over worlds, we need to be sure that the constants we substitute are in fact rigid designators. Moore (1984), following a proposal by Dana Scott, suggests that we should invoke a function, @, which returns an r.d. for any object in the universe of the frame. If we accept the existence of @, we can express the translation axiom for ALL as follows:

$$L_{ALL}: \ \forall\_W \ (TRUE(\_W, ALL(\_x', P')) \equiv \forall\_x(TRUE(\_W, P'|_{<@(\_x),\_x'>})))$$

To interpret this we have to think carefully about $P'|_{<@(\_x),\_x'>}$. It is a term which denotes the formula you would get by substituting an r.d. for the variable denoted by _x' in the formula denoted by P'. So $\forall\_x(TRUE(w_0, P'|_{<@(\_x),\_x'>}))$ would be true if and only if for every element of the universe of discourse the formula you obtained by substituting an r.d. of that element in the original was true in w_0. This interpretation is based on a version of the basic semantics of ∀ which says it relates directly to the universe of discourse, rather than going via the set of possible substitutions of constants for the bound variable in the way that we chose in Chapter 3, but it does not really make that much difference. The essential point is that since L_{ALL} involves quantification over worlds, we are going to have to make use of object language terms whose denotation does not vary across worlds, in other words we are going to have to appeal to some function such as @ which will provide us with r.d.'s - either an r.d. for each object in the universe of discourse or one for each constant of the object language, depending on the exact details of the chosen semantics for ∀.

The axiom for SOME is similar:

$$L_{SOME}: \ A\_W(TRUE(\_W, SOME(\_x', P')) \equiv E\_x(TRUE(\_W, P'|_{<@(\_x),\_x'>})))$$

Indeed, in the interests of conciseness we could have omitted it, taking ∃_x to be an abbreviation of ¬∀_x¬, and SOME(_x', P') to be a function which denoted the same formulae as that denoted by NOT(ALL(_x', NOT(P')))). We can show the equivalence as follows:

1 TRUE(_W, NOT(ALL(_x', NOT(P'))))
2 ¬TRUE(_W, ALL(_x', NOT(P')))   (by L_{NOT})
3 ¬∀_xTRUE(_W, NOT(P'|$_{<@(\_x),\_x'>}$))   (by L_{ALL})
4 ¬∀_x¬TRUE(_W, P'|$_{<@(\_x),\_x'>}$)   (by L_{NOT})
5 ∃_x(_W, P'|$_{<@(\_x),\_x'>}$)   (by definition of ∃)
6 TRUE(_W, SOME(_x', P'))   (by L_{SOME})

Adding L_{ALL} and L_{SOME} enables us to talk in the meta-language about first-order formulae, and hence to use any available first-order theorem prover to prove theorems about the validity of formulae of first-order modal logic. The proofs can be rather long winded, with a considerable amount of effort expended on translating the object language formulae into meta-language terms, but there is nothing mysterious about them.

We now have a choice of two approaches to automatic theorem proving for modal logic. The extended connection method uses indices to indicate the implicit constraints on possible worlds, and employs special purpose extensions to unification to check that these constraints are satisfied. Reification uses perfectly standard first-order techniques to prove things about the relations between formulae and sets of possible worlds. The choice between these techniques seems rather clearer than was the case for FOPC. If you already have a theorem prover for FOPC (which might itself be based on the connection method for FOPC), and you are not particularly concerned about how long it takes to prove things, you may as well use reification. The axioms are easy enough to write down, so if you already have a satisfactory first-order theorem prover you are more or less ready to start right away. If you do not already have such a theorem prover, or if you do care about the speed of derivations, then the connection method is almost certainly preferable. The advantage lies in the fact that proofs about the accessibility relation R do not require all the machinery of FOPC. For the logic K, everything we actually want to know about R can be embodied in attempts to unify descriptions of worlds. Even for T and S4 we only need to extend this by checking for reflexivity and transitivity - tasks which can be done much more quickly by special purpose procedures than by invoking all the machinery of FOPC. The connection method approach exploits the fact that R can be dealt with much more rapidly than is the case for general problems of FOPC. Indeed, the connection method provides a decision procedure for propositional modal logic, whereas the approach via reification and first-order reasoning about the semantics of formulae may quite possibly fail to terminate when asked to prove things which are not valid.

5.4 Reasoning about knowledge

Now that we have shown how to adapt the theorem proving techniques of Chapter 4 for modal logic, we can turn to the applications of this language as a representation language. Its main application is as a basis for reasoning about knowledge and action. As Moore (1980, 1984) has pointed out, intelligent systems need to reason about more than just the current state of the world. They need to reason about possible states it might be in, and they need to reason about their own and other people's knowledge about those states. This is particularly true for programs which are to take part in coherent dialogues in natural language. Such programs have to be able to reason about what is general common knowledge among members of their community, in order to avoid either telling them things at too great a level of detail or leaving out essential explanatory material. They also have to be able to reason about the knowledge the other person may have as a result of the preceding stages of the dialogue. Even in contexts not involving dialogue it can be necessary to reason about the state of one's own knowledge or that of another person. It is, for example, impossible to ring someone up on the telephone *unless you know their number*. A plan to ring someone up, therefore, may include actions which will enable the planner to find out the relevant phone number, perhaps by looking in the telephone book. Even apparently straightforward physical tasks such as driving a car from A to B may require knowledge, for instance of the roads that connect A and B. Furthermore, some of that knowledge may be unavailable at the point when the journey is being planned - it is impossible to refine a plan for a journey down to its finest details before beginning it, since you cannot know the road conditions, the colour the traffic lights will be when you come to them, and so on until you are actually executing it.

Since what we need is the ability to reason about our knowledge, it seems like a good idea to start by trying to see if any of the logical formalisms we know of provide a good model of this sort of reasoning. We will see that the formalisation of reasoning about knowledge is even more idealised than the formalisation of simple reasoning about the world that we have seen so far, but it will at least give us a starting point.

We start with some idealised observations about knowledge:

(i) If someone knows P and they also know P → Q, they know Q. This is clearly an idealisation. It means, for instance, that anyone who knows how to do arithmetic also knows that there is no biggest prime number, since the fact that there is no biggest prime number follows from the axioms of arithmetic. It would probably be better to take the view that if someone knows P and P → Q then they could work out Q. For the moment, however, we will accept the idealised version.

(ii) You can't know things that are not true. This is indeed true, though the situation is often muddied by the fact that you may think you know something when in fact you only believe it. It is the fact that only true things can be known that permits you to infer things from overhearing other people talk about them - if you hear someone in the hall say *It may not look as though it's raining, but when you get out there you'll find that it is* you can infer that they know it is raining outside, and therefore that it must be true that it is raining outside. You often cannot find out whether you know something or merely believe it, but if you do know it then it must be true.

(iii) Anyone who knows something knows that they know it. This again is an idealisation, as can be seen by considering what happens if you apply it to its own results. Since I know that most horses can swim, it would seem to follow that I know that I know most horses can swim, and that I know that I know that I know most horses can swim, and so on to any required depth. As with (i), it would be more realistic to say that anyone who knows something could work out that they knew it, without assuming that they do so automatically.

(iv) Everybody knows (i) to (iii). It is this fact that enables us to participate correctly in arguments. If I want to prove Q to you by showing you that P and P → Q are both true, then I am relying on the fact that I know you already accept (i) above. Similar arguments can be constructed for (ii) and (iii), and even for the axioms of FOPC and for (iv) itself.

These observations are idealisations, and like all idealisations they will lead to trouble if accepted without question. They do, however, provide a framework within which we can consider formal treatments of reasoning about knowledge, in the same way that FOPC provided a framework for simple real world knowledge.

Suppose we formalise these observations, using a two-place predicate KNOWS to denote the relationship between the knower and the known fact:

K_K: KNOWS(A, P → Q) → (KNOWS(A, P) → KNOWS(A, Q))

T_K: KNOWS(A, P) → P

$S4_K$: KNOWS(A, P) → KNOWS(A, KNOWS(A, P))

NEC_K: KNOWS(A, AX), where AX is any instance of K_K, T_K or $S4_K$, or is an axiom of FOPC.

We now have an axiomatisation of how knowledge works. We will call the logic we get by accepting these axioms *epistemic modal logic* (EML). The axioms look very similar to the axioms K, T and S4 of modal logic, together with the consequences of the rule of necessitation, apart from the presence of an argument which relativises each of them to a particular knower. We should therefore be able to adapt our theorem proving techniques for modal logic so that they will support reasoning about knowledge, or at any rate reasoning about the idealised version of knowledge characterised by these axioms.

5.4.1 *Connection method proofs with epistemic modal logic*
To adapt the connection method for standard modal logic we added indices to formulae in order to mark their status in terms of the worlds they were true in. For epistemic modal logic, indices carry information about the knowers involved in the construction of worlds. We therefore need to alter the definition of indices, and adapt the axioms about □, as follows:

An *index for EML* is either a basic index or a complex one. A *basic index for EML* is a 2-tuple of the form <P,I>, where P is a variable or constant denoting a person and I is a variable or constant denoting a world. A *complex index for EML* is a term of the form $succ(I_1, I_2)$, where I_1 is a basic index and I_2 is an index.

If P:I is an indexed formula where P is of the form ¬KNOWS(A, Q), then it should be replaced by the indexed formula ¬Q:succ(<A,w>, I), where w is some new constant. The motivation behind this rule is the idea that if A does not know Q to be true in the world described by I then A ought to be able to imagine a world in which Q is false. This world that A could have imagined is denoted by w. The index contains a mention of A to make sure that we know who it is that did not know Q.

If P:I is an indexed formula where P is of the form KNOWS(A, Q), then it should be replaced by the indexed formula Q:succ(<A,_W>, I), where _W is a new variable. This is just like the last rule, except that we use a variable _W to capture the idea that Q is true in every world that a is capable of imagining.

We illustrate this approach to EML by proving KNOWS(a, KNOWS(b, P)) → KNOWS(a, P), a result which can be used as the backbone of a lot of reasoning about how language works. The matrix we would derive from the negation of this formula is as follows:

$$\boxed{P} \quad succ(<a,\_W_1>,succ(<b,\_W_2>,w_0)) \qquad \boxed{\bar{P}} \quad succ(<a,w_1>,w_0)$$

The sole path, between P and $\bar{P}$, contains a connection which is acceptable if the required relationship holds between $succ(<a,\_W_1>,succ(<b,\_W_2>,w_0))$ and $succ(<a,w_1>,w_0)$. This will be the case if we are using an interpretation of the relationship which requires it to be transitive, which we will be since $S4_K$ clearly requires transitivity.

We need the more complicated indices in order to avoid inferring that KNOWS(a, Q) follows from KNOWS(a, P → Q) and KNOWS(b, P), whilst still permitting it to follow both from KNOWS(a, P → Q) and KNOWS(a, P), and from ∀_x(KNOWS(_x, P → Q)) and ∀_x(KNOWS(_x, P)). A formula such as ∀_x(KNOWS(_x, P)) should be read as saying that everybody knows P, or in McCarthy's more picturesque phrase, "any fool knows P". We will end this section by setting up the matrix for this last example, leaving it to the reader to check that all paths through this matrix contain connections for which the required unifications can be done satisfactorily.

$$\boxed{\begin{array}{c}\bar{P}\\Q\end{array}} \quad succ(<\_x,\_W_1>,w_0) \qquad \boxed{P} \quad succ(<\_x,\_W_2'>,w_0) \qquad \boxed{\bar{Q}} \quad succ(<a,\_W_3>,w_0)$$

5.4.2 *Reified epistemic modal logic*

It should be clear by now that we could adapt the reified approach to reasoning about modal logic to deal with EML in exactly the same way that we adapted the connection method, extending the accessibility relationship R to be a 3-place predicate, with an extra argument denoting a person, and including a translation axiom for statements about knowledge as follows:

$$L_{KNOWS}: \quad \forall \_a \forall \_p \forall \_W_1 (TRUE(\_W_1, KNOWS(\_a, \_p))$$
$$\equiv \forall \_W_2 (R(\_a, \_W_2, \_W_1) \rightarrow TRUE(\_W_2, \_p)))$$

It should be unnecessary to provide much detailed discussion of this axiom. The earlier discussion of L_{NEC}, together with the treatment of the EML version of the connection method, should give a clear indication of how a standard FOPC theorem prover could use a reified version of EML to support reasoning about knowledge. Even the reasons for deciding on whether to use the connection method or reification for reasoning about knowledge are exactly as they were for ordinary modal logic - use reification if you already have a good theorem prover for FOPC and are not particularly concerned about speed, use the connection method if you are starting from scratch or if speed is important to you.

We will shortly move on to consider the relationship between knowledge and action, where it may turn out that the reified approach has significant advantages. Before we leave EML itself, however, it is worth considering the relationship R which it depends on. The axioms about R are supposed to describe the semantics of the modal logic of knowledge itself. This might lead to the supposition that this axiomatisation gives some insights into the meaning of *knows* which was lacking in the connection method approach. On reflection, however, it is clear that the relationship R holds between a person and two worlds exactly when the person's state of knowledge is insufficient for distinguishing between the two worlds. The definition of R is thus parasitic on some characterisation of knowledge, rather than being an explication of it. The introduction of R is a means of exploiting the known behaviour of the semantics of modal logic as an aid to theorem proving, and tells us no more about what knowledge really is than we knew already.

5.5 Combining knowledge and action

We have so far considered the application of a version of modal logic to reasoning about knowledge. Moore, however, laid considerable emphasis on the interaction between knowledge and action. We can need knowledge in order to perform actions (for instance you would need to know my phone number in order to be able to phone me); and we can perform actions which will provide us with knowledge (you can look up my number in the phone book). Moore's paradigmatic problem concerns the nature of tests - how can my knowledge that if a piece of litmus paper is red it must have been dipped in an acid solution enable me to plan to find out whether a given solution is acid by dipping litmus paper in it? It is obviously a sound plan. The difficult thing is formalising how it might have been constructed.

The key to this problem lies in an observation we made earlier on when we looked at various accessibility relationships between worlds. Among the interpretations we considered was the possibility that W' was accessible from W if W could be turned into W' by the performance of an action by robot. This relationship is reflexive and transitive. and hence we ought to be able to discuss it in terms of S4 modal logic or something like it. For this particular task it seems more natural to talk about relations between worlds than to try to find an analogue of □. The obvious way to characterise the preconditions and effects of an action is to talk about propositions that must be true in a world if the action is to be feasible, and propositions that will be true in any world which results from performing it. We can, for instance, translate a STRIPS-like (Fikes & Nilsson 1971) specification of the action of putting one thing on another into a description of the world before and after the action:

STRIPS specification of PUT-ON

            put-on(A, X, Y)
            preconditions:
                clear(Y), holding(A, X), above(X, Y)
            add-list:
                on(X, Y)
            delete-list:
                clear(Y), above(X, Y)

Possible worlds specification of PUT-ON:

$\forall\_w_1 \forall\_w_2 \forall\_a \forall\_x \forall\_y$ result(put_on($\_a$, $\_x$, $\_y$), $\_w_2$, $\_w_1$)
$\quad\quad \rightarrow$ (TRUE($\_w_1$, $\neg\exists\_z$(on($\_z$, $\_y$))))
$\quad\quad\quad$ & TRUE($\_w_1$, holding($\_a$, $\_x$))
$\quad\quad\quad$ & TRUE($\_w_1$, above($\_x$, $\_y$))
$\quad\quad\quad$ & TRUE($\_w_2$, on($\_x$, $\_y$))
$\quad\quad\quad$ & TRUE($\_w_2$, $\neg$above($\_x$, $\_y$)))

This should not be surprising, given that the STRIPS notation was originally proposed as a shorthand for McCarthy and Hayes' (1969) *situation calculus*, which was itself a possible worlds approach to temporal reasoning. We will return to the situation calculus in the next chapter, which is specifically concerned with temporal reasoning. The point to note here is that the STRIPS notation can be translated extremely easily to a form which closely resembles the reified version of EML. The preconditions are propositions which must be true in the world in which the action was performed, the effects are propositions which must be true in the world which results from performing it. The possible worlds version, in fact, is rather more compact than the STRIPS version since we can do away with dual predicates like clear and on, or holding and hand-empty, since by using formulae like $\neg\exists\_z$(on($\_z$, $\_y$)) in place of clear($\_y$).

The main advantage of using the possible worlds analysis of actions is that we already have a possible worlds analysis of knowledge. We thus have a single framework within which we can treat both topics. We can even describe actions which bring about knowledge, or whose preconditions require some agent to possess knowledge. We can, for instance, provide a precise characterisation of the preconditions of the action of telephoning someone:

$\forall\_w_1 \forall\_w_2 \forall\_x \forall\_y$ result(phone($\_x$, $\_y$), $\_w_2$, $\_w_1$)
$\quad\quad \rightarrow \exists\_n \forall\_w_3$ (R($\_x$, $\_w_3$, $\_w_1$)
$\quad\quad\quad \rightarrow$ TRUE($\_w_3$, phone_number'(@($\_n$), @($\_y$))))

Spelt out, this means that for $\_w_2$ to be the sort of world that would result from $\_x$ phoning $\_y$ in $\_w_1$, then there must be an $\_n$ which is $\_y$'s phone number in any world $\_w_3$ which is compatible with what $\_a$ knows in $\_w_1$. To get a full characterisation of telephoning, of course, we would have to include a specification of the effects as well. For the moment, though, our main interest is in the way the possible worlds analysis of actions can be combined with the possible worlds analysis of knowledge to provide a description of an action whose preconditions include some piece of knowledge.

This is very appealing. We can construct plans using the possible worlds analysis of action simply by trying to prove that a world in which our goal was true is accessible via a chain of relations of the form result(<action>, <world1>, <world2>). If we keep track of how the proof gets constructed we should end up knowing what sequence of actions will lead to the construction of a satisfactory world. To incorporate statements about knowledge, either as effects or preconditions, we just allow action descriptions to mention the predicate R which is used to deal with agents' knowledge. Moore illustrates this with an analysis of planning to dip a piece of litmus paper in a solution to find out if the solution is acid. The essentials of the action of dipping litmus paper in a solution are captured by the following formula:

$$\forall\_w_1 \forall\_w_2 \forall\_a \forall\_x (\text{result}(\text{dip}(\_a, \text{paper}, \_x), \_w_2, \_w_1)$$
$$\rightarrow ([\text{TRUE}(\_w_1, \text{acid}(\_x)) \rightarrow \text{TRUE}(\_w_2, \text{red}(\text{paper}))]$$
$$\& \neg \text{TRUE}(\_w_1, \text{acid}(\_x)) \rightarrow \text{TRUE}(\_w_2, \text{blue}(\text{paper}))]))$$

This says that if $\_w_2$ is the sort of world which would result from $\_a$ dipping a piece of litmus paper in the solution $\_x$ in $\_w_1$, then if $\_x$ was an acid in $\_w_1$ then the litmus paper will be red in $\_w_2$, and if it was not then the litmus paper will be blue in $\_w_2$. Suppose we have an agent John who wants to know whether or not the solution S_1 that he has in front of him is an acid. We can describe his goal by describing a world in which it is satisfied, which we can do with the formula $\text{TRUE}(\_w_3, \text{knows}(\text{John}, \text{acid}(S_1)) \vee \text{knows}(\text{John}, \neg\text{acid}(S_1)))$. Constructing a plan to satisfy this goal is now a matter of attempting to prove that the existential quantification of this formula follows from our general knowledge of the world. Without going into all the details, it ought to be clear that we can prove that such a world exists. It is the world which would result if John were to dip a piece of litmus paper in S_1, so long as he is capable of distinguishing between red and blue litmus paper.

It seems likely that the reified approach will prove better than the approach via the connection method when we are trying to combine two possible worlds models. The connection method was appropriate for tasks where there was only one modal operator, since its dense encoding of the implicit relations between worlds supported carefully tailored variations on unification. When there are two accessibility relationships to be dealt with, as is the case when we want to combine analyses of knowledge and of action, the connection method encoding may well be too dense. The complexity of the structure of possible worlds which needs to be considered for this combined task may just be too great to be easily embedded in indices which are to be dealt with by extended unification algorithms. It is clearly possible, given that the connection method indices are just ways of encoding constraints on possible worlds, but in the new context it may no longer possess the advantages we claimed for it earlier on.

5.5.1 *Quantifying-in and rigid designators*

We remarked earlier on that the decision on whether or not to accept the Barcan formulae (the ones about whether quantifiers can be pushed through the operator □) had consequences for whether or not different possible worlds could contain different objects. We have to reconsider this when we want to use modal logic for reasoning about knowledge. We will start the discussion of the particular problem that arises in this context by considering a well-known example introduced by Quine. Quine pointed out that the sentence *Ralph knows that someone in this room is a spy* has two interpretations. It may be taken as saying that Ralph knows that one of the people present is spy, but that he does not know which of them it is. Perhaps he has found a miniature camera on the floor by the bed, and assumes that it has fallen out of the pocket of one of the coats that are piled up in a mess on top of the bed. On the other hand, he may know exactly who the spy is, perhaps because he found them looking through his desk. The distinction between the two readings seems to be captured very neatly by saying that the first sentence is equivalent to *Ralph knows there is a spy in this room but he does not know who it is* whereas the second is equivalent to *Ralph knows there is a spy in this room and he does know who it is*. We can capture this distinction perfectly satisfactorily in our epistemic modal logic. The first reading is knows(Ralph, ∃_x(present(_x) & spy(_x))), and the second is ∃_x(knows(Ralph, present(_x) & spy(_x))). We want these two to remain distinct, since they describe distinct situations. This is easy enough so long as we accept that spy is not a rigid function.

Let us now return to our specification of the preconditions for telephoning someone, namely:

$$\forall\_w_1 \forall\_w_2 \forall\_x \forall\_y \; result(phone(\_x, \_y), \_w_2, \_w_1)$$
$$\rightarrow \exists\_n \forall\_w_3 \; (R(\_x, \_w_3, \_w_1)$$
$$\rightarrow TRUE(\_w_3, phone\_number'(@(\_n), @(\_y))))$$

We see here that the condition is stated in terms of a rigid designator for _y's phone number. It is an attempt to capture the idea that _x can phone _y if there is an object which _x knows to be _y's phone number. When we couch this in terms of epistemic modal logic we find that the interpretation in terms of an r.d.

is all that is available to us. The description we used when we introduced r.d.'s said that they were terms which denoted the same objects in all possible worlds. We see that the arithmetic expression 1048576 is an object of this kind, and that it would be a suitable candidate for substitution into the given formula. This, clearly, is the kind of thing that this analysis is aimed at. Unfortunately the arithmetic expression 2^{20} is also a perfectly good r.d. for the same object, yet it is quite unlikely that you would be very pleased if I told you my phone number was 2^{20}. You might be able to cope if you happened to have a calculator with you, but it is easy enough to think of arithmetic expressions which are perfectly well-defined but inordinately difficult to compute (the 30'th prime number bigger than 100000, for instance). This indicates that the precondition for telephoning someone ought not just to refer to an r.d., but to a rather special kind of r.d., namely one whose appearance carries the information we need in order to carry out the act of dialling.

This example shows that in order to make use of our knowledge of which things have which properties we may need more than just an r.d. On the other hand, we may be able to act effectively on our knowledge of the existence of an object satisfying a property without having an r.d. at all. Suppose, for instance, that I know that if you detect a fire when you are at work you should phone the security officer who is currently on duty, and that the duty officer's phone number is 03-333. If I detect a fire, I can combine my knowledge about what you should do in that situation and my knowledge of the duty officer's phone number in order to construct an appropriate plan, namely ring 03-333 and tell whoever answers that there is a fire. In ordinary language we would want to say that I know who I should phone, namely *the duty security officer*. On the other hand this is not an r.d. for me - I may never have met any of the university's security officers, I may have met them without knowing that they were security officers, or I may know them all extremely well but not know who is on duty tonight. The non-rigid designator carries all the information that is required in the context, and may be more appropriate than some expression such as the duty officer's name which is, more or less, an r.d. We can see this again with the use of natural language referring expressions such as *closing time* when establishing the setting for a story. *I went into a shop near closing time* may be more informative than *I went into a shop at 7:20*, despite the fact that *closing time* is not a rigid designator whereas *7:20* is.

The approach to reasoning about knowledge, and about knowledge and action, has had a great deal of influence and a reasonable degree of success, particularly in the area of natural language processing. It seems to be rather flawed when we come to examine the crucial nature that rigid designators play in reasoning about existentially quantified statements about knowledge. This shows up in the preponderance of examples about phone numbers and safe combinations - objects for which there is a canonical r.d. which is what you want if you want to know "what they are". There has been comparatively little progress in finding alternatives to this. The approaches we have seen so far, however, suffer from another problem for which alternative solutions have been proposed. This is the problem of *consequential closure*: that if someone knows something they also know all its consequences. We have already seen one obvious example of this, namely that according to the theories we have considered to date anyone who knows the basic laws of arithmetic also knows that there is no largest prime number. There are many other manifestations of this problem. Another fairly significant example is that with the current theories it is very hard to express, and make use of, the fact that you know that someone else is less capable of reasoning than you are. We will end this chapter with a consideration of one attempt to circumvent the problems that arise from consequential closure.

5.6 Belief structures

Konolige (1986) argues that the approach to reasoning about knowledge via modal logic is wrong in two respects. Firstly, it is wrong to try to do anything at all with knowledge. The only things we are ever sure of having are beliefs, so that reasoning about what we or other people think should be done in terms of beliefs rather than knowledge. Secondly, it is a mistake to try to deal with beliefs (or indeed knowledge) by using a single monolithic reasoning system. What we should do instead is to construct a series of systems embedded within one another. Each system should represent a *belief structure*, i.e. a collection of beliefs about what is true and about how to derive new truths from old ones (Konolige calls them *deduction structures*, to emphasise the role of the embedded inference rules. The name belief structure, on the other hand, emphasises their tentative nature). Note that although belief structures only contain beliefs, the people they belong to will generally be under the impression that they contain truths.

Belief structures, then, contain sets of formulae (which are believed) and inference rules. They may also contain other belief structures. It is the presence of embedded belief structures which enables us to reason about other people. Consider the following belief structures (the notation is intended as an informal first attempt. We will develop a more formal version later):

Belief structure 1.
Formulae:
      $\forall\_x(\text{fairy}(\_x) \to \neg\text{mortal}(\_x))$,
      $\forall\_x(\text{dead}(\_x) \to \text{mortal}(\_x))$,
      dead(Oberon)
Inference rules:
      MP: from P and $P \to Q$ infer Q.
Embedded structures:
      NONE

Belief structure 2.
Formulae:
      NONE
Inference rules:
      MP: from P and $P \to Q$ infer Q.
      MT: from $\neg Q$ and $P \to Q$ infer $\neg P$
      NEG: from P infer $\neg\neg P$
      COPYING: if P is in belief structure 1, infer P.
Embedded belief structures:
      OWNER(Self, belief structure 2),
      OWNER(Lesley, belief structure 1)

It should be clear that the formulae and rules of structure 1 fail to support the derivation of ¬fairy(Oberon). The rule MP, which structure 1 does contain, would support the derivation of mortal(Oberon), but the inference would have to stop there. Structure 2, on the other hand, does have everything that is needed in order to work out that Oberon is not a fairy - the rule of copying in structure 2 would give it access to all the formulae available inside structure 1, and its own inference rules have been carefully tailored to be just what is needed to complete the inference.

It should be equally clear that structure 2 is intended to support inferences such as *Lesley doesn't know that Oberon isn't a fairy* and *I know that Lesley doesn't know that Oberon isn't a fairy*. The fact that our intention in setting up structure 2 is obvious, however, does not mean that we have a clear formal specification of how it is supposed to work. We need to move from an informal, but suggestive, notation to a formal language with well-defined semantics and inference rules.

Konolige proposes a language L_{Bq} (for *quantified belief language*) which extends FOPC with a notation for indicating belief. This notation simply prefixes the name of an agent to a formula, for instance [Ros]∀_x(cat(_x) → greedy(_x)) is intended to have the interpretation *Ros believes all cats are greedy*, and [Allan][Ros]∀_x(cat(_x) → greedy(_x)) is intended to have the interpretation *Allan believes Ros believes all cats are greedy*. The extension of the language to include this operator is not a very dramatic step. The hard work comes in providing a semantics and a proof theory to back it up. The semantics is rooted in belief structures of the kind we have sketched. A belief structure consists of a set of formulae (its *basic beliefs*), a set of inference rules (its *deductive machinery*), and a function ρ from people to belief structures (its *belief map*). The semantics of formulae of L_{Bq} can be given in two stages:

(i) a belief structure <BELIEFS, RULES, ρ> models a formula of the form [A]F, where F contains no instances of the belief operator, if and only if the belief structure returned by its belief map for A is a model of F. In other words, you should think someone believes something if it follows by the rules which you think they believe in from the basic belief set that you impute to them. The intention here is that statements about other people's beliefs should reflect what you would get if you pretended that you were them.

(ii) a belief structure <BELIEFS, RULES, ρ> models a formula F of any other form if and only if it follows from BELIEFS, together with any formulae of the form [A]F' which are modelled by <BELIEFS, RULES, ρ>, via ρ. In other words, a belief structure models anything which can be derived from the beliefs it has explicitly listed or from things which arise by virtue of rule(i).

There are two things to note about the second part of this definition. Firstly, it makes no reference to a valuation, or to any connection to the real world or any set of possible worlds. This is inevitable, and indeed perfectly reasonable, given that Konolige is firmly committed to the notion that beliefs need not be true, and need not even be coherent or consistent. Whether or not you believe something is simply a matter of whether it follows from your basic set of beliefs by arguments which you regard as valid. Secondly, this part of the definition of the semantics of L_{Bq} seems to reintroduce the very thing we were trying to avoid, namely consequential closure. Konolige argues that what he has allowed here is a much weaker notion, namely *deductive closure with respect to a set of inference rules*.

The inference rules can easily be couched in terms which provide a resource limit on the complexity of proofs, for instance a belief structure could have an inference rule that said that you could apply three resolutions but no more.

Konolige argues strongly that belief structures can most appropriately be described in terms of sequent rules. The point here is that we want to be able to talk about structures within which only a subset of the normal rules of FOPC hold. We might, for instance, want to be able to delete the rule of *modus tollens* (that from P → Q and ¬Q you can infer ¬P). This is fairly straightforward using sequent notation, but much less easy to deal with in a Hilbert-style axiomatisation - what, for instance, would we have to do to the axiomatisation we gave in Chapter 2 for Prop$_{hilbert}$ in order to do away with modus tollens? This suggestion may be a bit too sweeping. If, for instance, I want to impute to some agent a belief structure whose deductive machinery is linear input resolution with a depth bound of 100, surely the best way to express this is in terms of resolution.

Further consideration of this leads us to some rather difficult questions. The general problem can be illustrated with an example. Suppose that we have a belief structure that is meant to embody the beliefs of a novice PROLOG user who is thinking about a program they have written. It seems very natural to suppose that they will think about their program, together with the PROLOG system they are running it on, as an agent with a set of beliefs. In other words, their belief map ought to contain a belief structure which reflects their views on how the PROLOG system will interpret their program. It is quite common for PROLOG programmers (both novices and experts) to have models of the way PROLOG derives conclusions which are perfectly accurate but which they themselves are unable to apply to specific cases. The simplest situation in which this might arise is if the programmer has a perfect model of PROLOG's inference mechanisms, but is incapable of mimicking it for more than a dozen steps. To take another case, I might know that Lesley believes in modus tollens and is capable of applying it, but I might be incapable of applying it myself. If that were the case, I would be unable to work out what I thought Lesley believed, since I would know that there were computations she might do with the data available to her which I was unable to do. It is not important here to ascertain whether or not I believe it. If I disbelieve it, but am nonetheless capable of applying it, I could work out what the consequences of Lesley's beliefs would be for her. If I believed it, but could not apply it for myself, I could not apply it when pretending to be Lesley either.

Konolige's theory does solve some of the problems associated with the direct interpretation of modal logic as a formalism for talking about knowledge. In particular it provides a way of talking about people whose abilities to perform inferences are different as well as about people whose basic beliefs are different. There still seems to be a problem in distinguishing between people's ability to use inference rules and their belief in their validity. In particular, there does not seem to be any mechanism for describing someone who believes that someone else has a particular set of inference rules but who is unable, themselves, to apply them (and is perhaps even aware of their own inability). This is, of course, a problem which did not even arise until we had Konolige's analysis to help us talk about people with different deductive powers, but now that we have it we seem immediately to need something more.

There are two other places where the theory of belief structures leaves some work to be done. The first is that Konolige identifies knowledge with true belief - that somebody knows something if they believe it and it is true. This does not seem to be adequate. Certainly for you to know something you must believe it and it must be true, but there is surely more to it than that. It is not obvious exactly what more is required, but there is definitely more work to be done here. The current theory also makes little progress with the problems we discussed above about quantifying-in. This remains an important open area.

There have been numerous other attempts to formalise the rules for reasoning about knowledge and belief, for instance (Said 1985, Hintikka 1962, Castaneda 1967). Some may improve on the ones we have considered here in various ways, but the theories we have considered do at least provide a flavour of the sorts of thing being done in this area. We therefore leave the topic of knowledge and belief in the hope that we have at least provided the background for assessing alternatives, and turn in the next chapter to theories of reasoning about time.

CHAPTER SIX

TEMPORAL REASONING

The second area in which standard FOPC turns out to be inadequate is that of reasoning about time. The two most important tasks for which we need to be able to reason about time are natural language understanding and plan generation. If we are to understand natural language we need to be able to understand the significance of tense markers - what, for instance, is the relationship between *I will have done it* and *I was going to do it*? If we are to construct plans then we need to be able to reason about what is going to be true when, and in particular about what things are going to remain true when we perform some action and what things are going to change. There are three separable approaches to the formalisation of temporal reasoning. (i) We can use a version of modal logic, with modal operators for FUTURE and PAST. These operators are standard modal operators, though their interpretations have to be carefully constrained if they are to induce normal modal logics. Using these operators we can interpret our first example sentence above as FUTURE(PAST(do(I, it))) and the second as PAST(FUTURE(do(I, it))). (ii) We can develop a language for talking either about instants of time or about intervals of time as objects. This reflects a tendency which is present in natural language use, as can be exemplified by the phrase *About the time the door-knob broke*, which contains an expression referring to a specific instant in time. (iii) We can use a language in which the effects of actions can be described as changes in what is true in some situation, as we did with the reified logic of actions in Chapter 5. We will review attempts to deal with time from all three points of view.

6.1 Modal logics of time

6.1.1 *Propositional modal logics of time*
We start by trying to provide axioms for a modal propositional logic of time. As
with the modal logics of Chapter 5, we will actually use the propositional part of
FOPC, so that the transition to first-order temporal logic is made easier, and so
that we can use the whole of FOPC in situations where we do not actually need
any temporal operators. The simple operators FUTURE and PAST (for future and
past) are not adequate. They do not even induce a normal modal logic, let alone
an analogue of any of the richer theories. From FUTURE(A) and FUTURE(A $\rightarrow$
B) we cannot infer FUTURE(B), since nothing in the premises constrains the
future times at which A and A $\rightarrow$ B are true to overlap. To take a simple
example, consider the English sentences *At some time in the future Liverpool will
win the league* and *At some time in the future Liverpool will not win the league.*
It is clearly possible for both of these to be true - if, for instance, Liverpool win
the league next year but fail to retain their title in the following season. The
natural interpretation of the two sentences as formulae of a modal logic would be
as FUTURE(win(Liverpool, league)) and FUTURE(¬win(Liverpool, league)),
from which we could immediately derive a contradiction if the logic based on
FUTURE were normal. Similar arguments show that any logic based around
PAST must also fail to be normal. There are also no very interesting relationships
between PAST and FUTURE. We cannot, for instance, infer
PAST(FUTURE(A)) from FUTURE(PAST(A)) or vice versa. To get anywhere
we need to add two further operators, A_{FUTURE} and A_{PAST}. $A_{FUTURE}(A)$ is
supposed to mean *A will Always be true in the Future*, $A_{PAST}(A)$ is supposed to
mean *A was Always true in the Past* (they are often called G and H, but it seems
impossible to remember whether G should mean *always in the future* or *always
in the past*). Once we have these we can start to get some useful results.

Firstly, they both induce normal modal logics. Consider the following
axioms.

TIME0: any axiom of FOPC is an axiom.

TIME1$_{FUTURE}$: $A_{FUTURE}(A) \rightarrow ([A_{FUTURE}(A) \rightarrow A_{FUTURE}(B)] \rightarrow A_{FUTURE}(B))$

TIME1$_{PAST}$: $A_{PAST}(A) \rightarrow ([A_{PAST}(A) \rightarrow A_{PAST}(B)] \rightarrow A_{PAST}(B))$

TIME0, TIME1$_{FUTURE}$ and TIME1$_{PAST}$ capture properties of what we mean by
always true, and can be accepted as axioms. We also have an intuitively
acceptable axiom relating FUTURE and A_{PAST} to the present, and a similar one

for PAST and A_{FUTURE}.

$TIME2_{FUTURE}$: $A \rightarrow A_{PAST}(FUTURE(A))$
$TIME2_{PAST}$: $A \rightarrow A_{FUTURE}(PAST(A))$

$TIME2_{FUTURE}$ says that if something is true now, then at any time in the past it must have been going to be true later. It picks out the present as the point that past time was leading to. Since I am now typing this sentence, it has always been true that at some time (which turns out to be the present) I would type it. $TIME2_{PAST}$ similarly says that anything which is true now is always going to have been true. $TIME2_{FUTURE}$ and $TIME2_{PAST}$ seem to imply that the present is the only possible future for past time and the only possible past for future time. We should perhaps have been more careful about what we said FUTURE and PAST meant. The axioms we have so far work equally well if we interpret FUTURE(A) as saying *A may be true in the future* and PAST(A) as saying *A may have been true in the past*. $TIME2_{FUTURE}$ and $TIME2_{PAST}$ are as consistent with these readings as with the ones that say FUTURE(A) is *A will be true* and PAST(A) as *A was true*.

Before we go on to consider axioms which characterise FUTURE and PAST more precisely we should note that since we generally accept that the basic laws of logic hold in all worlds and at all times, we can supplement the axioms we have so far with the general inference rule of modus ponens, and with specialised versions of necessity which say that if AX is an axiom then $A_{FUTURE}(AX)$ and $A_{PAST}(AX)$ are both axioms as well. A_{FUTURE} and A_{PAST} clearly both induce versions of the modal logic K. The next move is to add some more interesting axioms about FUTURE and PAST.

$TIME3_{FUTURE}$: $FUTURE(FUTURE(A)) \rightarrow FUTURE(A)$

$TIME3_{FUTURE}$ says that if at some future time A is something which will be true in the future, then it is currently something which will be true in the future. On either of our interpretations of FUTURE, the only way for this to fail is for it to be the case now that A is never going to be true at any time in the future, but for there to be a future time or possible future time at which A is going to be true at some (possible) future time. This seems to contradict our intuitions about time so strongly that we seem to be forced to accept $TIME3_{FUTURE}$ as a valid formula. The analogue for a past version of $TIME3_{FUTURE}$ looks equally valid - anything which used to have been true surely continues to have been true.

TIME3$_{PAST}$: PAST(PAST(A)) → PAST(A)

The axioms we have seen so far have been fairly uncontroversial, and have also failed to distinguish between past and future, in that all axioms about FUTURE have had counterparts which are concerned with PAST, and all axioms about A$_{FUTURE}$ have had A$_{PAST}$ counterparts. The next axiom we will consider is both arguable and asymmetric with respect to past and future. It is an attempt to capture the intuition that there is only one past:

TIME4$_{PAST:}$ (PAST(A) & PAST(B))
     → [PAST(A & B) ∨ PAST(PAST(A) & B) ∨ PAST(A & PAST(B))]

In other words, if A and B were both true in the past, then one of three situations must obtain. (i) At some past time they were both true together. (ii) At some past time B was true and A had previously been true. (iii) At some past time A was true and B had previously been true. We can contrast this with what happens if we know that FUTURE(A) & FUTURE(B) is true, with the interpretation of FUTURE as *is true at some possible future time*. With this interpretation of FUTURE we get the rather startling result that *I am going to chop this apple into either two or three identically shaped pieces* translates as FUTURE(chop(me, apple, 2)) & FUTURE(chop(me, apple, 3)) - that the situation in which I chop it into 2 pieces and the one in which I chop it into 3 are both possible future states of the world. It is clear that

   FUTURE(chop(me, apple, 2) & chop(me, apple, 3))
     ∨ FUTURE(FUTURE(chop(me, apple, 2) & chop(me, apple, 3))
     ∨ FUTURE(chop(me, apple, 2) & FUTURE(chop(me, apple, 3))

does not hold, since the two actions are mutually exclusive - I cannot do them both at the same time, and doing either precludes me from doing the other.

The introduction of TIME4, and the seeming inadmissibility of a future oriented version of it, stems from one particular way of thinking about NOW. TIME4 is supposed to capture the fact that everything which has happened is fixed, that there is only one linear sequence of past times, but that the future is open and that decisions we take now can lead us down different time lines. It is very far from obvious that either of these assumptions is true. The assumption that the past is fixed seems to be contradicted by the fact that we frequently have to reason about different possible pasts to explain the current state of the world. Suppose, for instance, I come into work to give a lecture and I find that none of my students have turned up. I can construct various different explanations. One is concerned with the present, namely that I am in the wrong place or it is the wrong time. The others will typically be concerned with different possible pasts - that my previous lectures have been so boring that no-one is prepared to come any more, or that there has been a hurricane which blocked all the roads, so that no-one was able to get in, or other possible past events which have made it impossible for anyone to attend. I may have some feeling that one of them is the REAL past, but in order to think about them, and to come to some conclusion about which is the real one, I have to be able to consider a range of possible pasts. On the other hand, although I feel that in any given situation I can consider a number of actions I or other people might take, and the alternative possible futures they might lead to, I still have a gut feeling that only one of those futures is going to become the REAL future.

TIME4, then, seems to be an axiom which we might accept or reject for both PAST and FUTURE, depending on our purposes. We need to reject it for FUTURE if we are trying to work out a plan to bring about a desired state of affairs, since we need to consider a range of different futures. But we similarly need to reject it for PAST if we are trying to construct explanations of present situations. Such explanations may have important consequences for our future actions. If, for instance, I decide that the real past is one in which my lectures were so boring that people refused to come any more, my future actions would be different from what they would be if I decided that it had been a hurricane which prevented them from attending. In a way I have the same freedom in constructing the past as I have in constructing the future, since I can make a fairly free choice about which of these explanations I want to believe, if not about which of them is actually true. Accepting TIME4 for either PAST or FUTURE fits with our gut feeling that there is real world, with a real past and a real future, but it is not all that clear how useful it is.

The remaining axioms are concerned with questions about how many states of the world there are.

TIME5: $A_{FUTURE}(A) \rightarrow FUTURE(A)$
         $A_{PAST}(A) \rightarrow PAST(A)$

TIME5 says that anything which will be true at all future times will indeed be true at some future time, and anything which was true at all past times was indeed true at some past time. The intention here is to prevent people talking about the first (or last) instant of time, at which there would have been all sorts of things which had been true at all previous (or subsequent) times, simply by virtue of the fact that there were no such times.

TIME6: FUTURE(A) → FUTURE(FUTURE(A))
        PAST(A) → PAST(PAST(A))

TIME6 says that if there is a time in the future when A will be true, then there is an instant between now and then when it will still be in the future, and similarly for things which used to be true. The notion that between any two instants I_1 and I_2 there is a third, I_3, is referred to as the *denseness* of time.

   TIME5 seems to be difficult to dispute. Even if you consider such events as the big bang in which the physical universe as we know it was created, or the state when the entropy of the universe is infinite, it seems intuitively reasonable to ask about what happened before or afterwards. The laws of physics may, in fact, force us to accept these as beginning and end points to time, but for most purposes it seems reasonable to accept TIME5. TIME6 is more open to question. If we think about times as instants which can be given names (1:35 pm on Wednesday 17 November 1987, for instance) then we probably do want to imagine that between any two such instants there is another one. If we think about times in terms of changed states of the world, as we shall later on, we probably will not want to posit instants in between changes.

6.1.2 *First-order modal logics of time*
The collection of axioms above gives us the machinery for reasoning about propositions modified by temporal operators under a variety of assumptions about the nature of time - does it branch forwards, does it branch backwards, is it dense, does it have end points, and so on. We would like to extend this so that we could talk about temporally qualified first-order formulae. As with our previous encounters with first-order modal logic, the problems that arise are associated with the persistence and naming of objects in different situations. The situation with respect to temporal theories is, if anything, worse than it was with the previous theories, since temporal statements frequently talk about things being created or destroyed. As Steel (1985) has pointed out, current AI planning techniques, which are closely related to theories of time, are ill-suited to tasks such as making omelettes. To describe the differences between the state of the world before we started making our omelette and the state after it is made, we would need to be able to talk explicitly about the fact that beforehand there were some eggs, which subsequently disappeared, and that afterwards there was an omelette which had not been present to start with. We therefore have the same problem that we always had, namely that to talk about things that were true of an

object at different times we need a rigid designator for that object which will denote it reliably and uniquely at all times; but we now have also to contend with a distinction between the fact that an object existed sometime during the history of the universe and the fact that it exists at some specific time. There seems to be no option but to introduce a predicate EXISTS which can be true or false of objects at different times. We could use ∃ to indicate that the object referred to is present at some time and place in the universe of discourse, EXISTS to indicate when and where it is present. With this we could give a rough characterisation of the fact that a one-egg omelette is going to be made as follows:

$$\exists\_x \; \exists\_y([egg(\_x) \; \& \; omelette(\_y) \; \& \; EXISTS(\_x)$$
$$\& \; \neg EXISTS(\_y) \; \& \; FUTURE(EXISTS(\_y) \; \& \; \neg EXISTS(\_x))])$$

In other words, _x is an egg, _y is an omelette, _x exists now, _y has not yet been made, _y is going to be made and _x is going to disappear. Steel raises a number of other awkward questions of the same kind - how, for instance, should we describe the action of making an N-egg omelette. None of them have as yet been given very elegant answers. As far as we can we will follow most writers on temporal logic and ignore these problems. In situations where we cannot ignore them, we will fall back on rigid designators for referring to objects in different contexts, and for dealing with quantifying-in to temporally qualified expressions; and we will use the predicate EXISTS for talking about the creation and destruction of objects over time.

6.2 Reification of temporal logic

The axioms of the previous section provide an account of various different views of what time is and how it works. They are, however, fairly awkward to compute with. One way to make them more manageable, and at the same time to get a better feel for what they really mean, is to consider the properties of their possible worlds semantics. If we can get a precise first-order characterisation of the semantics of the various combinations of temporal axioms, we can use a standard first-order theorem prover for reasoning about them, or perhaps develop a suitable version of the connection method. We may also be able to extend our analysis of time by imposing further constraints on the possible worlds semantics, or by investigating properties which were not immediately apparent from the initial axiomatisation of FUTURE, PAST, A_{FUTURE}, and A_{PAST}.

The set of worlds and accessibility relationship that we used as the basis for the semantics of standard modal logic needs to be turned into a set of time points and an order relationship when we want to consider temporal logic. Since we are going to want to talk about formulae being true or false at particular times, it is convenient to assume that time points are in fact models of FOPC in the same way that possible worlds were. The meanings of formulae which are not temporally qualified are then given in terms of the standard semantics for FOPC with respect to these models. We will denote a *temporal frame* with a set of time points/worlds T and an order relationship BEFORE by <T, BEFORE>. We will use the notation <T, BEFORE> $\models_t$ A to indicate that the frame <T, BEFORE> models the formula A at time t. With this notation we can give the semantics of the temporal operators with the following rules:

TIME$_{SEM}$1: <T, BEFORE> $\models_t$ FUTURE(A) if and only if <T, BEFORE> $\models_{t'}$ A for some t' such that BEFORE(t, t').

TIME$_{SEM}$2: <T, BEFORE> $\models_t$ PAST(A) if and only if <T, BEFORE> $\models_{t'}$ A for some time t' such that BEFORE(t', t).

TIME$_{SEM}$3: <T, BEFORE> $\models_t$ A$_{FUTURE}$(A) if and only if <T, BEFORE> $\models_t$ A for all times t' such that BEFORE(t, t').

TIME$_{SEM}$4: <T, BEFORE> $\models_t$ A$_{PAST}$(A) if and only if <T, BEFORE> $\models_t$ A for all times t' such that BEFORE(t', t).

These are very precise characterisations of the relations between the temporal operators and property of being modelled by a frame at a time. We have couched them in English in order to emphasise that these are not rules of temporal logic. They are statements about it. We could have stated them as translation axioms between a (temporal) object language and a first-order meta-language, as we did for the modal logics of Chapter 5. We will not go into all the details of this procedure for temporal logics, but it should be clear how we would do it. If we did then we could use standard first-order theorem proving techniques for dealing with our temporal logic.

The axioms up to TIME2$_{PAST}$, together with rules of inference MP and NEC$_{TIME}$, induce a logic whose theorems correspond exactly to the set of formulae which are true at all times in all temporal frames. This is clear for TIME0, TIME1 and TIME2, which characterise normal modal logics, since they make no use of the fact that the relationship between worlds is an order relationship. Adding TIME2$_{FUTURE}$ and TIME2$_{PAST}$ simply exploits the fact that FUTURE and A$_{PAST}$ make exactly complementary use of the order relationship, as do PAST and A$_{FUTURE}$, so that it should come as no surprise that they are well matched by the set of temporal frames (note: this is nothing like a proof that TIME0 to TIME2$_{PAST}$ induce a complete and consistent logic with respect to the set of temporal frames, it is just a hint of the direction in which such a proof might be found).

The remaining axioms are captured by putting constraints on the order relation, just as the axioms T, S4 and B were captured by putting constraints on the accessibility relationship between possible worlds. We could call any logic modelled by a temporal frame with no constraints on the order relationship a *normal temporal logic*, by analogy with normal modal logics, but the accepted term seems to be *minimal temporal logic*. The axiom TIME3$_{FUTURE}$ corresponds to a constraint on BEFORE to the effect that if BEFORE(t, t') and BEFORE(t', t'') both hold, then so does BEFORE(t, t''). TIME3$_{PAST}$ corresponds to the constraint that if BEFORE(t', t) and BEFORE(t'', t') both hold then so does BEFORE(t'', t). We can choose whether or not we want to impose these constraints, exactly as we can choose whether or not we want to accept TIME3$_{FUTURE}$ and TIME3$_{PAST}$.

TIME4$_{PAST}$ requires the constraint that if t' and t'' are both BEFORE t, then one of three conditions holds. t' and t'' may be the same, or t' may be BEFORE t'', or t'' may be BEFORE t'. This constraint forces all times to be preceded by a sequence of earlier times, though it does not rule out the possibility of non-overlapping collections of times. Even with this constraint, we could have a time frame that looks like the following:

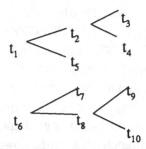

This is a finite time frame which satisfies all the constraints we have seen so far. In particular, although it satisfies the constraint that time does not branch backwards, there is no single point t_0 which precedes all other times, since t_1 and t_6 are not related to each other at all. It is perfectly possible for this to happen with infinite time frames as well as with finite ones.

It is clear that if we wanted to accept TIME4$_{FUTURE}$, the axiom that says that there is only one possible future as well as only one possible past, we could introduce a dual constraint on the relation BEFORE.

The constraints we have seen so far have been like the ones we saw for the accessibility relationships of modal logic, in that they have concerned properties of the relationship rather than of the set of worlds. To capture the remaining temporal axioms that we have looked at we need to talk about properties of the set of times, rather than of the order relationship itself. For the two versions of TIME5, for instance, we have to constrain the set not to contain times FIRST and LAST such that there is no time t for which BEFORE(t, FIRST) holds, and no time t' for which BEFORE(LAST, t') holds. For TIME6 we need to insist that if t and t' are times such that BEFORE(t, t') holds then there is another time t'' such that BEFORE(t, t'') and BEFORE(t'', t') both hold. These are all claims about what times may or may not exist. The constraints relating to TIME5, for instance, require the set of times to be infinite, and the constraint relating to TIME6 requires it to be dense.

The constraints induce interesting relationships between FUTURE and PAST. In unconstrained temporal frames, there are virtually no reliable connections between them. The obvious one, that FUTURE(PAST(A)) ≡ PAST(FUTURE(A)), has a counter-example in the following temporal frame.

If we suppose that <{t$_1$, t$_2$, t$_3$}, BEFORE> ⊨$_{t2}$ A, then clearly <{t$_1$, t$_2$, t$_3$}, BEFORE> ⊨$_{t2}$ PAST(FUTURE(A)) and also <{t$_1$, t$_2$, t$_3$}, BEFORE> ⊨$_{t3}$ PAST(FUTURE(A)), but nowhere does it model FUTURE(PAST(A)). We therefore have a model in which PAST(FUTURE(A)) is true at some time but FUTURE(PAST(A)) is true nowhere, so it cannot be the case that PAST(FUTURE(A)) ≡ FUTURE(PAST(A)). This corresponds to the fact that the English sentences *I will have done it* and *I was going to do it* are not equivalent.

The constraint that time should not be allowed to branch backwards, however, does support a relation between PAST and FUTURE, namely that FUTURE(PAST(A)) → PAST(FUTURE(A)). For suppose that for some frame <T, BEFORE>, some time t in T, and some formula A, <T, BEFORE> ⊨$_t$ FUTURE(PAST(A)) holds. From the semantics of FUTURE and PAST we can infer the existence of times t' and t'' such that <T, BEFORE> ⊨$_{t'}$ PAST(A) and

<T, BEFORE> ⊨$_{t''}$ A, where BEFORE(t, t') and BEFORE(t'', t') both hold. We then know, from the constraint on BEFORE that prevents time from branching backwards, that one of t=t'', BEFORE(t, t'') and BEFORE(t'', t) must hold. Suppose we are in the situation where BEFORE(t, t'') holds, as in:

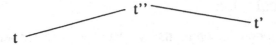

So long as t is not the first point in the history of the universe, there must be a further time t''' BEFORE t, and hence BEFORE t''. Since t''' is BEFORE t'', we have that <T, BEFORE> ⊨$_{t'''}$ FUTURE(A), and then since t''' is also before t we can then conclude <T, BEFORE> ⊨$_t$ PAST(FUTURE(A)). We can carry out more or less the same argument if t and t'' are the same time point, so all we have to consider now is the case where t'' is BEFORE t, i.e.

In this case we have to posit a time t''' which is BEFORE t''. Since A holds at t'', we know that FUTURE(A) holds at t''', and hence, since t''' is also BEFORE t, we know that PAST(FUTURE(A)) holds at t, i.e. <T, BEFORE> ⊨$_t$ PAST(FUTURE(A)). We thus see that if time is constrained not to branch backwards, and if there is no point in time which has no preceding points, then FUTURE(PAST(A)) → PAST(FUTURE(A)) is valid. The point at which we used the fact that time could not branch backwards was in inferring that t and t'' must be ordered with respect to one another; we needed the fact that there was no first moment when we posited a point t''' which was before both of t and t''.

It is obvious that for PAST(FUTURE(A)) → FUTURE(PAST(A)) to be valid time will have to be constrained not to branch forwards either. There seems little point in going through all the details again. The crucial point of this section is that constraints on the ordering relation on time points have a major influence on the formulae which will be valid, and that certain interesting formulae can only be shown to be valid under very specific combinations of such constraints. As far as theorem proving about temporal logics is concerned, the complexity of the constraints on the order relation suggests that it is likely to be easier to derive first-order theorems about validity than to try to devise a specialised version of the connection method, or to use any other direct mechanisation of temporal logic. This is particularly true in contexts where you may want to investigate the consequences of different combinations of constraints, for instance using one version of temporal logic to work out what WILL happen if you perform a particular sequence of actions, and another version for working out what MIGHT happen given all the possible actions somebody else might take.

6.3 The situation calculus

The approaches to temporal reasoning that we have seen so far seem to regard time as something which has its own existence, and to which events and actions can be related. One thing happens before another if the time at which the first happens is before the time at which the second happens. Even if nothing happens, time still passes. For many purposes, however, we are interested in chains of events, rather than in sequences of instants. In the context of AI planning systems, for instance, what matters is the changes to the world that are brought about by specific actions. Most of these systems use a framework for reasoning about time based on McCarthy and Hayes' (1969) *situation calculus.*

The situation calculus is based, naturally enough, on a notion of situation. A situation is taken to be something like a snapshot of the world. It is a collection of statements which are all true at the same time. The notation of the situation calculus is very similar to that of the reified modal logic of actions described in Chapter 5. It is simply a version of predicate calculus in which predicates have one more argument than would normally be expected, where the extra argument is the name of a situation. We include an extra set of constants, S_0, S_1, ..., which are intended to have situations as their values, and we replace each N-place predicate of FOPC by an N+1 place predicate with the same name. To say, for instance, that Cherry is hungry in situation S_0, we would simply write hungry(Cherry, S_0). S_0 is the name of a situation. The semantics of the situation calculus is given, as usual, by providing a frame consisting of a collection of standard models of FOPC and a relation (which is in fact a partial order) between them. A *situation frame* consists of a collection of situations, a valuation function which assigns a situation from the set to each of the constants S_i, and an order relation. The semantics is then given by the following rules:

SIT1: If P is an N-place predicate of FOPC, a_1, ..., a_N are constants of FOPC, and S_i is a situation constant, then $P(a_1, ..., a_N, S_i)$ is a formula of the situation calculus. The situation frame <SITUATIONS, V_s, BEFORE> is a model of $P(a_1, ..., a_N, S_i)$ if and only if $V_s(Si) \vDash P(a_1, ..., a_N)$.

SIT2: If F is a formula of the situation calculus made up out of simpler formulae connected by one of the logical operators v, &, →, ¬, ∀ and ∃, then the rules for determining whether some frame models it are the same as usual (e.g. <SITUATIONS, V_s, BEFORE> $\vDash$ A $\vee$ B holds if and only if <SITUATIONS, V_s, BEFORE> $\vDash$ A or <SITUATIONS, V_s, BEFORE> $\vDash$ B, and so on).

There are no operators specifically concerned with talking about relations between situations. Instead we have characterisations of actions which describe the relations between situations in which they are executed and situations which result from their execution. The action of picking up a block, for instance, would be described by the following:

$$\forall\_S_1 \forall\_S_2 \forall\_x(\text{pickup}(\_x, \_S_1, \_S_2) \rightarrow$$
$$\text{holding}(\_x, \_S_1) \And \neg \exists\_y(\text{on}(\_y, \_x, \_S_1))$$
$$\And \exists\_z(\text{on}(\_x, \_z, \_S_1) \And \neg\text{on}(\_x, \_z, \_S_2))$$
$$\And \text{FRAME-AXIOMS})$$

This is very much the same as the description we had in Chapter 5 for the same action. There has been a slight change in notation, in that situations are supplied as arguments to predicates rather than via the meta-language predicate T, but it does not really make an enormous difference. What has changed is the inclusion of the final component of the situation calculus version, the *frame axioms*. Frame axioms are collections of statements about things that do NOT change when you perform an action.

The need for frame axioms is not restricted to the situation calculus. Any formal analysis of reasoning about actions will have to take account of the fact that most actions have only a very small number of effects. It is tempting to deal with this problem by saying that the description of an action should include all the changes that it brings about, so that the frame axioms amount to saying that nothing else changes. We cannot state that nothing else changes concisely in a first-order language, but it is certainly possible to state it verbosely. For every N-place predicate P not mentioned in the original statement, we would have to add a conjunct of the form:

$$\forall\_x_1 \ldots \_x_N(P(\_x_1, \ldots, \_x_N, \_S_1) \equiv P(\_x_1, \ldots, x_N, \_S_2))$$

For predicates which were mentioned in the effects of the action we would have to be careful to ensure that the new conjunct explicitly ignored the particular entities which were affected by the action, so that the predicate on, for instance, would need the following conjunct:

$$\forall \_x_1 \forall \_x_2 (\_x_1 \neq \_x \ \& \ \_x_2 \neq \_z \rightarrow [on(\_x_1, \_x_2, \_S_1) \equiv on(\_x_1, \_x_2, \_S_2)])$$

This would be tedious, but would be effective so long as we only had a finite number of predicates to deal with. In the context of the situation calculus we can take the following shortcut. Suppose we start out with a collection of statements we know to be true in some situation S_0, and we accept the *closed world assumption* (CWA) that anything which we do not know to be true is false. To take a concrete example we will imagine that we know that the world contains a table T and three blocks A, B and C, and that in S_0 A and B are both on the table and C is on top of A. We record every predicate and set of arguments that we know to be true in S_0, marking the situation and the fact that it is known to be true. In the concrete example this amounts to setting up the following database:

on(A, table):   <S_0 true>
on(B, table):   <S_0 true>
on(C, B):   <S_0 true>

As usual we characterise actions by sets of preconditions and effects, with the FRAME-AXIOMS left empty. We then try to work out what would be true in a situation S_1 which arose from performing some action in situation S_0. To imagine the situation that would arise from performing an action we add the effects of the action to our database. Suppose we performed the action of picking up C in the example world. The database would be changed to the following:

on(A, table):   <S_0 true>
on(B, table):   <S_0 true>
on(C, B):   <S_1 false> <S_0 true>
holding(C):   <S_1 true>

We have mimicked the order relation that holds between S_0 and S_1 by treating the records of truth values associated with particular predicate-argument combinations as stacks. Suppose, for instance, we want to see if on(C, B) is true in some situation. We look down the stack of values associated with on(C,B) until we come to an entry whose situation component is the same as, or earlier than, that of the situation in which we are interested. Is on(C,B) true in S_1? No, because the first entry we come across in the stack of values for on(C,B) is <S_1 false>. S_1 is clearly the same as or earlier than S_1, since it is S_1, and the associated truth value is false. Is on(B, table) true in S_1? Yes, since the first appropriate entry we come across for it is <S_0 true> - S_0 is earlier than S_1, and the associated truth value is true.

This is more an implementation technique than an argument about the nature of time or action. It is a very dense way of recording changes in the truth values of propositions. It furthermore provides very rapid access to the truth value of a proposition in the most recently created situation, since all you have to do is look at the stack of associated values. If the stack is empty then the CWA tells you that the proposition must be false in the given situation, otherwise its truth value is simply the one recorded in the top entry. If, therefore, you accept the CWA and the *universal frame axiom* that nothing which is not explicitly mentioned in the description of an action is changed by it, then this implementation of the situation calculus provides rapid access to the truth values of propositions in different situations.

Both the CWA and the universal frame axiom can lead to trouble. Problems arise with the CWA if it is possible to acquire new knowledge about the world, since whenever you discover a new fact you may have to revise any conclusions you had drawn on the basis of your previous assumption that it was false. This is particularly awkward when working with actions which can bring about knowledge, since you may be able to find out in S_1 some fact about S_0 which you did not know in S_0, and which the CWA would therefore have led you to disbelieve of S_0. The universal frame axiom will introduce problems if actions can have indirect consequences of actions as well as direct ones. Suppose, for instance, that we had the following rule:

$$\forall\_S(\text{empty-hand}(\_S) \equiv \neg \exists\_x(\text{holding}(\_x, \_S)))$$

In other words, your hand is empty exactly when you are not holding anything. If we wanted to know whether or not hand-empty held in some situation we would have two ways of finding out. We could inspect the database to see whether it contained a relevant entry; or we could use the inference rule, which would lead us to inspect the database for entries to do with holding things. The two are likely to lead to conflicting answers. In the present case, inspecting the initial database for an entry about hand-empty would, via the CWA, lead to the conclusion that it was false. Inspecting it to discover the value of $\exists\_x(\text{holding}(\_x, S_0))$, however, would lead to the conclusion that this was false, and thence to the conclusion that hand-empty(S_0) itself was true. Which should we choose?

At first sight, it is tempting to suggest that whenever we want to update the database to reflect the construction of a new situation we should include all the consequences of the changes as well as the changes themselves. This, unfortunately, may lead to unlimited amounts of computation. Working out the

consequences of changing the truth value of a single statement is a completely
open-ended problem. Even if we restrict our attention to formulae whose truth
values are already recorded in the database, there is no bound on the amount of
work involved in investigating the consequences of changing the truth value of a
single statement. In the worst case, simply seeing whether one statement whose
value is recorded in the database is affected by a single other change will lead to a
non-terminating computation.

The obvious alternative is to distinguish between *primary predicates*, which
can appear in action descriptions, and which can therefore appear in formulae
which appear in the database, and *secondary predicates*, whose values depend on
the values of primary ones. This is rather an artificial solution, but nothing else
seems to be even feasible. The *frame problem*, i.e. the problem of finding a way
to cope with the fact that most actions leave most things unchanged, is a
pervasive problem when reasoning about time and action. We have highlighted it
in this section because the situation calculus seems, at first sight, to provide a
way of making it more manageable. Any other approach we take to reasoning
about actions is going to have to find a solution to this problem. The most
successful formalism available so far for dealing with it is the *default logic* of
Section 7.3.1, but this is also rather difficult to deal with computationally. None
of the other approaches in the current chapter cope as well as the situation
calculus, but as we have just shown, the treatment within this approach is also
badly flawed.

6.3.1 *The event calculus*
Kowalski (1986) proposes an alternative to the situation calculus in which facts
are indexed by intervals during which they are true, rather than by points of time
at which they become true. The theories we have seen so far have taken the view
that the best way to talk about time is as a set of instants. Events happen at
particular times, and their consequences are then true at all subsequent times until
other events cause them to be no longer true. From this point of view, an *interval*
is a closed, dense connected set of instants (in other words it contains all the
instants between two end points). It is possible to turn this view round, taking
intervals as the primitive building blocks of a theory of time, and instants simply
as the names for the end points of intervals. Kowalski's *event calculus* does
exactly this. An operator called HOLDS, which is analogous to the operator
TRUE of Chapter 5, is introduced to denote that some statement holds during
some interval. HOLDS(owns(John, book1), I_0), for instance, would have the
intended interpretation that the person called John was the owner of the book
denoted by book1 during the interval I_0. Specifications of actions and

spontaneous events now contain clauses which initiate and terminate intervals. There is a general inference rule called the *initiation rule* (INIT), which enables you to infer the existence of intervals during which things hold from the fact that an event which brings them about has been performed:

INIT: $\dfrac{\text{HAPPENS}(e),\ \text{INITIATES}(e, r)}{\text{HOLDS}(r,\ \text{AFTER}(e, r))}$

In other words, if we know that some event e happens, and we know that e is an event which would bring about the fact r, then we can infer the existence of an interval AFTER(e, r) during which r holds. The interval has to be indexed both by the event name e and the result r, since a single event may bring about several results which subsequently persist for different lengths of time. We will want to be able to refer explicitly to these intervals, so we need to be able to distinguish them by noting what it is that is known to hold during them. The double occurrence of r in the expression HOLDS(r, AFTER(e, r)) may seem redundant. Kowalski, in fact, drops the first occurrence, abbreviating the expression to HOLDS(AFTER(e, r)), but though this is more compact it does seem to be significantly more confusing.

Once we have INIT, we can write down descriptions of actions in terms of what they initiate. Selling something to someone, for instance, would have as part of its description the following statement:

$\forall\_x \forall\_y \forall\_z \forall\_e\ [act(\_e, sell)\ \&\ buyer(\_e, \_x)\ \&\ seller(\_e, \_y)\ \&\ goods(\_e, \_x)]$
$\rightarrow \text{INITIATES}(\_e, owner(\_y, \_z))$

In other words, if _e is an act of selling, where _x is the person who is selling something, _y is the person to whom it is sold, and _z is the thing being sold, then _e initiates the result that _y is the owner of _z. The use of predicate names for naming roles that entities play in events is just like any other use of predicate names - the relationship between _e and _x, for instance, is just like any other relationship we have seen, such as being on top of something, or being true in a world, or whatever. The notion that events are simply entities like any others can cause some problems, notably with properties concerning the manner in which the event occurred. Davidson (1980) considers a number of such problems in the context of event based interpretations of natural language sentences such as *John ate all the peaches slowly*, where we have to distinguish between John eating each individual peach very quickly, but taking a long time about eating all of them because there were so many, and John taking a long time over each of them individually. If we postpone worrying about these issues for the moment, we can see that if we had a description of a specific selling event, then the general description of sales together with the rule INIT would enable us to infer the existence of an interval in which we knew the ownership of the object which had been sold, as follows:

1 act(E1, sell)
2 buyer(E1, Mary)
3 seller(E1, John)
4 goods(E1, bike26)
5 $\forall\_x \forall\_y \forall\_z \forall\_e$ [act(_e, sell) & buyer(_e, _x) & seller(_e, _y) & goods(_e, _x)]
          → INITIATES(_e, owner(_y, _z))
6 INITIATES(E1, owner(Mary, bike26) (MP on 1,2,3,4,5)
7 HOLDS(owner(Mary, bike26), AFTER(E1, owner(Mary, bike26)) (INIT on 6)

We also need to be able to talk about events which cause things to cease to be true. Kowalski introduces a predicate, TERMINATES, which holds between an event and a fact if the event brings it about that the fact will cease to be true. Selling, for instance, entails that the seller of the goods ceases to own them, as well as that the buyer begins to own them:

$\forall\_x \forall\_y \forall\_z \forall\_e$ [act(_e, sell) & buyer(_e, _x) & seller(_e, _y) & goods(_e, _x)]
          → TERMINATES(_e, owner(_x, _z))

We need a rule called TERMIN, parallel to INIT, for introducing the interval before the performance of an action which terminates some state of affairs.

TERMIN: HAPPENS(e), TERMINATES(e, r)
            ─────────────────────────────
            HOLDS(r, BEFORE(e,r))

INIT and TERMIN suffice to enable us to infer the existence of intervals during which particular statements are true. We do not as yet have any way of talking about relations between intervals, and hence have no way of working out what will be true when. In the example of John selling Mary his bike, we know from INIT and TERMIN that he owned it in the interval denoted by BEFORE(E1, owner(John, bike26)) and that she owned it in the interval denoted by AFTER(E1, owner(Mary, bike26)). But apart from the fact that the names of these intervals include the suggestive predicates BEFORE and AFTER, we do not actually know anything about the relationship between them. Even if we did assume that we had axioms which specified the ordering between them, there is nothing in what we have seen so far to enable us to infer that HOLDS(owner(John, bike26), AFTER(E1, owner(Mary, bike26))) is not true. It seems as though we need a set of time points again; a way of relating intervals to events by date-stamping them; and the following *persistence axiom*:

$$\forall\_e\forall\_r\forall\_t\forall\_n \ ([HOLDS(AFTER(\_e, \_r))$$
$$\& \ DATE(\_e, \_t) \& \_t < \_n$$
$$\& \ \neg\exists\_e'\exists\_t'(HAPPENS(\_e')$$
$$\& \ TERMINATES(\_e', \_r) \& \ DATE(\_e', \_t')$$
$$\& \ \_t < \_t' \& \_t' < \_n)] \rightarrow HOLDS\text{-}AT(\_r, \_n))$$

This axiom makes reasonable sense. It says that _r will hold at time _n if something has happened which would cause it to be true, and nothing has subsequently happened which would make it false again. It may even be that careful organisation of the way such rules are represented, and of the way that specific events are indexed, will make it easy to work out whether or not some fact is true at some particular time. The extremely casual presentation that Kowalski (1986) provides us with, however, leaves rather too many matters open to inspire confidence. Among these are (i) the particular axioms which govern the relations between intervals, events and their dates, and the structure of the set of time points; (ii) a throwaway remark about the need to maintain the consistency of the set of propositions believed to be true during an interval, as though this were not in itself an undecidable problem; and (iii) the cavalier approach to the relations HOLDS and HOLDS-AT. As we have already noted, these relations are extremely reminiscent of the predicate TRUE of the reified approach to modal logic. It seems likely that we will have exactly the same problems dealing with questions about when we can infer HOLDS-AT(A ∨ B, n) or HOLDS(∃xP, n) as we had with reified modal logic. It is therefore disingenuous of Kowalski to suggest that "... of all the alternative approaches, modal temporal logic has seemed to have the least to offer". The event calculus is of interest because of the insights it provides into the use of intervals in a simple framework for planning, but it does not absolve us from careful analysis of the relations between intervals, events and instants. We therefore end this chapter with a consideration of the kind of axioms that will be needed to make an interval-based approach as precise as the point-based approaches we considered at the start.

6.4 Points or intervals?

It seems as though sometimes we need to think about time as though it were made up of a succession of instants, and sometimes as though the basic building blocks were extended periods. It is probably not appropriate for us to try to work out whether time really is made of instants or chunks. The real nature of time, if there is such a thing, is more the concern of physicists than logicians. If there is an answer to this question it is probably to be found somewhere in quantum theory and general relativity, along with the answers to questions about the real nature of space. Our concern here is to find ways of thinking about time that work in a reasonably wide range of everyday circumstances. As an example of the tension between the "real" nature of time and our everyday conception of it, we note Reichenbach's (1971) suggestion that time cannot reliably be seen to be linearly ordered, on the grounds that the mathematical description of the behaviour of anti-matter can most easily be seen as a description of ordinary matter moving backwards through time. This should not be allowed to overrule the assumption that for everyday purposes we should accept that time is properly ordered, and that *before* and *after* are meaningful words.

If we accept, however, that the axiomatic treatments of time we are considering are in fact just conveniences, to be used for reasoning about everyday problems but not to be taken too seriously, then it is inappropriate to get into heated debates about whether point-based sets of axioms are better than interval-based ones or vice versa. We should note that points are convenient for some tasks, and intervals for others. We should further take care that our analysis of the relations between the two types of object makes sense, and that we provide enough machinery to enable us to describe everything we need to describe, and leave it at that. The question is not whether our theory of time is right - we know in fact that it is not - but whether it enables us to draw useful conclusions.

We end this chapter, then, with a look at some questions raised by Allen (1984) and McDermott (1982) about the kind of thing we need to be able to describe, and with Allen's characterisation of the relations between points and intervals. Allen and McDermott discuss three major distinctions which we need to be able to make but which are hard to capture within the frameworks we have discussed so far. The first of these is raised by McDermott in the context of anticipating the effects of our plans. Suppose we consider St. George, looking at a scene containing a ravenous dragon and a sacrificial damsel. He employs his ability to reason about future events and comes to the conclusion that the dragon will shortly devour the damsel. He doesn't want to see this happen, so he forms a plan to save her by killing the dragon. He now reviews his vision of the future and sees that the damsel is no longer in any danger, and hence he need not do anything to save her. This reassures him considerably, since he was not at all sure that he would be able to kill this fearsome animal, and he is greatly relieved that he does not have to try. The flaw in this reasoning, of course, is that he has failed to distinguish between two alternative possible futures, one in which he kills the dragon and the damsel is safe, and one in which he takes no action and she is eaten. We have already accepted that for some purposes it is useful to think about time as though there were a number of alternative futures, even though only one of them is going to be realised. The lesson of our story about St. George is that we ought to be careful to categorise alternative futures according to the events which we envisage happening, and to distinguish between constructing a plan to bring about some goal and intending to act it out.

The next problem concerns the characterisation of actions which seem to have no effects. These can be extremely passive actions, such as staying in bed all morning, or more active ones which simply bring us back to where we started, such as running to Brighton and back, or complex ones which ensure that nothing happens, such as standing where I am in order to prevent you from seeing the stolen microfiche on the table behind me. We could probably get some sort of characterisation of staying in bed all morning in Kowalski's event calculus, since Kowalski's intervals are characterised by some identifying proposition. An interval for Kowalski is not just the set of time points between some start and finish points, it is that set of points plus some collection of propositions that are true during them. The interval with end points 9:00am and 1:00pm during which Allan was in bed is not the same interval as the one with the same end points during which Ros was in the garden, and we could describe Allan's "action" of staying in bed all morning by referring to the existence of the relevant interval. This will not work so easily if we want to describe the interval during which Ros ran round Preston Park three times. There is no obvious single proposition which is true all the time she was doing it, so we cannot refer to an interval characterised by start and end points and a characteristic proposition. We might perhaps propose a property of running-thrice-round-Preston-Park, and posit that it was true of Ros during the specified interval, but it hardly seems very helpful. To make any real progress we need to be able to talk about the instants that make up the interval. If we can do that, then we can specify the characteristic property of this interval by:

∃_I([∀_t(member(_t, _I)
    → (HOLDS-AT(_t, running(Ros))
    & HOLDS-AT(_t, in(Ros, Preston-Park))))]
& ∃_t_1∃_t_2∃_t_3(_t_1 ≠ _t_2 & _t_1 ≠ _t_3 & _t_2 ≠ _t_3
    & HOLDS-AT(_t_1, at(Ros, entrance(Preston-Park))
    & HOLDS-AT(_t_2, at(Ros, entrance(Preston-Park))
    & HOLDS-AT(_t_3, at(Ros, entrance(Preston-Park))
    & ∀_t_4[member(_t_4, _I) & _t_4 ≠ _t_1 & _t_4 ≠ _t_2 & _t_4 ≠ _t_3]
        → ¬(HOLDS-AT(_t_4, at(Ros, entrance(Preston-Park))))))))

The predicates we have used here seem rather more acceptable than the absurd running-thrice-round-Preston-Park. The formula we have constructed is fairly complex, but each bit of it seems necessary, so we have to accept that descriptions of events like this probably will be fairly complex. The crucial thing to note about it, though, is that it makes essential use of both points and intervals, and of the relations between them.

The case of null actions with effects, such as standing where I am in order to prevent you seeing what is behind me, can be treated in much the same way. If we accept that → captures the notion of cause correctly, then the action of standing still to stop you seeing the microfiche is something like the following:

∃_I∀_t(member(_t, _I) → [HOLDS-AT(_t, standing(Allan))
                        & HOLDS-AT(_t, at(Allan, LOC1))])
& (at(Allan, LOC1) → ¬(seeing(Reader, μ-fiche)))

Of course the interpretation we have been giving to → is not what we usually mean by causation, so that to get a more adequate analysis of this action we need to include a more adequate notion of cause. But it is not the analysis of time that is at fault here. If we knew what it meant for one thing to cause another, we could replace at(Allan, LOC1) → ¬(seeing(Reader, μ-fiche)) by CAUSES(at(Allan, LOC1), ¬(seeing(Reader, μ-fiche)). If we knew what CAUSES meant, this would be a pretty accurate description of the specified action.

The final general point raised by McDermott and Allen is the need to distinguish between *state-like* and *event-like* intervals. A state-like interval is one where each sub-interval is of the same type as the interval as a whole. The interval defined as the period between 9:00am and 1:00pm during which I am in bed is like this. The interval between 9:10am and 9:15am is just like the larger interval except that its end points are closer together. This is in contrast to the interval we would refer to as *the period during which Stevenson wrote Treasure*

Island. This seems like a coherent concept, and we would like to be able to refer to it in our logic of time just as much as we would like to be able to refer to the period I spent in bed. It is clear that this new interval is not state-like. Whatever it is that characterises the period during which Stevenson wrote Treasure Island is definitely not true for any lesser interval. To talk about this interval we would probably want to be able to refer explicitly to its end points:

$$\exists\_I(\forall\_t(BEFORE(\_t, start(\_I)) \to \neg\exists\_x(\_x = page(1, \text{T-Island})))$$
$$\& \ \forall\_t(AFTER(\_t, end(\_I)) \to \exists\_x(\_x = page(234, \text{T-Island}))))$$

The idea that we can represent the statement that Stevenson has not started writing Treasure Island by saying that its first page does not yet exist, and the statement that he has finished writing it by saying that its final page does exist, is obviously very crude. It does, however, bring out the essential difference between the two kinds of interval. One is defined by properties of its end points, the other by properties that are shared by every intermediate point.

The moral of this discussion is that it is indeed important to be able to talk fluently about both points and intervals, and to understand the relationship between them. Allen takes the view that intervals are rather more complicated than points, so that correct axiomatisation of their properties is going to be rather harder. It may be that the axioms for points will follow immediately from the axioms for intervals, but even if they do not they are unlikely to impose any new structure which conflicts with the structure imposed by the interval axioms. If we go the other way, providing axioms for points before axioms for intervals, we may find that we made a decision about how we thought about points without realising all its consequences, and only subsequently find that this conflicts with something we want to say about intervals. Allen has provided several alternative axiom sets for intervals. There seems little point in giving a detailed rehearsal of any particular set. The descriptions in Allen (1983, 1984) are as adequate as any other axiomatisation we have seen, but they do not make any radically different recommendations. It is perhaps worth noting that in these reports Allen suggests that we should do away with time points entirely, arguing that it is easier to think solely in terms of intervals, but allowing intervals to be arbitrarily short. This decision may turn out to be difficult to square with the need to attach dates to beginnings and ends of intervals - certainly all the worked examples in Allen (1984) are in terms of abstract intervals, with no reference to specific times.

6.5 Review of temporal logics

It is striking that the theories of temporal logic we have seen leave so many choices open. None of them can realistically be claimed to be descriptions of what time is *really* like, and it is hard to find very strong grounds for choosing one over another. Points or intervals? Branching or nor branching? Continuous or discrete? There does not seem to be any absolute reason for supposing that one decision is better than another. It may, however, be possible to make a rational choice once you have considered the characteristics of the specific problem you are working on. The event calculus, for instance, might turn out to be a good choice if you are trying to solve a planning problem where the available actions can be described in terms of effects and preconditions. It might be useful to think of time as branching backwards if you are trying to work out how you got into the situation you find yourself in. It might be that you do not want to think about time as being dense if you are trying to reason about the behaviour of programs (Gabbay 1987). Casting these theories in terms of axiom sets gives them a spurious air of authority. They are not descriptions of the nature of time. It is better to think of them as abstractions which may or may not prove suitable to a particular problem domain or a particular style of reasoning. You can pick or choose as you like, so long as you make sure that you have compared the supposed advantages of the theory you pick with the detailed properties of your current task. Above all, it should always be remembered that the simpler the axiom set, the more likely you are to be able to actually arrive at useful results using a reasonably orthodox inference engine.

CHAPTER SEVEN

NON-MONOTONIC REASONING

7.1 Monotonic and non-monotonic inference

We have seen a number of ways in which classical logic may be adapted or extended to make it more suitable for our purposes. These alternatives to the classical theory have differed in a variety of ways, but they have all shared one of its major properties, namely *monotonicity*. A theory is monotonic if the addition of new knowledge about the world can increase, but not decrease, the set of inferences which can be drawn. In all the theories we have seen so far, if a conclusion Q follows from a set of sentences $P_1 \dots P_n$, then it will also follow if we add a new sentence P to the set.

Monotonicity follows directly from either of the basic characterisations of logic, either as the study of valid arguments, or as the study of entailment. Looking at logic as the study of valid argument, monotonicity can be taken as saying that if $P_1 \dots P_n \vdash Q$ then $P, P_1, \dots, P_n \vdash Q$. The standard description of an argument or a proof specifies conditions under which a formula may be used as a step. These conditions refer to monotonic properties of the formula, namely whether it is an instance of an axiom or is a member of the set of assumptions. Neither of these conditions can possibly be falsified by the addition of new assumptions, so anything which counted as a valid proof or argument with respect to the old set of assumptions must still do so with respect to the augmented set. If we are concerned with entailment rather than proof, then monotonicity amounts to saying that if, for any model M, $M \vDash P_1 \& \dots \& P_n$ implies $M \vDash Q$, then $M \vDash P \& P_1 \& \dots \& P_n$ also implies $M \vDash Q$. To see that this generally holds, we can consider the set of models of the original assumption set. Clearly anything which is a model of the extended set is also a model of the original, and hence is also a model of the conclusion. It is worth noting in passing that even if we add the negation of the conclusion or the negation of one of the assumptions, the original argument will still hold. Formally, if $P_1, ..., P_n \vdash Q$ then $\neg Q, P_1, ..., P_n \vdash Q$ and also $\neg P_i, P_1, ..., P_n \vdash Q$ (where i is between 1 and n).

It seems, then, that all the standard ways of thinking about logic lead to monotonic systems. Once a set of assumptions has been shown to entail a conclusion, the only way to get rid of the conclusion is to delete one of the assumptions. There are, however, a number of mundane contexts in which we may want to use inference rules for which this property cannot be guaranteed. The purpose of the current chapter is to survey the situations in which we may need to use non-monotonic inference rules; to consider the formal properties of such rules as far as they are understood; and to present concrete mechanisms for coping with the practical problems which arise when we need to use them.

7.2 Uses of non-monotonic rules

7.2.1 *Uses of non-monotonic rules: explorations*
In any sort of problem solving, it is essential to be able to explore the consequences of different hypotheses about the world. A theorem prover trying to solve the three blocks problem needs to be able to explore the different cases for the possible colour of the middle block; a language processing program trying to analyse the sentence *They refused them a permit because they were communists* will have to explore the consequences of different assumptions about the referents of the pronouns; a fault finding program for circuit boards will have to try out different combinations of hypotheses about where the fault might lie.

In a number of domains, specific techniques have been developed for ensuring that conclusions arrived at under one set of hypotheses are still available when these are replaced by appropriate alternatives. Chart parsing, for instance, enables language processing programs to access structures built up in the course of alternative overall analyses. The connection graph discussed in Chapter 4 makes clauses derived in the course of one attempt at a solution available in any subsequent attempts. Such special purpose algorithms can greatly improve the performance of systems which have to perform non-deterministic searches of large spaces. It is, however, easy to construct examples where the special purpose techniques do not apply, but where it is clear that results derived under one set of hypotheses should be passed into contexts where a different set hold. Suppose, for instance, that you were trying to work out why your car would not start. You might start by exploring the hypothesis that the ignition key was faulty. To test this you would turn the key. If the engine turned over at this point, you could conclude that there was nothing wrong with the ignition key, and furthermore that there was nothing wrong with the battery. This extra inference would remain available to you when you came to investigate alternative possibilities - having tested the ignition key, you would have no further need to test the battery, and you would be able to use the conclusion about the battery in any other tests you did decide to try.

The point to note here is that there is no need for you to be committed to any particular hypothesis until you have found good evidence for it. Even if you are merely exploring possibilities, you may make inferences which you want to re-use when you come to consider alternatives. In specific cases such as parsing or theorem proving you may be able to find carefully tailored representations and algorithms which can help you; in general you will need ways of working with non-monotonic inferences.

7.2.2 Uses of non-monotonic rules: defaults

There are also frequent cases where intelligent systems need to work with propositions to which they are committed, but which can nevertheless be falsified. The most blatant examples of arguments which may be undermined by the addition of new knowledge occur in systems whose knowledge is supposed to reflect the current state of the world. In any such system, any chain of inference based on the facts as they are known at the moment may be undermined by information about changes to the world. If, for instance, I decide I can afford to buy a new pair of shoes, my reasoning will have to be revised if I discover I have lost my wallet. A plan to have a picnic, based on the fact that the sun is shining, would have to be changed if it started to rain. A program which classified people as being in credit or debt should change its classification in response to new information about transactions on their bank account, and should revise any inferences based on the previous classification.

These examples generally seem to be instances of the frame problem. The reasoning in the first example could be sketched as follows: *I have enough money now to buy a new pair of shoes. I see no reason why I should have any less money when I get to the shops. Therefore when I get to the shops I shall have enough money to buy a pair of shoes.* Similarly, the reasoning in the second example is something like: *If it's sunny, a picnic is a good idea. It's sunny now, so it should be sunny later. Therefore we can have a picnic later.* In such examples, the chain of reasoning nearly always depends on an assumption of the form *P is true now, therefore P will be true later.*

To get by in everyday life, we need to make assumptions of this form, and then to be able to cope with the consequences when the assumption turns out to be ill-founded. We also need to be able to make a variety of other types of assumption. Knowledge representation schemes for AI frequently include ways of stating assumptions. Type hierarchies embody assumptions about properties of typical tokens of the type, so that a rule of the form *All birds can fly* can be used with the fact *X is a bird* to infer *X can fly*. Inferences of this form are non-monotonic, since subsequent discovery of the fact *X is an ostrich* would lead to retraction of *X can fly*, even though it is itself quite consistent with the premise *X is a bird* which was used to justify the inference. Default slot fillers of the sort found in frame based representations embody similar assumptions. A default slot filler such as elephant(_X) → colour(_X, grey) can be used to infer the conclusion colour(Nellie, grey) until such time as concrete evidence that Nellie is in fact pink is discovered.

7.2.3 *Uses of non-monotonic rules: beliefs and contradictions*
In most existing AI systems, non-monotonic inferences usually occur either when the system is exploring hypotheses which it has no *a priori* grounds for distinguishing, or when it has used some default rule on the grounds that it has no reason not to. In the first case the system has no commitment to any particular hypothesis, in the second its commitment is sanctioned by observed regularities about the world. People, in fact, also get involved in non-monotonic inferences where they do have a commitment to their hypotheses, but do not have any strong sanction for this commitment, in other words, when they believe things. Beliefs can come about from a variety of sources - simple mistakes, as in believing that I paid you back the money you lent me; unifying assumptions, such as believing in the existence of God; misinformation, as when someone tells you (intentionally or not) that you have ten minutes to catch your train when in fact you only have five; and so on. What they have in common is that they can be falsified by later evidence, so that any inferences based on them may have to be retracted. As AI systems become more complicated we have to face the fact that they will probably come to have all these sorts of belief as well as the relatively principled ones they have now. Mechanisms for coping with complex sets of falsifiable inferences will be required even if we can solve the problems associated with problem exploration and default reasoning.

Belief systems, of all types, are prone to inconsistency. In any classical context, this would be seen as a grave problem, since it is well known that any inconsistent set of propositions suffices to justify any conclusion whatsoever. Any formal treatment of non-monotonic inference systems must provide an account of how to deal with inconsistencies - how to recognise them, how to resolve them, and how to distinguish sound inferences within an inconsistent system from unsound ones. Consider the following set of propositions: A, C, A → B, C → D, ¬(B & D), A → E, C → E, E → F. Taken as a whole these are inconsistent, since from A and A → B we can infer B, from C and C → D we can infer D, but from ¬(B & D) we know that B and D cannot both be true. What we would like our analysis of this set of propositions to do is enable us to realise that there is a problem; to pinpoint our options for resolving it (i.e. retract any of the first five propositions); and yet to ensure that any inferences using F are retained, since the derivation of F will remain valid no matter how we resolve the inconsistency. The task splits into two parts: formal analysis of when we are justified in believing something, and development of practical mechanisms for managing our sets of beliefs and inferences.

7.3 Formal properties of assumption based reasoning

Non-monotonic inferences may arise from a variety of causes. As outlined above, we may make inferences based on our accurate current knowledge of the world, only to have to revise them when the world itself changes. In this case we are faced with practical problems about which of our conclusions need to be revised and which can be retained. There are not, however, any theoretical problems about the nature of the justifications - the inferences were perfectly sound and orthodox, it is just that the world has changed. We may also make inferences on the basis of pure, unjustified beliefs. Again we have a practical problem when we are forced to concede that one of our beliefs is untrue, so that any conclusions which depend on it must be revised. And again there is no theoretical problem - beliefs can turn out to be false, and there is no need for us to try to do anything about it in the logic.

We have also seen that non-monotonic inferences can arise when various sorts of default rule are used. These rules seem to behave systematically. They have a coherent interpretation, there are formal inference steps involving them, and we can make judgements about them such as showing that some set of defaults has no coherent interpretation, or that some other set inevitably entails some conclusion no matter what assumptions you make. It seems worth trying to develop a logic of such rules, i.e. a precise formulation of their semantics, a precise set of inference steps for them, and a set of meta-theorems showing that the inference steps accurately reflect the semantics. The main attempts to provide such logics are Reiter's (1980) *default logic* and McCarthy's (1980) theory of *circumscription*, which are reviewed in the next two sections.

7.3.1 *Default logic*
Reiter introduces a notation for default rules as follows:

<u><basic preconditions> : ◇(refutable preconditions)</u>
conclusion

A *default rule* of this sort is to be read as saying *if the basic preconditions are all true, and none of the refutable preconditions are known to be false, then you can infer the conclusion*. This is a very general form for a default rule, and it is hard to imagine any cases which it fails to capture.

Reiter concentrates on a specialisation of this form, namely on rules of the form *if A is consistent with what you know, assume A is true*. Rules of this form have two attractions: they are by far the most common form of assumption used in AI systems, so that any treatment of them will have wide applicability; and they are reasonably amenable to formal analysis. Before we move on to the formal analysis, it is worth looking briefly at some typical uses of defaults to show that they are all, in fact, easily converted to this more restricted form.

Type hierarchies: the rules in generalisation hierarchies are typically of the form *to see if P(_x) is true, find the lowest type T in the hierarchy such that either P or ¬P is known to be true of tokens of T, and such that _x is known to be a token of T*. The hidden assumption is that it is consistent to assume that _x will inherit P or ¬P from type T if _x is not known to belong to any lower type which specifies for P. In other words, you should do property inheritance whenever it is consistent to do so.

Default slot fillers: these barely need further comment. A default value for a slot in frame-like representation is nothing more than a value which is assumed whenever it is consistent to do so.

Closed world assumption: the closed world assumption amounts to saying that if you can consistently believe ¬P (i.e. if you cannot prove P) then you can assume ¬P. The CWA has many problems associated with it. To take just one, consider a biconditional such as (i) single(_X) ≡ ¬married(_X). This seems to be completely equivalent to (ii) married(_X) ≡ ¬single(_X). Using the CWA with (i) on an individual whose marital status you knew nothing about would lead you to conclude that they were single, whereas using it with (ii) would lead you to conclude they were married, even though the worlds in which (i) is true are identical to the ones in which (ii) is. Despite all its problems, the CWA is widely used in AI systems. The interesting thing from our current point of view is that it has exactly the form we are interested in - *if P is consistent with what you know then assume P* - and hence can be treated by the methods described below.

The form of rule we are interested in, then, is formalised by requiring rules to fit the following pattern:

$$\frac{\text{<preconditions>} : \diamond\text{(conclusion)}}{\text{conclusion}}$$

or more briefly as <preconditions>:$\diamond$(conclusion)/conclusion, where $\diamond$ is the possibility operator of Chapter 5. A *normal default rule* like this is intended to be read as saying that if the preconditions are true as far as you know, and the conclusion is consistent with the rest of what you know, then you can infer that the conclusion is true. For example, block(_X): $\diamond$(clear(_X))/ clear(_X) says that any block which is not known to have anything on it can be assumed to be clear. Note that the precondition restricts the rule to blocks - it says nothing about items which are not blocks. Similarly elephant(_X):$\diamond$(colour(_X, pink))/colour(_X, pink) is a rule which allows you to infer that an arbitrary elephant is pink unless you have concrete evidence that it is not. The last example we shall give here provides a concise statement of a complete set of frame axioms for the situation calculus:

$$\frac{\text{holds(P,S) \& after(S, S') : } \diamond\text{holds(P,S')}}{\text{holds(P,S')}}$$

This says that any fact which was once true (held in a situation S) can be assumed to continue to be true (hold in later situations S') until something makes it untrue. Note that this concise statement of the general frame axiom may hide very large amounts of computation - the fact that something can be said concisely does not mean that it is necessarily easy to compute.

7.3.2 *Extensions of a default theory*
The formal treatment of default logic proceeds by giving an analysis of the semantics of default theories and then providing a proof theory and theorem proving techniques to support the semantics. Before we consider the details of the semantics, we consider the intuitions that they might be expected to capture.

A default theory is taken to consist of two parts, namely a set of standard assumptions (the basic theory) and a collection of normal default rules (the defaults), written as a pair <T, Δ>. What would we like such a pair to mean?

The basic theory contains a set of ordinary sentences of FOPC. The only reasonable interpretation for these is the standard one, namely that no matter what else is or is not the case these sentences at least are true of the world. What do the defaults mean? They are suggestions about things which you may want to believe in addition to the basic theory, so long as it is consistent for you to do so. It is tempting to try to interpret them as rules which specify what you do believe, rather than just as outlines for what it is reasonable for you to include in your belief set. However, if we recast our earlier example as a default theory we see that it does not fully determine the set of possible beliefs. <{A → B, C → D, ¬(B & D), A → E, C → E, E → F}, {:◇(A)/A, :◇(C)/C}> is a default theory which contains two defaults, one saying that if you can consistently believe A then you should believe it and the other saying the same for C. We can consistently apply either of these default rules. Applying the first leads to a description of the world in which A, B, ¬C, ¬D, E and F are all known to be true, applying the second to a description in which ¬A, ¬B, C, D, E and F all hold. The previous discussion of this example shows that we cannot apply both of them at once, since we would then have B, D and ¬(B & D); but there are no grounds for choosing between them.

Considering this example, we can see that there are two options for a semantics for default theories. We might choose the set of all the different ways of consistently choosing default rules to apply, so that in our example we would end up with two sets of sentences, namely {A, B, ¬C, ¬D, E, F} and {¬A, ¬B, C, D, E, F}. This would mean using the semantics as a way of characterising 'reasonable belief' - it would be reasonable to believe something if it were a consequence of one of these sets of sentences. The other option would be to try to find the set of propositions which hold no matter which of the consistent sets of default rules was applied - in the example this would just be the set {E, F}. It is hard to see any *a priori* grounds for choosing between these forms for the semantics. There are, however, clear practical grounds for choosing the first. To answer the question "Is it reasonable to believe X?" all you have to do is find some way of applying the defaults which entails X. To answer the question "Am I forced to believe X?" you have to find all consistent ways of applying the rules, show that they all entail X, and furthermore show that you have indeed considered all the options. In terms of computational resources there is no contest.

The semantics of a default theory, then, are given in terms of structures which capture the notion of applying rules from the default component to extend the basic theory. Such a structure, called an *extension*, provides a description of a way that the world might be, given the facts that are known for certain and the defaults that might apply.

It is clearly desirable that any extension be consistent. Extensions are to be interpreted as ways the world might be, and we are not usually prepared to countenance inconsistent sets of sentences as possible descriptions of the world. What other properties should they have?

It is reasonable to require that extensions should also be deductively closed. If P and P → Q are both in an extension of some theory, then according to the theory it is possible for both P and P → Q to be part of some description of the world. If the world fits that description then Q must also be true of it, which is exactly what would happen if the extension were deductively closed. Deductive closure amounts to requiring that extensions be as complete as possible with respect to the theory.

Reiter further argues that any default rule which is consistent with the rest of the extension should be applied. The justification for this relies on interpreting a rule like P:◇(A)/A as saying that if P is true and you can consistently infer A then you must infer A, not just that under those circumstances you can infer it. This seems to be right. ◇(A) itself already says that you can include A in your belief set if you want, so the only way that the default rule can add anything is by demanding that you add it, rather than just allowing you to. To put it more concretely, consider the following default theory:

<{isa(Cherry, cat)},
  {isa(_X,cat):◇(likes(_X, fish))/likes(_X,fish)}>.

(Cherry is a cat, cats usually like fish). We would not want TH({isa(Cherry, cat)}) (i.e. the *theory*, or set of logical consequences, of the set {isa(Cherry, cat)}) to count as an extension for this theory, since it ignores part of the content of the original theory. Although the default part of a theory may not completely constrain the way the world must be, it does provide some extra information, and we would want our extensions to capture this extra information. The way to do this is to take TH({isa(Cherry, cat), likes(Cherry, fish)}) as the extension instead - that according to what we know Cherry is a cat and she does like fish.

7.3.3 *Formal semantics for default theories - extensions*

The formalisation of these conditions can be captured by the following definition. We define an operation Γ on sets of sentences as follows. Given a default theory $<W, \Delta>$ and a set of sentences S, $\Gamma(S)$ is the smallest set of sentences satisfying the following three properties:

(i) $W \subseteq \Gamma(S)$ ($\Gamma(S)$ contains all the basic facts and rules)

(ii) $TH(\Gamma(S)) = \Gamma(S)$ ($\Gamma(S)$ is deductively closed).

(iii) Suppose A: $\diamond B1, ... \diamond Bn / w$ is a default from Δ. Suppose further that A is in $\Gamma(S)$, and none of the $\neg Bi$ are in $\Gamma(S)$. In other words, the basic preconditions of the rule are included, and there is nothing to say that the others are inconsistent. Then w should also be in $\Gamma(S)$. This condition corresponds to the argument that all allowable rules should be applied.

A set of sentences E is a complete characterisation of a way for the world to fit the default theory if and only if $E = \Gamma(E)$. This is what it means to be an extension of the theory.

The operator Γ is defined in a highly non-constructive way. The definition might conceivably suffice for checking whether some set of sentences was in fact an extension of a given theory, though it is not easy to see how. It is certainly not enough to give a feel for how to construct an extension for a given theory. The first step in this direction comes from the following construction. Given a default theory $<W, \Delta>$, we define a series of sets of sentences E_i as follows:

$E_0 = TH(W)$ (we just start out with the basic theory)

$E_{i+1} = TH(E_i \cup \{A: (P:\diamond A/A) \varepsilon \Delta, P \varepsilon E_i, \diamond A \varepsilon E\})$ (the i+1-th step introduces the consequents of default rules whose basic preconditions are satisfied in the i-th step)

$E = \cup E_i$ (the final step joins up all the pieces so far).

This looks more like a way of generating extensions, but it is still rather non-constructive. The problem is that the definition of E_k refers to E, which is not constructed until after all the individual E_i have been constructed, including all the ones that come after step k. The basic definition of what extensions are like, and the semi-constructive characterisation, provide the basis of a reasonable semantics for default theories. With these notions we can give an account of the meaning of a set of rules in terms of sentences which are in particular extensions.

An extension is a perfectly ordinary set of first-order sentences, so its semantics is given by standard model theory. The default nature of the theory is captured by the fact that there may be several extensions of a given theory, so that the theory may be seen to have different consequences depending on different ways of elaborating the extensions. The notion of a default proof will also be founded on the semi-constructive characterisation of an extension, so that the proof theory will correspond appropriately to the semantics. Before we move on to develop the proof theory, we should look at some examples of theories and their extensions, and note some significant properties of extensions.

Example 1:
<{A → B, C → D, ¬(B & D)}, {:◇(A)/A, :◇(C)/C}> is the theory we have seen several times so far. It has two extensions, namely TH({A, B, ¬C, ¬D, A → B, C → D}) and TH({C, D, ¬A, ¬D, A → B, C → D}). We can use the semi-constructive characterisation to generate these as follows:

   (i) Start with TH({A → B, C → D}) (we cannot start with anything less).
   (ii) Pick a default rule whose preconditions are satisfied, say :◇(A)/A.
   (iii) There are no more default rules whose conclusions can be included. There is another default rule whose preconditions are satisfied, namely :◇(C)/C, but if we include it then we will get an inconsistency. Therefore the iterative part of the construction is terminated.
   (iv) We now have to check the satisfiability precondition of the rule we used in (ii) does not conflict with anything in the putative extension. This amounts to showing that it is not the case that A, A → B, C → D, ¬(B & D) ⊢ ¬A, which we can easily do, by checking truth tables, for instance.

Example 2:
There is not too much point in multiplying examples, but it may be worth looking at one involving easily interpretable predicates:

The theory is

   <{¬(sunny & raining),
    (spring & windy) → raining,
    in(England), spring},
    {[in(England) & spring : ◇(raining) / raining],
    [in(England) & spring : ◇(windy) / windy],
    [in(England) & spring : ◇(sunny) / sunny]}>.

In the obvious interpretation, the basic theory says that it cannot be rainy and sunny at the same time; that if it is spring time and it is windy then it will be raining; and that the time/place co-ordinates of the world being discussed is England in the spring. The default part says that in England in the spring it is always reasonable to assume that it is rainy, and windy, and sunny, unless you have grounds for believing otherwise. The theory has two extensions, namely TH({¬(sunny & raining), (spring & windy) → raining, in(England), spring, raining, windy}) and TH({¬(sunny & raining), (spring & windy) → raining, in(England), spring, sunny}). In other words, if you are in England in the spring it is either sunny or it is both windy and raining.

Counter-example:
It is worth noting that not all default theories have extensions. Indeed, there is a very simple default theory with no extension, namely <{B, A → C}, {:◇(A)/¬A, :◇(¬A)/A}>. To see that this cannot have an extension, consider what a set of sentences E would have to be like to be an extension of this theory. Suppose ¬A is not in E. From this we can infer that the satisfiability part of the first default rule is OK, so ¬A must be in E after all, in other words that it cannot be the case that ¬A is not in E. A similar argument shows that A must also be in E. However, if A is in E then so is ¬¬A (since this is a consequence of A, and E is deductively closed). This is the condition for showing that the conclusion of a default rule which depends on ¬A should not be inferred, so the construction of the extension was not valid in the first place. Note: this argument shows that the theory has no extension, not that any extension it may have is inconsistent. There is no set of sentences satisfying the definition of extension for this theory, no matter whether you allow both A and ¬A in or not.

There is, however, nothing whatsoever wrong with the basic component of the theory. Nothing in the argument mentioned any of the basic facts, which must therefore be irrelevant. The problem arises purely from the default rules.

This example is fairly pathological. Nonetheless, if a theory as simple as this can fail to have an extension, despite the consistency of its basic component, then we should be wary when we come to build more complex theories.

7.3.4 *Properties of extensions*
Reiter demonstrates a number of properties of extensions in an attempt to show that they are well-behaved objects that capture our intuitions appropriately. The most important ones for us are the following:

(1) If a theory has an inconsistent extension, that is its only extension. Note that there is a difference between having an inconsistent extension and failing to have an extension at all. Our example above had no extension, whereas $\langle \{A\}$, $\{:\diamond(B)/\neg A\}\rangle$ has an extension, namely $\mathrm{TH}(\{A, \neg A\})$, which is inconsistent.

(2) Although general default theories may fail to have extensions, normal default theories (that is, ones where all the default rules are of the form $A :\diamond(w)/w$) are guaranteed to have them (though even so they may be inconsistent).

The proofs of these results are given in Reiter (1980). They are fairly tedious, and not particularly enlightening, so we omit them here.

7.3.5 *Proofs in default theories*
We now have a reasonable semantics for 'believable assumptions', based on the notion of extensions. For the theory to be at all satisfying, we also need a notion of proof.

A *default proof* of P from $\langle T, \Delta\rangle$ is a sequence of sequences of formulae satisfying certain conditions. The essence of the notion is that each sequence should be a proof, possibly involving the conclusions of default rules. The first sequence should be a proof of P, the second a proof of the normal preconditions of all the default rules used in the first, ... the $i+1$-th a proof of the normal preconditions of the default rules used in the i-th ... until we finally get one which uses no default rules. Furthermore, we have to check at the end that the default rules we used were in fact consistent with each other. Formally, a default proof of P from $\langle T, \Delta\rangle$ is a sequence of sequences S_i satisfying the following conditions:

S_0 is a proof of P from T and $\{D_{0,1}, D_{0,2}, ...\}$ where $P_{0,i} : \diamond(D_{0,i})/D_{0,i} \varepsilon \Delta$. In other words, each $D_{0,i}$ is the conclusion of some default rule.

S_1 is a proof of $P_{0,1}$ & $P_{0,2}$ & ... from T and $\{D_{1,1}, D_{1,2}, ...\}$ where $P_{1,i} : \diamond(D_{1,i})/D_{1,i} \varepsilon \Delta$. So S_1 is a proof of all the preconditions of the defaults used in S_0

...

S_k is a proof of $P_{k-1,1}$ & $P_{k-1,2}$ & ... from T alone.

This shows how the proof of P is built up from the basic theory. No default rule gets used unless we have a proof that its basic preconditions hold. We have, however, said nothing about the refutable preconditions. To make sure that the proof is sound we have to include the following extra condition:

$T \cup \{D_{i,j}\}$ is consistent.

The individual stages of this process are "just" first-order problems, so we could use any standard first-order theorem prover (such as the ones in Chapter 4) to construct them. The process as a whole, however, has two properties which mean that mechanising it is likely to be significantly harder than mechanising ordinary theorem proving. Firstly, we not only have to construct a series of proofs, we have to ensure that the last one we construct makes use of no default rules. We could add heuristics such as removing a default rule from the theory as soon as it had been used. This would guarantee that any sequence of proofs would terminate with one which used no defaults, since eventually all defaults would get eliminated, but only at the cost of possibly failing to find proofs which would have been found without the restriction. This is bad enough, but even when we have found a candidate sequence of proofs we have to check the consistency of the default preconditions. This amounts to checking that we cannot derive the negation of any of them. This is a semi-decidable problem tacked on the end of a series of tasks each of which is itself semi-decidable. The conclusion that we reach about the task as a whole is our most pessimistic one yet - the problem is not just semi-decidable, but is, in fact, fully undecidable. We have no way of writing a program which is guaranteed eventually to find a default proof if one exists.

This result is depressing in the general case. We should note, however, that just as the standard result on semi-decidability does not stop us finding proofs and counter-examples in a wide variety of practical problems couched in standard FOPC, it often happens that we can find default proofs in particular cases. We end by providing an example (adapted from (Reiter 1980)):

Consider the theory $<W, \Delta>$ given by

W: $C \rightarrow X$, $(A \& B) \rightarrow E$, $E \vee X$, $X \rightarrow F$

Δ: $\delta 1 = E \vee F : \diamond(A \& F) / A \& F,$
  $\delta 2 = A : \diamond(B) / B,$
  $\delta 3 = A \& E : \diamond(C) / C$

The following is a default proof of X from this theory.

(1) X follows from C $\rightarrow$ X and the conclusion of $\delta 3$, namely C.

(2) $\delta 3$ has a single standard precondition, namely A & E. A & E can be derived from the conclusions of $\delta 1$ (A & F) and $\delta 2$ (B), together with (A & B) $\rightarrow$ E. We now need the preconditions of $\delta 1$ and $\delta 2$, namely E $\vee$ F and A & E.

(3) These follow from E $\vee$ X, X $\rightarrow$ F and the conclusion of $\delta 1$ (A & F). E $\vee$ F follows directly from E $\vee$ X and X $\rightarrow$ F. A follows from the conclusion of $\delta 1$, E from (A & B) $\rightarrow$ E plus A (already proved) and B (conclusion of $\delta 2$), and A & E follows immediately once we have proofs for each conjunct.

(4) The sole precondition of $\delta 1$ is E $\vee$ F, whose derivation from E $\vee$ X and X $\rightarrow$ F makes no use of default rules, so the first part of the proof is now complete.

The proof is now checked to make sure that all the default rules we used were consistent with each other and the basic rules: this amounts to checking that C $\rightarrow$ X, A & B $\rightarrow$ E, E $\vee$ X, X $\rightarrow$ F, A & F, B and C are consistent, which can easily be done by checking truth tables or semantic tableaux ▦

This proof was fairly tedious. In particular, the fact that we had to use $\delta 1$ twice just to prove A on different steps seems like more work than we would like. Nonetheless, there was nothing really very difficult about it, and it should be quite straightforward to adapt a standard theorem prover to carry out a sequence of steps of this sort.

7.3.6 *Circumscription*

Reiter's default logic provides a precise characterisation for one sort of non-monotonic reasoning which is commonly used in AI systems. The analysis provides all the material we require to refer to a formal language as a "logic", namely precise specifications of the semantics and proof theory, and some indication of how to mechanise the process of finding proofs. Default logic covers a range of non-monotonic inference rules, including, in particular, a form of the closed world assumption. In terms of default logic, we suggested above that the CWA could be stated as :$\diamond(\neg P)/\neg P$ (*if you can't prove P, assume* $\neg P$), and we showed that two apparently equivalent formulae (*single($\_X$)* $\equiv$ $\neg married(\_X)$ and *married($\_X$)* $\equiv$ $\neg single(\_X)$) could lead to different conclusions given this form of the CWA. The CWA is important enough, and problematic enough, to have received several attempts at formalisation. McCarthy (1980) in particular tries to deal with it within a theory called *circumscription*.

McCarthy's initial concern is with people who attempt to solve puzzles by cheating. It seems typical of puzzles (and exam questions) that everything which is relevant to the puzzle is explicitly stated. For example, in the classical missionaries and cannibals problem, a solution which posited a bridge downstream would not seem acceptable, even though it is not explicitly stated that there is no such bridge. Similarly, criticism of an orthodox solution to the effect that the boat might not be usable, or that it might not have oars, or that the current on the river might be too fast for the missionaries to row back to the point they started from, and so on, would not be regarded as valid criticism (*).

It seems that puzzles are typically circumscribed. Nothing which is not explicitly mentioned either needs, or is allowed, to be considered. McCarthy argues that this is, in fact, a general facet of problem solving for real life tasks as well as for toy puzzles, and that the CWA is just a version of problem circumscription. In most problem solving, we generally constrain the problem we are trying to solve by pre-specifying what is and is not to be seen as relevant. In solving the missionaries and cannibals problem, for instance, we do not use a default rule to the effect that rowing boats can be used for crossing rivers unless they are leaky, or lack oars, or don't have enough seats, or ... We proceed rather by simply assuming that rowing boats *can* be used for crossing rivers. If you were asked to explain your solution to this problem, you would not usually refer to all the exceptional reasons why the boat might not be suitable, and then show why you could afford to ignore them. You would simply say that you would use the boat.

---

* For those who have not met this problem, it concerns a group of N missionaries and M cannibals, who are on the bank of a river. They need to cross the river, using a rowing boat which is moored in their vicinity. The problem is that the boat only holds three people, and that if at any point there are more cannibals than missionaries on either bank of the river or in the boat then the cannibals will eat the missionaries).

McCarthy's concern, then, is to provide a logic within which he can specify how to circumscribe predicates in advance, so that the actual task of problem solving is not cluttered up with irrelevant caveats about possible exceptions. This logic has to provide a way of making statements of the form *The only items which satisfy property P (which may be hard to check) are those which are explicitly known to satisfy P' (which should be easier)*. In the case of the boat in the missionaries and cannibals problem, P might be *is a usable boat* (which is subject to all the constraints of not leaking, etc.) and P' might be *is a boat* (which can be checked directly).

Clearly, a problem solution based on the fact that something satisfies P' may fail if it is subsequently discovered that P' does not entail P. However, as a way of reducing a complex problem involving all sorts of unlikely contingencies to a simpler one involving nothing but the obvious standard cases, this is a promising move.

The theory is based on a *circumscription operator*, CIRC, which circumscribes a predicate within a formula. The formula within which a predicate is circumscribed is intended to function as an upper bound on the set of objects that satisfy the predicate. We are going to want to use it as the basis for inferences about items which do not satisfy the predicate, by arguing that the circumscription does not cover them and therefore the predicate cannot be true of them. The circumscription of P in A, written $\text{CIRC}_p(A)$ is the following schema:

$$[A(P/\Phi) \ \& \ \forall\_x((\Phi(\_x) \rightarrow P(\_x))] \rightarrow \forall\_x(P(\_x) \rightarrow \Phi(\_x)).$$

$A(P/\Phi)$ denotes the formula you would obtain by replacing all occurrences of P in A by Φ. This schema is equivalent to a range of formulae, each derived by substituting a one-place predicate or a formula with a single free variable for Φ. How does it capture the notion we are looking for? The first thing to realise is that it is completely vacuous for values of Φ for which $[A(P/\Phi) \ \& \ \forall\_x((\Phi(\_x) \rightarrow P(\_x))]$ is false. In this case, the implication comes out as true no matter what the value of $\forall\_x(P(\_x) \rightarrow \Phi(\_x))$, simply by virtue of the semantics of $\rightarrow$. The only interesting case is when $[A(P/\Phi) \ \& \ \forall\_x((\Phi(\_x) \rightarrow P(\_x))]$ is true. In other words, when Φ is a formula which entails P, and which shares with P the property of being characterised by A. Under these circumstances the conclusion of the circumscription states that Φ holds for everything that P holds for, so that if you want to prove that something does not satisfy P you can simply prove that it fails to satisfy Φ instead. We will illustrate the use of circumscription with some examples, starting with one from the blocks world.

Example 1: suppose we had a problem whose statement mentioned that A and B were both blocks, i.e. isblock(A) & isblock(B). We would like to take this as an indication that A and B are the only blocks to be considered. Consider the circumscription of isblock in (isblock(A) & isblock(B)). The definition of CIRC shows that this is

$$[(\Phi(A) \ \& \ \Phi(B)) \ \& \ (\forall\_x(\Phi(\_x) \rightarrow isblock(\_x)))] \rightarrow (\forall\_x(isblock(\_x) \rightarrow \Phi(\_x)).$$

As it stands this schema does not help very much. We need to choose a useful value for Φ. Suppose we try member(_x, [A B]) (assuming we have appropriate axioms for the definition of member). Substituting this for Φ we obtain:

$$[(member(A, [A \ B]) \ \& \ member(B, [A \ B]))$$
$$\& \ \forall\_x(member(\_x, [A \ B] \rightarrow isblock(\_x)]$$
$$\rightarrow (\forall\_x(isblock(\_x) \rightarrow member(\_x, [A \ B]))$$

It is clear that the basic axioms of FOPC, plus the definition of member and the statement that isblock(A) & isblock(B), will suffice to derive the antecedent of this implication. We are therefore able to say:

$$\{problem \ specification\} \cup \{CIRC_{isblock}(isblock(A) \ \& \ isblock(B))\}$$
$$\vdash (\forall\_x(isblock(\_x) \rightarrow member(\_x, [A \ B]))$$

We can use this result to prove things like:

$$\{problem \ specification\} \cup \{CIRC_{isblock}(isblock(A) \ \& \ isblock(B))\}$$
$$\vdash \neg isblock(C)$$

which we could not have proved without the circumscription.

This example illustrates the major points about working with circumscriptions. The choice of circumscription was entirely straightforward. We simply chose to circumscribe the predicate we were interested in (isblock) within the most specific formula which specified what objects satisfied it (isblock(A) & isblock(B)). The difficult part of the process was choosing a value for Φ which had the required properties, namely that as far as we knew it was co-extensive with the relevant predicate, and that we could easily check and prove negative result about it. There are two important differences between isblock(_x) and member(_x, [A B]). Firstly, the range of _x's for which isblock(_x) is true can be varied by adding or deleting facts about the world to the problem specification, whereas the only way we could change the range of _x's for which member(_x, [A B]) is true would be by changing the definition of member. Secondly, the axioms defining the meaning of member will be bi-implications, so that we can prove not only that some things do fit the predicate, but also that other things do not. It is not possible to prove ¬isblock(C) simply from the absence of a statement to the contrary, whereas we can prove ¬member(C, [A B]).

Example 2: for the second example we will consider the property of *usable boat* discussed above. We start by introducing axioms for a number of new predicates:

istool:
    $\forall$_x(isboat(_x) → istool(_x))
    $\forall$_x(ishammer(_x) → istool(_x))
    $\forall$_x(isvoltmeter(_x) → istool(_x))
    ...

usable, unusable & marked:
    $\forall$_x(usable(_x) ≡ ¬unusable(_x))
    $\forall$_x(marked(_x, faulty) → unusable(_x))

We now consider the circumscription of unusable in $\forall$_x(istool(_x) & ¬unusable(_x)). This is:

[$\forall$_x(istool(_x) & ¬Φ(_x))
    & $\forall$_x(Φ(_x) → unusable(_x))]
        → $\forall$_x(unusable(_x) → Φ(_x)).

Substituting marked(_x, faulty) for Φ(_x) leads to

[$\forall$_x(istool(_x) & ¬marked(_x, faulty))
    & $\forall$_x(marked(_x, faulty) → unusable(_x))]
        → $\forall$_x(unusable(_x) → marked(_x, faulty)).

From the relationship between usable and unusable, we can transform this to

$$[\forall\_x(istool(\_x) \,\&\, \neg marked(\_x, faulty))$$
$$\&\; \forall\_x(marked(\_x, faulty) \to unusable(\_x))]$$
$$\to \forall\_x(\neg marked(\_x, faulty) \to usable(\_x)).$$

The second part of the antecedent is known generally to be true, by the axiom that relates marked(_x, faulty) and unusable(_x). Furthermore it is generally true for any formulae P, Q, R that

$$Q, (P \,\&\, Q) \to (Q \to R) \vdash P \to R.$$

Applying this result to the analysis above, we see that

$$\forall\_x(\neg marked(\_x, faulty)), CIRC_{unusable}\,\forall\_x(istool(\_x) \,\&\, \neg unusable(\_x))$$
$$\vdash \forall\_x(istool(\_x) \to usable(\_x)).$$

We now have a generally applicable result for all problems involving tools, which says, in effect, that if nothing in the problem specification mentions that a particular tool is faulty then you can infer that it is usable. There is one small unjustified step in this inference. We have to assume that someone reading a problem like the missionaries and cannibals will be prepared to include $\forall\_x(\neg marked(\_x, faulty))$ as part of the problem statement, even though it is not strictly available from its literal content. With this assumption, it is clear that the problem specification will allow us to use isboat(_x) wherever we might strictly have needed to use (isboat(_x) & usable(_x)) (isboat is just a special case of istool, by the axioms above).

   This analysis of usable in terms of the absence, from the problem specification, of explicit statements about faults was fairly intricate. It does not look like the sort of thing that could easily be automated. The general result, however, is a very straightforward looking rule of inference which could easily be used within an AI system, so long as the system was capable of extracting the formula $\forall\_x(\neg marked(\_x, faulty))$ from the problem specification.

Example 3: for our last example of circumscription, we will return to the asymmetry between married(_x) ≡ ¬single(_x) and single(_x) ≡ ¬married(_x) that we discussed earlier. We introduce a new predicate, registered(E, D), which holds if there is a database entry for the event E at time D. registered is related to married by the following axiom:

$\forall\_x[(\exists\_y\exists\_d([registered(marriage(\_x, \_y), \_d) \lor registered(marriage(\_y, \_x), \_d)])$
$$\to married(\_x))].$$

We introduce a further predicate, REG, simply to make the discussion less cumbersome:

$REG(\_x,\_y,\_d) \equiv registered(marriage(\_x,\_y),\_d) \lor registered(marriage(\_y,\_x),\_d)$

The axiom above can then be rewritten as

$\forall\_x([\exists\_y\exists\_d(REG(\_x,\_y,\_d))] \to married(\_x)))$.

If we circumscribe married in this, we get:

$[\forall\_x[\exists\_y,\_d(REG(\_x,\_y,\_d))] \to \Phi(\_x)] \& \forall\_x(\Phi(\_x) \to married(\_x))]$
$$\to \forall\_x(married(\_x) \to \Phi(\_x))$$

Substituting $\exists\_y\exists\_d(REG(\_x,\_y,\_d))$ itself for Φ leads to:

$[\forall\_x\exists\_y\exists\_d(REG(\_x,\_y,\_d)) \to \exists\_y\exists\_d(REG(\_x,\_y,\_d)))$
$\quad \& \forall\_x([\exists\_y\exists\_d(REG(\_x,\_y,\_d))] \to married(\_x))]$
$$\to \forall\_x(married(\_x) \to \exists\_y\exists\_d(REG(\_x,\_y,\_d)))$$

The first conjunct of the antecedent is trivially true. The second is the axiom relating marriage registration to marital status, so it can also be trivially proved, so we end up with:

$\forall\_x\exists\_y\exists\_d([registered(marriage(\_x, \_y), \_d)$
$$\lor registered(marriage(\_y, \_x), \_d)] \to married(\_x)),$$
$CIRC_{married} A\_x\exists\_y,\_d([registered(marriage(\_x, \_y), \_d)$
$$\lor registered(marriage(\_y, \_x), \_d)] \to married(\_x))$
$\vdash \forall\_x(married(\_x) \to \exists\_y\exists\_d([registered(marriage(\_x, \_y), \_d)$
$$\lor registered(marriage(_y, _x), _d)])$

The circumscribed formula says that someone is married only if there is a record of their wedding. Hence the closed world inference from $married(\_x) \equiv \neg single(\_x)$ ought to be $single(\_x)$ unless there is information to the contrary.

The last two examples have required us to introduce extra predicates ("marked" and "registered") whose status appears to be a bit different from the other predicates mentioned in the problems. These extra predicates seem to refer somehow to properties of the problem, rather than properties of the individuals referred to within it. This is a common pattern with circumscription. The appropriate formula for circumscribing a predicate, and the formula that is used to instantiate the resulting schema, are chosen with reference to the structure of the problem itself - what information is available, what predicates can be inferred to have null extensions on the basis of the form of the problem, and so on. The result of circumscription is a transformed problem which should be more easily amenable to automated deduction processes than the original. The process of circumscribing is far harder, but can often be done once for a substantial range of different problems.

McCarthy (1980) and Davis (1980) consider the formal properties of circumscription, and show that it is sound with respect to a semantics couched in terms of *minimal models*. The definition of minimal models depends on an ordering on standard models defined as follows:

M is a sub-model of M' in P (written $M \leq_p M'$) if M and M' assign the same interpretations to all symbols except P, and the set of n-tuples that M assigns as the interpretation of P is a subset of the one that M' assigns it.

A model M is then minimal in P with respect to a formula A if (i) $M \vDash A$, and (ii) for all other M' such that $M' \vDash A$, if $M' \leq_p M$ then M' = M. In other words, any model of A which gives the same interpretation as M to the symbols other than P must give P an interpretation which includes the interpretation given by M. We write $A \vDash_p q$ if q is true in every model M which is minimal in P with respect to A. The main result concerning circumscription is that it is sound with respect to minimal entailment, i.e. if $A \vdash_p q$ then $A \vDash_p q$. It is also very clear that it is non-monotonic: simply adding isblock(C) to the axiom set in example 1 will cause

{problem specification} $\cup$ {CIRC$_{isblock}$(isblock(A) & isblock(B))}
    $\vdash \neg$isblock(C)

to fail.

7.3.7 *Preferential models*

There have been numerous other attempts to extend FOPC to cover various kinds of default and assumption based reasoning, e.g. McDermott (1980). The two we have covered are as well-developed and coherent as any, and between them they give a good indication of the difficulties you encounter and the clarification you can hope to gain. There seems little point in surveying yet more minor variations on the theme. We will therefore end this section by discussing a semantics for non-monotonic logics in general, proposed by Shoham (1987) in the course of an important discussion of causality. The significant point, for us, about Shoham's work is that it provides a framework for comparing a wide range of alternative non-monotonic logics. It is not that he proposes a particularly interesting specific logic, but that he shows us how to think about non-monotonic logics in general.

Shoham's suggestion is that we should present the semantics of non-monotonic logics in terms of a *non-monotonic frame*, i.e. a set of standard models and a partial ordering. This should not sound too radical at this point. It is, after all, exactly what we did when defining the semantics of the temporal logics in Chapter 6. What is new in Shoham's treatment is that we now regard only some of the models in the frame as being significant for the semantics. A member M of a non-monotonic frame $<W, \leq>$ *preferentially satisfies* a formula A if M satisfies A and there is no model M' which satisfies A and for which $M \leq M'$ holds. If M preferentially satisfies A we write $M \models_\leq A$. Preferential satisfaction emphasises the role of the partial order. The hope is that we can find a natural order in the intended interpretation of our non-monotonic logic. If we can, preferential satisfaction should enable us to talk about what is true in all worlds allowed by the statements we have made in the logic. If we recall Reiter's semantics for default logic in terms of extensions, it is clear that the definition of an extension involved constructing an ordered series of objects, and then thinking about the object that you would get if you somehow leapt to the end of the series. Shoham's notion of preferential satisfaction in a non-monotonic frame is clearly very closely related.

The notion of preferential satisfaction is supposed to provide a semantics for any non-monotonic logic. The difficult part, of course, is working out what ordering relationship is appropriate to the particular logic you are interested in. Shoham considers three specific non-monotonic logics, namely a version of Moore's (1984) autoepistemic logic and the two logics we have seen in the current chapter. We will examine the order he chooses in order to get an interpretation of circumscription. As far as the other two are concerned, we will just note that the order he chooses for autoepistemic logic is fairly natural, but that he has considerable difficulty constructing a relationship which will work for default logic.

For circumscription, we define the order between models as follows. Suppose we have circumscribed with respect to some predicate P. Then we have an order relation $\leq_p$ between models. For $<W, V> \leq_p <W', V'>$ to hold, (i) W must be a subset of W', (ii) V(R) and V'(R) must be identical for any predicate R except P itself, and (iii) V(P) must be a subset of V'(P). This, as Shoham points out, is almost indistinguishable from McCarthy's own notion of a minimal model. Shoham's contribution is to have realised that the use of minimal models as a semantics for circumscription is in fact a special case of a general approach to the semantics of non-monotonic logics, namely that you should try to find an order on models which matches your non-monotonic inference rules, and then deal mainly with models which are maximal with respect to the ordering.

We have now seen enough examples of non-monotonic logics to have a reasonable grasp of the kinds of problem area where they are useful, and the kinds of proof theory and model theory which make up such logics. We now move on to practical matters of implementation associated with such theories.

7.4 Truth maintenance

The theories considered so far in this chapter enable us to construct chains of inference which hold under the circumstances which obtained when they were constructed, but which may need revision when the circumstances alter. It is clear that there are two other very common situations in which we have to worry about chains of inference which may become unsound as circumstances alter. The first is the obvious one, which we noted earlier, where the database of facts on which the inference is based represents the real-time state of the world. In this case it is evident that since the world is subject to change, entries in the database will also be subject to change and hence inferences based on these entries will need to be monitored for changes in status. The second case is also extremely widespread in AI. This concerns programs which explore problem spaces, and which base their inferences on hypotheses which they are trying out during the course of their explorations.

In all these cases, we have a bookkeeping problem: which of the inferences we have made so far are still valid? The remainder of this chapter surveys some attempts to solve this problem. We shall discuss them all in terms of hypotheses which can be asserted or withdrawn, i.e. as though we were only considering the case where we have a system exploring a problem space by trying out hypotheses. This is for convenience only. The discussion transfers immediately to any of the other cases.

The first solution is simply to throw away all the inferences we have made so far as soon as we change a hypothesis. This is clearly a safe, sound solution. If we do this we will never be tempted to use the conclusion of an invalidated chain of reasoning, since we will have thrown away the results of all earlier inferences. It is also a most unattractive solution. Inferences can take a considerable amount of work to establish, and often remain valid (or become revalidated) during the course of numerous alterations to the set of current hypotheses. The mechanisms we shall discuss in the remainder of the chapter all attempt to retain as many of the results of previous work as possible without allowing any inferences which have become invalid since their initial derivation to be re-used. It is worth noting, though, that the performance of any such mechanism must be compared with the trivial solution of throwing everything away as soon as a hypothesis is added or subtracted.

The solutions we will be considering are, in order of increasing complexity and increasing power, fact garbage collection (Steele & Sussman 1977), justification-based truth maintenance (Doyle 1980) and assumption-based truth maintenance (de Kleer 1986). Again these are particular representatives of methods which have been developed by a number of different people. Other examples could have been chosen to make the point just as well, but no better.

7.4.1 *Fact garbage collection*
The first improvement on simply throwing away everything when the hypothesis set changes is to throw away everything whose justification is invalidated by the change to the hypothesis set. If we keep a link between hypotheses and inference chains, we can easily see which conclusions depend on which hypotheses. When a hypothesis is retracted then we just delete all the inference chains which depend on it.

This can be very easily implemented as follows:

(i) Whenever you construct an inference chain you should collect together all the hypotheses that were used (this can be done by inspecting the inputs to inference steps to see whether they are hypotheses, facts or the results of previous inferences. In the last of these cases, the hypotheses on which the input itself depends should be added to the collection). At the end of the inference, the conclusion should be added to the database, with pointers to it from each hypothesis that was used in its derivation.

(ii) If you want to know if something is true you should first look in the set of derived facts (if you do not, you will not gain anything from keeping them).

(iii) When a hypothesis is abandoned, you must delete all its consequences. This can be done by following all the pointers associated with the hypothesis and deleting the formulae you find at the other end.

This might be all we need to do. It is clearly better than the previous solution, since the results of inferences are cached for as long as they are known to be sound. It has two major advantages over almost any alternative (including the two we are going to examine next): it is easy to implement, and it incurs very little processing overhead. The only costs are a test for the status of the input to an inference step, the construction of a list of hypotheses on which a conclusion is based, and the work involved in deleting facts from the database. These advantages could outweigh the extra facilities provided by more complex systems, which generally entail considerably more work.

There are, however, two ways in which this model might be thought to be inadequate. Firstly, it is still too drastic. It is quite possible for a hypothesis to be retracted as one line of analysis is abandoned, only to be reinstated later on as another part of the space is explored. With the algorithm outlined above, any inference chain which has had one of its underlying hypotheses retracted is thrown away forever, so that when the hypothesis is retried the inferences that used it must be built from scratch again. The second problem with this very basic model is that it is inadequate for handling contradictions. In particular, difficulties arise with it if we have rules of the sort discussed in Section 7.2 whose validity depends on the absence of specified information. The extension of the basic model to cover these cases is fairly straightforward, but there is enough extra complication to warrant treating it separately.

7.4.2 *Justification-based truth maintenance*
The first way of extending the basic model is exemplified by Doyle's (1980) *truth maintenance system* (TMS). This system, like the assumption-based TMS that we consider in the next section, is based on the view that an intelligent system consists of two pieces - a problem solver, and a bookkeeper. The problem solver draws conclusions from the current beliefs, while the bookkeeper looks after knowing what the current beliefs actually are. This division of labour has the usual benefits: the problem solver can be implemented to work as effectively as possible within the desired logic, while the bookkeeper can be designed as an

efficient manipulator of data structures, without any concern for their interpretation. Furthermore, if the bookkeeper is designed to work without any intimate ties to the underlying logic then it ought to be possible to use the same system with a variety of different problem solvers, each working with a different logic. This notion of portability of components is an elusive dream in AI, but if it were ever achieved it would provide significant benefits, and anything which will make it more achievable should be encouraged.

The problem solver itself is not our concern here. The TMS performs the bookkeeping part of the task, largely without interpreting the structures on which it is doing its work. The problem solver provides justifications for beliefs, in a form which is suitable for manipulation by the TMS, and the TMS monitors the status of those justifications and hence of the beliefs. The problem solver can provide the TMS with new justifications for beliefs; it can ask it about the current status of a belief; and it can ask to be informed whenever two beliefs, which it knows to be inconsistent, are both believed at the same time. The TMS, however, has very little idea what any of the structures it is manipulating mean. If the problem solver provides it with unsound chains of inference it will maintain them just as well as it would if they were sound.

The TMS has three main tasks. (i) It has to look after the addition of new justifications. The problem solver supplies justifications for conclusions, which the TMS will subsequently use to work out whether or not a particular fact is currently believed. It can easily happen that the conclusion that the problem solver has just provided a justification for already had an alternative justification. If this happens the TMS should ensure that the new one is considered as an addition to the set of ways in which the conclusion can be believed, rather than as a replacement. (ii) It should garbage collect the consequences of retractions. The problem solver will not typically retract justifications, but it may well retract the hypotheses which back them up. The most notable difference between the TMS and the simple fact garbage collector discussed above is that the TMS does not destroy the data structures representing invalidated justifications. The structures which the TMS uses for representing conclusions contain a field representing their status (as currently believed or disbelieved). For the TMS, the effect of retracting the hypotheses behind some chain of inference is to change the status field of the conclusion, rather than to destroy it entirely. This enables it to reinstate the conclusion automatically if the underlying hypotheses are later reinstated. (iii) The TMS also watches explicitly for contradictions. This part of its task does require it to have some knowledge of the background logic used by the problem solver. It does need to know that if it has justifications for both P and ¬P then it should take care that they are never both accepted at the same time. It could be argued that the problem solver should be responsible for noticing that justifications for both formulae have been derived, and that it should warn the TMS about them explicitly. It seems easier to make the TMS itself responsible for it. It is probably acceptable to build this amount of logical machinery into the TMS, since it is hard to conceive of a formal calculus in which both P and ¬P can be tolerated at the same time. It should be noted, though, that there are complex reasoning systems which can function quite satisfactorily whilst believing inconsistent sets of propositions, namely human beings. It turns out that the TMS' treatment of contradictions is one of the points where it can be criticised.

7.4.3 *Representation in the TMS*

The TMS works on two main types of data structure, namely *nodes*, which represent propositions, and *justifications*. A node is a triple of the following form:

    <name {justifications} status>

The name is a symbol generated by the TMS for its own internal use. Since propositions can appear in each other's justifications, the TMS needs some way of referring to them. It might be that a direct pointer would be a more efficient way of doing it, but it would also make human inspection of the system far harder. A unique name for each node enables a programmer to follow what is going on, without introducing gross inefficiencies into the operation of the system. The status is one of IN and OUT (for in or out of the current belief set). It should be noted that IN and OUT do not correspond directly to TRUE and FALSE. In particular, they allow the situation where neither P nor ¬P is currently believed to be described. It can happen, in fact, that both P and ¬P are believed, although the TMS generally tries to resolve such situations as soon as they arise. The justifications are a set of structures, each of which is a pair of the form:

    <in-list out-list>

The in-lists and out-lists are themselves lists of nodes. Each pair represents the hypotheses underlying a particular justification for the given node. The in-list part of a justification is rather like a material implication. If all the nodes in the in-list of some justification are IN, then the conclusion of the justification should also be IN.

If justifications consisted only of in-lists, it would be hard to see how they could be used to represent anything other than standard material implications. The addition of the out-list provides more flexibility. The out-list contains a list of nodes none of which must be IN if the justification is to hold. Note that this is not the same as requiring that all the entries in the out-list must be OUT. The out-list provides facilities for justifications of the sort discussed in Section 7.2, namely ones which depend on lack of evidence about some contra-indication. The difference can be seen by considering the following pair of examples:

<single(john) {<[] [married(john)]>} ???>

<single(jack) {<[¬(married(jack)] []>} ???>

The justification in the first of these has married(john) as a member of its out-list. This means that it is based on the default rule that anyone not known to be married should be assumed to be single. This justification would be valid so long as married(john) did not itself have a valid justification, i.e. so long as we have no evidence that John is in fact married. The second example has ¬married(jack) as a member of its justification's in-list. It will be valid exactly when we have concrete evidence that Jack is not married. The situations in which the two justifications hold are different, and the circumstances in which they would be retracted reflect the different underlying rules about marriage. Note that if both justifications had been concerned with John's marital status, there would have been a single node with two justifications:

<single(john) {<[¬(married(john)] []>
          <[] [married(john)]>} ???>

This node would be IN if either justification held, i.e. either we knew for sure that John was not married or we did not have any information either way.

The structure of the in- and out-lists reflects the different ways conclusions may be justified. It is worth noting the following characterisations:

Axioms: an axiom has a justification with its in- and out-lists both empty. Axioms should not depend on anything. They should not require the presence of other propositions, nor should they depend on the absence of others.

Monotonic inferences: normal inferences of FOPC simply depend on the truth of their antecedents. Although the conclusion of such an inference can be retracted if one of its antecedents ceases to hold, there is nothing which could be added which would directly cause its retraction. If a set of nodes contained nothing but axioms and conclusions of ordinary inferences of FOPC, then nothing would ever get retracted. The conclusions of such inferences are represented by nodes whose justifications have empty out-lists.

Assumptions: an assumption is something which is accepted in the absence of evidence to the contrary. Clearly the way to represent "something to the contrary" is as an entry in the out-list of a justification. Inferences based on the normal default rules of Reiter's logic, for instance, would lead to the construction of nodes of the form:

$$\text{<conclusion } \{<[\text{preconditions}] \ [\neg\text{conclusion}]>\} \ ???>$$

Nodes and justifications, together with some indexing scheme for linking propositions to their representative nodes, make up the structures used by the TMS for representing belief sets. What does it do with them?

7.4.4 *Processing in the TMS*
Most of the work done by the TMS is fairly straightforward. As noted above, its main tasks are to assimilate new justifications; to propagate their consequences for other justifications, marking them as IN or OUT if the new justification makes it appropriate to do so and then propagating the effects of these new changes in turn; to detect and handle contradictions; and to return the current status of a proposition when asked for it by the problem solver. The last of these tasks is clearly trivial. To find out the status of a proposition, the TMS simply looks in its proposition:node index to find the right node, and then returns the value of its status field. There is nothing more to be said, except to remark that this part of the system, at least, could hardly be made more efficient.

Most of the work is in assimilating new justifications, and particularly in propagating their effects. The first move is easy enough. The representations of the conclusion and the propositions in the justification are replaced by the names the TMS uses for them. This is done just by accessing its index, and if there is no entry there for a proposition then a new name is generated and entered in the index. If the conclusion already has a corresponding node, the new justification is added to its set of justifications, otherwise a new node with this justification alone is created. The new justification is checked for validity. This is done by simply checking the status of each node in its in- and out-lists to make sure that all the in-list nodes, and none of the out-list ones, are IN. If the justification is found to be currently invalid, there is nothing further to be done. If it is a justification for a brand new conclusion, the status of the node is set to OUT. Since nothing ever depends on nodes being OUT (only on whether they are or are not IN) this cannot affect the status of any other node, so there are no effects to propagate. The same is true if the conclusion for which this is a new justification was already OUT, since the new justification clearly does not change its status. Even if the conclusion was previously IN, the addition of a new invalid justification has no effect, since adding a new invalid justification to a node which currently has a different valid justification will not change its status to OUT.

The same argument applies if the new justification is valid but the conclusion was already IN. The new justification has no effect, so there is nothing to propagate. The only time that anything has to be done is when we get a new valid justification for a conclusion that previously had either no justification at all or only invalid ones. In this case the node representing the conclusion either changes status to IN, or is in fact a brand new IN node. In this case there may two types of effect to propagate:

(i) there may be a node somewhere which is currently OUT, but which has a justification which lacks only the current node to become valid. For instance, if the current node were

$$\text{<NODE}_1 \text{ } \{<[] []>\} \text{ IN>}$$

there might be a node like:

$$\text{<NODE}_2 \text{ } \{... <[\text{NODE}_1 \text{ NODE}_3] [\text{NODE}_4]> ...\} \text{ OUT>}$$

The situation here is that NODE_1 is a newly created instance of an axiom, and hence is IN with no in-list or out-list. NODE_2 is some node which is currently OUT, which has among its justifications one which depends on NODE_1 and NODE_3 being IN and NODE_4 not being IN. If it so happened that NODE_3 was IN at the time the new one came into being, and NODE_4 was not, then the addition of NODE_1 with status IN would validate this justification, so that NODE_2 should have its own status switched to IN. It is important to note that NODE_2's change of status might itself have consequences to be propagated, for instance if there were another node

$$<NODE_5 \{... <[NODE_2 \ NODE_3] \ []> ...\} \ OUT>$$

and so on until the node whose status has switched has no further effects.

(ii) there may be a node somewhere which is currently IN, but which has a justification which has the current node in its out-list. For instance

$$<NODE_6 \{... <[NODE_3] \ [NODE_1]> ...\} \ IN>$$

(where again we assume that $NODE_3$ is currently IN). The situation is slightly more complex in this case than it was in the previous one. This justification is clearly no longer valid, and hence is no longer grounds for maintaining $NODE_6$'s status as IN. It might be, however, that $NODE_6$ has some other justification which is still valid. If we looked more closely at the other elements of its set of justifications, we might have found that $NODE_6$ was, for instance,

$$<NODE_6 \{<[NODE_3] \ [NODE_1]> <[NODE_2] \ []>\} \ IN>$$

where $NODE_2$ was currently IN. In this case, we would not want to switch its status to OUT, since it does still have at least one valid justification, and hence should still be IN. Only if it turns out that it has no other valid justifications should we switch its status. If we do switch its status, then we have to propagate the effects in an exactly dual way. Any node which has the current one in the out-list of some justification, and which is currently OUT, should be reassessed to see if the fact that the current node was IN was its own only reason for being OUT. Any node which is currently IN, and has the current node in the in-list of its justification, should be reassessed to see if it has any other justifications which are currently valid.

This all sounds straightforward enough, though it seems likely that the propagation of effects may take some time to settle down. There are, however, some serious problems to beware of. The first point is that it is quite possible to establish circular chains of justifications which cannot be retracted by the basic propagation algorithm outlined above.

Suppose, for instance, the problem solver at different times constructed the following chains of justifications:

C: {} {X}   D: {} {Y}
A: {C} {}   B: {D} {}
B: {A} {}   A: {B} {}

The first chain is a justification of B on the basis of A, which is in turn justified by C, which is justified by the absence of X. The second justifies A on the basis of B, which is justified by D, which is justified by the absence of Y. There is nothing problematic about either of these chains of inference in isolation. Adding them to the TMS would lead to representations of A and B as:

<A [<{C} {}> <{B} {}>] IN>
<B [<{A} {}> <{D} {}>] IN>

Each of A and B has two different justifications. A, for instance, is justified in the first chain by C and in the second by B. If X were subsequently to have its status changed to IN, it is clear that C would become OUT (since X is in its out-list) and hence the first justification for A would become invalid. A, however, would remain IN, since its other justification is still OK. If Y now also had its status changed to IN, D would become OUT and hence the second justification of B would become invalid. But B would still have its initial justification, and hence would stay IN. At this point both A and B would be IN though neither of them has any *independent* justification.

Cases like this can easily arise. They need to be checked for explicitly, since the basic algorithm cannot detect them. The check is not hard to implement, since it is simply a matter of following pointers from a starting point until either you get back to where you started, in which case there is clearly a circularity, or there is nowhere else to go to, in which case there is not. It is fairly time consuming, but can be ameliorated by the realisation that you only need to search for circularities in the support of nodes which have just had justifications invalidated.

A worse sort of circularity can arise with nodes like the following pair:

(1) <A [<{B} {}> OUT> (2) <B [<{} {A}> IN>

Suppose (1) was already in the TMS, and (2) had just been added. Adding (2) would validate the justification for (1), since it has B in its in-list, so it would switch status to IN. This would invalidate the justification for (2), which has A in its out-list, so it would immediately become OUT. This would cancel the validity of (1), which would become OUT, thus reinstating (2) which would reinstate (1) which would cancel (2) which would ... This form of circularity is far more pernicious than the first sort, since instead of simply leaving the TMS with a node or two which are IN when they should be OUT it will completely dominate the system's behaviour, preventing it ever doing anything again. Fortunately, static checks for loops in the graph similar to the ones used for the first kind of circularity can be used to pick up these cases as well. However, in the first case the detection of a circularity simply indicates that one or more nodes should be switched from IN to OUT. In the second case the result of detecting a loop is to indicate that the problem solver has provided two inconsistent justifications, without providing any clues as to what should be done about it.

Detection of loops like these is not an insoluble problem, but it can be very time-consuming. If it is not done, the behaviour of this kind of TMS is unpredictable, possibly unsound, and possibly non-terminating. It may be omitted if you are absolutely certain that your problem solver will never produce justifications which can lead to circularities of this kind, but proving that circularities will never arise is substantially harder than keeping a dynamic watch for them either when justifications are added or when changes in status are propagated.

7.4.5 *Contradiction processing*
One of the most important uses of the TMS is for monitoring for the presence of contradictory hypotheses. It is perfectly possible for the TMS to contain nodes for both P and ¬P. In fact it is often useful for it to do so, since other justifications may depend on any of the four conditions P:IN, P:not IN, ¬P:IN, and ¬P:not IN. However, if at any time both P and ¬P are both IN there must be a problem somewhere. The TMS can be provided with a special node, called NOGOOD, as follows:

$$<\text{NOGOOD } \{<[P_1 \; \neg P_1] \; []> \; <[P_2 \; \neg P_2] \; []> \; ...\} \; ???>$$

NOGOOD has a justification for every other node that is ever created, consisting of that node and its dual. If the TMS has a NOGOOD, then the process of creating new nodes must clearly be extended to add entries to its justification set as appropriate. The treatment of NOGOOD is rather different from the treatment of other nodes. It is clear that NOGOOD should never become IN. A change in the belief set switches its status to IN only if there is an inconsistency in the underlying set of hypotheses. The TMS cannot tell which of the hypotheses should be retracted, since it does not know anything about what they mean. It can, however, produce a candidate list of retractable hypotheses for the problem solver to choose from, and hence resolve the conflict. It may or may not be worth noting the particular set of hypotheses that led to NOGOOD becoming IN as a further justification for NOGOOD. It is not essential, since if they are ever all reinstated at the same time then the particular combination of P_i and $\neg P_i$ that they invoked before will reappear, but it may save time.

7.4.6 *Conditional proof justifications*

The discussion above covers the main functionality of the TMS. Doyle (1980) also considers a different type of justification which he calls a *conditional proof justification* (CP-justification). The motivation for these seems to stem from a type of proof in FOPC called a conditional proof. The following example illustrates what a conditional proof looks like:

1	$A \rightarrow B$	(axiom)
2	$B \rightarrow C$	(axiom)
3	A	(hypothesis)
4	B	(from 1 and 3)
5	C	(from 2 and 4)
6	$A \rightarrow C$	(from 3 and 5)

The essential point about this proof is that it invokes a hypothesis at step 3 which disappears from the conclusion. The proof introduces A as a hypothesis, but the validity of the conclusion in no way depends on the truth of A.

Doyle suggests that a proof of this kind should be passed to the TMS in the form of a CP-justification such as

<(3) {1 2} {}>

This is be read as saying something like *this justification is valid if whenever 3 is IN so are 1 and 2*. The status of a node which depends on such a justification is extremely difficult to monitor, especially in situations where the antecedent part (i.e. 3 in the current case) is itself OUT. Should the justification be valid in this case or not? Doyle expends a considerable amount of effort discussing these justifications and suggesting tricks which can be used to monitor their validity. It may well be that this is completely wasted effort, since it is not at all clear what they should be used for. They certainly should not be used to deal with the sort of conditional proof which motivates the discussion. In the example above, the justification for A → C should definitely not mention A explicitly, even in the position that the CP-justification puts it.

7.4.7 *Assumption based truth maintenance*

The final step in this series of mechanisms for managing non-monotonic inference systems involves a slight change of emphasis. Again there are a number of presentations of very similar ideas to choose from here, and there seems little to indicate that the one we will use to illustrate the discussion (de Kleer 1986) is any better or worse than any of its competitors (e.g. McAllester 1978). The argument behind these refinements is that truth maintenance is a good idea, but that the original presentation takes a slightly inappropriate view. de Kleer particularly criticises the original analysis on the following grounds:

(i) it is over zealous in its efforts to resolve contradictions. Whenever a contradiction appears (i.e. when NOGOOD becomes IN), the original TMS drops everything until a culprit has been found and retracted. We saw in Chapter 3 that a full first-order theorem prover can prove anything whatsoever if its set of hypotheses contains a contradiction. That does not mean, however, that typical theorem provers actually generate proofs which undetectably depend on hidden contradictions in their hypotheses. Inconsistencies may well be tolerated if they are known about and we are careful not to allow any of our inferences to depend on them.

(ii) state switching is extremely expensive. Every addition or deletion of a justification forces a full round of propagating effects, with all the costs that this entails, especially in terms of watching out for circularities.

de Kleer recommends that we should concentrate on the assumptions underlying a conclusion, rather than the details of its justification. He further argues that the design of a TMS can be considerably improved if we think harder about the typical ways in which it gets used and try to optimise its performance on its major tasks. He identifies the main tasks of the TMS as follows:

(i) incremental addition and deletion of justification.

(ii) maintaining consistency.

(iii) querying the status of conclusions.

The main difference between this and the earlier characterisation is the realisation that justifications are added and deleted piecemeal, and that we are never interested in being told about all the effects of an individual change when it is made. What we care about is the status of specific individual conclusions after a series of changes to the current set of beliefs and justifications. de Kleer therefore concentrates on maintaining a representation of the belief set which can easily be queried for the status of any particular proposition at any time, rather than trying to keep propositions explicitly marked as IN or OUT. de Kleer does not keep a status field in the representation of each proposition, on the grounds that maintaining the status explicitly is a waste of effort for all the propositions whose status is not going to be queried under the current set of assumptions. Instead he calculates it on the fly, whenever it is actually required. It is conceivable that if the TMS is to be used in a context where changes to the belief set are very infrequent in comparison to queries about individual statuses, a TMS of the kind described by de Kleer will perform worse than the basic sort described above. de Kleer bases his analysis on the assumption that queries do not massively outnumber alterations to the belief set, and on the fact that his representation in fact allows extremely rapid calculation of the status of a node.

7.4.8 *Data structures in the ATMS*

The design of de Kleer's assumption based TMS (ATMS) depends on a carefully constructed set of data structures. The basic structures, as in the TMS, are nodes and justifications provided by an independent problem solver. In the ATMS a justification is a triple with the following components:

<consequent {antecedents} informant>

The consequent is just a name for a node, as in the TMS, and the antecedents are just a set of such names. Note that the antecedents are not split into in- and out-lists. The effect achieved by these lists in the TMS is dealt with rather differently in the ATMS. The informant is simply the problem solver's representation of the justification, to be used for debugging purposes and for any interactions with the problem solver, but meaningless to the ATMS itself.

de Kleer defines a new object, called an *environment*, which is simply a set of assumptions.

A *context* is defined as the theory of an environment given a set of justifications.

A node in the ATMS is again a triple, of the form

<description label {justifications}>

The description is the representation used by the problem solver, and is of no concern to the ATMS.

The label is the object from which the current status of the node is calculated. It is a set of environments whose context contains n. In other words, it is a set of sets of propositions each of which is known to entail n, so that if, and only if, the current set of beliefs contains one of the entries in the label, then n is known to be true.

The justifications are supplied by the problem solver. They are of no significance to the ATMS, though again we can use the form of the justification for a node to tell whether it is an axiom, or an assumption, or a derived proposition:

An axiom is something which needs no justification, and is true no matter what the current set of beliefs is. In other words it will look like <A {{}} {[]}>. An assumption is something which has no justification other than itself: <A {{A}} {[A]}>. Anything else must have a justification which depends on the presence of something else.

The main task of the ATMS is to make sure that the labels of all nodes satisfy the properties (defined below) of being *consistent, sound, complete* and *minimal* with respect to the current set of justifications. If it can do this then calculating the status of a node given a set of beliefs becomes almost trivial.

Consistent: this is just the usual meaning of consistent, namely that no environment in the label entails a contradiction.

Sound: a label of a node N is sound with respect to a set of justifications J if each entry in it suffices for a derivation of N from J. In other words:

$E \varepsilon$ label(N) entails $J \vdash E \rightarrow N$

Complete: a label of N is complete if it contains environments which provide for all possible environments which could provide the basis of proofs of N from J:

If J ⊢ E → N then there is some E' in label(N) such that E' ⊂ E.

Minimal: a label is minimal if none of its environments contain each other.

If E, E' are in label(N), then not(E ⊂ E') and not(E' ⊂ E)

If label(N) satisfies all these properties, then

J ⊢ E → N if and only if there is an E' in label(N) for which E' ⊂ E

If the label of a node has been maintained correctly, then checking whether it is true in a given situation is simply a matter of checking whether any of the environments in its label is a subset of the current set of beliefs. Given an appropriate representation for sets of beliefs, this can be done extremely quickly. The most important task for the ATMS, then, it is to ensure that labels are kept up to date and correct.

Before we move on to consider how labels are maintained, it is worth noting how the use of contexts and environments classifies the world.

A context C splits the set of propositions into three classes. For each proposition N, either N ε C, or ¬N ε C, or neither N or ¬N ε C.

A collection of environments splits the world into four classes - TRUE, FALSE, IN and OUT - as follows:

(i) TRUE(N) = N ε TH({ })
(ii) FALSE(N) = ¬N ε TH({ })
(iii) IN(N) if there is at least one consistent environment E such that N ε TH(E)
(iv) OUT(N) if there are no such consistent environments

Nodes can move from IN or OUT into any of TRUE, FALSE, IN or OUT, but once a node is in TRUE or FALSE it stays there. This classification resembles the kind of effect that was obtained in the TMS by using separate nodes for P and ¬P, and allowing each to have as its status either IN or OUT.

7.4.9 *Processing in the ATMS*

We said above that the critical task for the ATMS is to maintain the labels of its nodes correctly. How is this done?

The only time that anything has to be done is when a new justification is added. To create a new node, with no previous justification, you just add it to the database in such a way that you can retrieve it from its description via some sort of index. The label of such a new node just contains one set of nodes, namely the ones in its justification. Its set of justifications likewise just contains the one that is given.

To add a new justification for a proposition for which a node already exists, we have to retrieve the old node for the proposition and calculate its new label. The hard work comes when we try to calculate the new label.

The analysis proceeds by first considering how to get just any sound and complete label for a node from its justification, and then showing how to convert this to a minimal consistent one.

A sound and complete label for a justification can be obtained by simply taking the Cartesian product of the labels of the antecedents. As an example, consider the following case:

Suppose $\{G_3 [G_1 G_2] ...\}$ is a justification, where G_1 and G_2 are nodes whose labels are as follows:

$$\text{label}(G_1) = \{\{A \ B\} \ \{B \ C \ D\}\}$$

$$\text{label}(G_2) = \{\{A \ C\} \ \{D \ E\}\}$$

Then $\{\{A \ B \ C\} \ \{A \ B \ C \ D\} \ \{A \ B \ D \ E\} \ \{B \ C \ D \ E\}\}$ is a complete, sound label for G_3. Any set of propositions which entails both G_1 and G_2 must have one of the elements of this label as a subset. Furthermore, any set which has an element of the label as a subset must entail both G_1 and G_2, and therefore must also entail G_3. This is exactly what we need for this to be a complete, sound label for G_3.

If G_3 already had a label, which by hypothesis was complete and sound with respect to the previous set of justifications, then adding the new one to it would produce a label which was complete and sound with respect to the whole of the new set.

We still need to make the new label minimal and consistent. This can be done by deleting all entries which are subsumed by other ones and all entries which are subsumed by some known inconsistent label. One set of propositions, P, subsumes another, P', if all of P are true whenever all of P' are, which will be the case exactly if $P \subseteq P'$. Thus in our example, {A B C} subsumes {A B C D}, so that the given label should be converted to {{A B C} {A B D E} {B C D E}} to make it minimal. If none of these are subsumed by any known inconsistent sets, this label satisfies the requirements.

We are now in one of three cases:

(i) The new label is the same as the one the node already had. In this case there is obviously nothing more to do.

(ii) The consequent of the justification is in fact †. In this case we add the elements of the new label to a database of NOGOOD's, since we often need to search explicitly for inconsistent labels.

(iii) The consequent of the justification is something other than †. It should be given the new label, and the new label should be propagated through all consequents of the consequent. If the labels of any of these need updating, then this in turn has to propagated, and so on until no more changes are required. This could conceivably have repercussions on the current node, e.g. it could make some environments in the label could become inconsistent, but the structure of the space of nodes guarantees that it will eventually terminate, so we do not need to worry about circularities.

This could all be very inefficient. de Kleer, however, is very careful about the way he represents structures. If nodes are numbered as they are created, the critical operations can be performed extremely fast.

The first point is that since nodes are numbered, it is easy to write an indexing algorithm for the problem solver to access the node that represents a given proposition.

A more significant advantage of the numbering of nodes is that environments (which are finite sets of nodes) can be represented as bit strings. This means that the critical set operations - union, subset, and so on - can be performed by bitwise operations, which on present day machines are about as fast as anything you can do. This is a major source of speed up in the ATMS, though it really should not be taken as saying anything very interesting about non-monotonic inference systems.

de Kleer points out a number of other general points about efficient implementation of this kind of system. None of them are really specific to the ATMS, though all of them are good programming advice. His final comment on efficiency is to point out that by tailoring the ATMS so carefully to the tasks which he believes it will generally be used for, he has constructed a system which may perform poorly when used for other tasks. In particular, explicit retraction of justifications will be extremely inefficient, since the original form of the justification will have disappeared into the structure of label of the justified node. For this reason, rather than trying to retract a justification such as

$$<G_1 \{\{G_2\,G_3\}\} \{[G_2\,G_3]\}>$$

he prefers to add a subsequent justification like

$$<\dagger \{\{G_2\,G_3\}\} \{[G_2\,G_3]\}>.$$

This has much the same effect, since it makes $\{G_2\,G_3\}$ a justification for a NOGOOD, and hence stops it contributing to the label of G_1. It is achieved by the additive operators which have been carefully tailored to be fast, rather than by explicit deletion of the justification, which would be extremely awkward.

7.5 Non-monotonic reasoning: theory and implementation

In most areas of AI in which some form of logic has been used as a knowledge representation language, the logical formalism pre-dated the AI research which used it. In some cases, such as the use of possible worlds semantics for situation calculus, the formalism has been changed as a result of its application in the new domain, but in general the formalisms have been borrowed and developed by AI workers, rather than being invented by them. Non-monotonic inference, on the other hand, had received very little attention indeed prior to its use in AI systems. It seems as though quite a number of systems which required non-monotonic inferences had been written before anyone really understood that there was anything to worry about. People developed effective systems using the closed world assumption, using frames and defaults, and storing the results of inferences that were developed during the course of exploration of hypotheses which were themselves later abandoned. Only when these systems existed, and indeed worked, did people start to worry about what the formalisms they were using meant. We thus see that some of the decisions about the nature of the semantics of non-monotonic logic were taken in order to explicate what systems which were up and running were actually doing. The decision, for instance, to define extensions in terms of all the alternative consistent ways of choosing defaults, rather than in terms of the sentences that are always true no matter which defaults you apply, seems arbitrary as an attempt to make the nature of default reasoning clearer. It makes perfect sense, however, if we regard it as an attempt to clarify what systems using various sorts of rule were already doing.

The fact that the formal analysis of non-monotonic inference addresses the formalisms being used in AI systems, rather than trying to prescribe the correct way of thinking about such inference, is in no way a bad thing. It does, however, emphasise that the role of logic is to clarify the properties of particular languages. There is no such thing as the "correct" way of dealing with non-monotonic inference, any more than there was a "correct" way of dealing with time, or with knowledge. But there are tests which we can apply to any new proposals to ensure that they are at least well-behaved and sensible, and that people understand the consequences of using them.

CHAPTER EIGHT

PROPERTIES

The formal systems we have considered so far have all been concerned with objects and relations between objects. There has always been a distinction between our attitude to objects and our attitude to relations. We have been prepared to use variables for talking about unnamed objects, with quantifiers to indicate whether we are talking about all objects of a given kind or some specific object of that kind; and we have used predicate symbols for denoting properties of objects and relations between objects. We have not, however, used variables to stand for properties and relations, and we have not considered relations between relations.

There are two reasons why we might want to relax this restriction and countenance properties of properties, or quantification over properties. It might be that, as with the frame axioms of Chapter 6, we want to say something about statements in general which we could have said within the existing language, but which would have been extremely verbose. Suppose we had a problem specified in the situation calculus, and that the only predicates it mentioned were $P_1, ..., P_n$, where the largest number of arguments that any P_i took was N. We could have written down the universal frame axiom as

$$\forall S_1 \forall S_2 \forall x_1 ... \; \forall x_N [(P_1(x_1, ..., x_{i1}, S_1) \rightarrow P_1(x_1, ..., x_{i1}, S_2))$$
$$\& \; (P_2(x_1, ..., x_{i2}, S_1) \rightarrow P_2(x_1, ..., x_{i2}, S_2))$$
$$\& \; ...$$
$$\& \; (P_n(x_1, ..., x_{in}, S_1) \rightarrow P_n(x_1, ..., x_{in}, S_2))]$$

This is perfectly acceptable as a statement of the situation calculus, but it might turn out to be extremely verbose if n is a fairly large number. If we were allowed to quantify over predicates, on the other hand, we could just write it as:

$$\forall\_S_1 \forall\_S_2 \forall\_P[\_P(\_S_1) \rightarrow \_P(\_S_2)]$$

This says that for any two situations $\_S_1$ and $\_S_2$ and any statement $\_P$ about the world, if $\_P$ is true in $\_S_1$ then it is true in $\_S_2$. This is rather strong for a frame axiom, since what it says is that nothing ever changes, but it does at least provide some flavour of the sort of thing we might want to be able to say.

Using properties of properties, and allowing quantification over properties, in situations where only a finite number of properties are relevant is rather like using FOPC in a domain where there are only a finite number of individuals. It may be more concise than a more restricted language in which we have to refer to everything by name, but it does not in principle introduce any added difficulties. If the extended formalism did introduce insurmountable problems when we tried to compute with it, we could always translate it into the less powerful one and work with that. The database reduction technique we mentioned at the end of Chapter 4 did exactly that, recognising when some part of a problem couched in FOPC was in fact concerned only with a finite set of individuals and translating that part of the problem into propositional calculus instead. FOPC, however, is not always just a more concise notation for problems which could have been couched in terms of the propositional calculus. There are situations where we need the whole of FOPC, since there are situations in which the set of individuals we are concerned with is either known to be infinite, or is at any rate unbounded. When, for instance, we have a statement such as *Everyone who lives in America owns a car*, we know that the domain of individuals which *Everyone* is quantifying over is finite, but since we do not know exactly what finite set it is made up of we are forced to treat it as though it were infinite.

The results in Chapter 3 led us to conclude that if we really do need the whole of FOPC, and are not just using it as a shorthand for a long-winded but finite collection of statements of propositional calculus, then we may get into trouble when we try to use automatic theorem proving techniques. The same is true when we consider situations where we really need to talk about properties of properties. FOPC is semi-decidable. We can write automatic theorem provers which will construct a proof for any valid formula of FOPC, but which may embark on an infinite search for a proof if we ask them about an invalid formula. Once we have a language in which we can talk about properties of properties, we find that any theorem prover we might construct may fail to return when asked about valid formulae, as well as when asked about invalid ones. Indeed, we have to be rather careful in constructing our language to avoid paradoxical sentences such as *This sentence is not true* for which it is impossible to provide a coherent semantic analysis.

There have been a number of proposals for languages in which it is possible to talk about properties of properties, and to do quantification over properties. We will be concentrating on one, namely λ-*calculus*, but we should at least note the existence of others. The most important of these are the language of *set theory* and Turner's (1987) *property theory*. Set theory was developed in an attempt to construct a language within which to investigate the foundations of mathematics. Much of the work in set theory has been concerned with the nature of the axioms for constructing and manipulating sets. The first formulations of these axioms made it possible to describe paradoxical objects such as the set of all sets that are not members of themselves. Whitehead and Russell's (1925) *theory of types* tried to eliminate such objects by constructing a hierarchy of types and banning the construction of sets whose elements were of higher type than themselves. Other axiomatisations of set theory, e.g. Zermelo-Frankel set theory (Jech 1971), attempted to ban them by being careful about the form of expression which could be used for specifying the conditions for set membership. The axiom sets required for set theory are sufficiently complex for there to be considerable doubt about whether they are in fact consistent, and about whether some of them are actually consequences of others or whether they are genuinely independent. Godel (1940) developed a technique for constructing models of the main axioms, thus showing that they were consistent. Cohen (1966) showed how to force the existence of non-standard models in which selected axioms are false, thus showing that they are independent. This work, though fascinating in itself and of critical importance to the foundations of mathematics, has had very little influence in AI, and we omit it from the current text without feeling we have missed something which would help us with our attempts to understand the nature of intelligence. Turner's property theory may well turn out to be of rather more immediate importance to us, but since there are as yet no computational treatments of it there is little we can say about it here. It may be that it will be more tractable than the theory of λ-calculus on which we shall be focussing, but until more work has been done λ-calculus is the best we have.

8.1 λ-calculus

We start the discussion of λ-calculus by reviewing the semantics of FOPC. We have taken the view that the semantics of FOPC is given by a basic semantics which interprets the constants and predicate names, in terms of a model, and a set of rules which explain how the semantics of complex expressions are built up in terms of the semantics of the constituents. The part of this that we are going to look at again is the use of a model to interpret the constants and predicate names.

In the semantics we have used so   ır, a model consists of a universe W and a valuation function V which assigns a   :ember of W to each constant, and a set of N-tuples from W to each N-place predicate name. The pair <W, V> is then a model of the expression $P(a_1, ..., a_N)$ if the N-tuple $<V(a_1), ..., V(a_N)>$ is a member of V(P). We could look at this slightly differently, taking the view that the value of a predicate should be a function which, when applied to a set of individuals, returns either T or F. The intended meaning, clearly, is that this function should return T if the relation named by the predicate does hold between these individuals, and F if it does not. Every set has a *characteristic function* of this kind - a function which maps members of the set to T and non-members to F. It is not going to make much practical difference whether we base our semantics for FOPC on sets or on their characteristic functions. The connection between the two is so tight that you can just go through everything we did in Chapter 3 changing all references to sets to references to characteristic functions, and especially changing "membership of a set" to "having the value T returned by a characteristic function", and everything will come out the same.

Once we have couched our basic semantics of FOPC in terms of characteristic functions, though, the idea that we might be able to use other sorts of functions as part of the semantics of an extension of FOPC suggests itself. To see what is going on we will consider the 2-place predicate EATS which holds between two entities if one is a foodstuff that forms part of the diet of the other. In our usual semantics for FOPC, the interpretation of EATS would be a set of pairs {<[[squirrel]] [[nuts]]> <[[cow]] [[grass]]> <[[tiger]] [[people]]> ...}. The formula EATS(sparrow, crumbs) would be satisfied in any model <W, V> in which <V(sparrow), V(crumbs)> was a member of V(EATS). We can imagine taking the interpretation of EATS and deleting all entries which did not have sparrow' as their first element. The result of this would be a set of 2-tuples, and as such would be something which could be used as the interpretation of a 2-place predicate. It is, however, a highly redundant set of 2-tuples, since they all share the same first element. What about considering the set of 1-tuples you would get if you deleted this shared element? The result is a well-defined set of 1-tuples, and as such is a candidate as the interpretation of some 1-place predicate. But not just any old 1-place predicate. We know that it is intimately related to the interpretation of EATS and to the individual object sparrow'. It is in fact the set of objects that sparrows eat. λ-calculus provides us with a language in which we can express this kind of relation. We use λ rather as though it were a quantifier, to indicate what variables in an expression need to be bound, and what order to bind them in. The 2-place relation EATS, for instance, would be denoted by $\lambda\_x\lambda\_y(EATS(\_x, \_y))$. Informally we can read this as saying that this denotes a

2-place relation which is waiting for values of _x and _y to be supplied. The more specialised property of being something which sparrows eat would be denoted by λ_y(EATS(sparrow, _y)) - a 1-place property waiting for a value for _y.

The discussion so far has been rather informal. We have introduced the idea of a relation between the general relation of being something which some species of animal eats and being something which sparrows eat, and offered up a suggestive notation for capturing this relation. Suggestive informal notations are not what we need. The precise details of the semantics for λ-calculus may seem rather unintuitive at first. We will try to relate them to the informal ideas we have considered above as soon as we can.

The syntax of λ-calculus is just like that of FOPC, except that we now have the symbol λ which behaves syntactically just like ∀ or ∃, i.e. if P is a formula of λ-calculus and _x is a variable then λ_x(P) is also a formula of λ-calculus. As usual we give the semantics in terms of a model <W, V>. W, however, is no longer just a set of individuals. It will also include sets of individuals, and sets of sets of individuals, and sets of sets of sets of individuals, and so on. This means that constants can have the objects that we used to regard as properties as their values, that properties can apply to other properties (or even themselves), and that quantification can range over properties. In other words, our version of λ-calculus is *untyped*.

V is still a valuation function, but it is no longer restricted to assigning individuals to be the values of constants - constants can be assigned sets of individuals, or sets of sets of individuals, and so on. We will use the term *entity* to emphasise the fact that W contains sets, and nested sets, as well as individuals. For λ-calculus V should behave as follows:

(i) If b is a constant of the language, V(b) should be a member of the universe W of the model (remember that W now contains sets as well as individuals).

(ii) If P is a 1-place predicate of the language, V(P) should be a characteristic function, i.e. a function which returns T for objects to which P applies and F for ones to which it does not. We denote the fact that V(P) is a function from W to the set of truth values {T, F} by writing $V(P):W \rightarrow \{T, F\}$. W is the *domain* of the function V(P), {T, F} is its *range*. The set of all functions from W to {T, F} is denoted by $W^{\{T, F\}}$. As we remarked above, there is a very close relationship between characteristic functions and sets. We will be very cavalier when talking informally, and will switch between talking about sets and their characteristic functions with very little comment. When we want to talk formally, we will always use characteristic functions.

(iii) If P is a 2-place predicate, then V(P) should be a function from members of W to members of $W^{\{T, F\}}$. In our standard semantics for 2-place predicates, we assume that they will be evaluated in terms of two supplied entities. If we just supply one entity, then we are left waiting for another before we can calculate a truth value, which is exactly the situation we would have been in if we had originally been supplied with a 1-place predicate. Suppose P is a 2-place predicate and a is a constant, and that Π_a is the function which V(P) returns when applied to V(a), i.e. it is $[\![P]\!]_V([\![a]\!]_V)$. Our intention is that $\Pi_a([\![b]\!]_V)$ would return T exactly when our usual sort of model would have satisfied P(a, b). To take a concrete example, suppose we had a model of FOPC which included the following interpretation of the predicate MOTHER:

{<janet sam> <janet james> <janet michael>
<sue alex> <sue hannah>}

This would correspond to the following λ-calculus model:

{<janet {<sam T> <james T> <michael T> <alex F>
        <hannah F> <janet F> <sue F>}>
<sue {<sam F> <james F> <michael F> <alex T>
        <hannah T> <janet F> <sue F>}>
<sam {<sam F> <james F> <michael F> <alex F>
        <hannah F> <janet F> <sue F>}>
<james {<sam F> <james F> <michael F> <alex F>
        <hannah F> <janet F> <sue F>}>
 ... }

This is rather more verbose than the alternative representation, since we have had to include all the cases where the relationship of being someone's mother does not hold as well as all the ones where it does, but it contains essentially the same information. In the first case we can find out whether Janet is Sue's mother by seeing whether the pair <janet sue> is in the set of 2-tuples given as the interpretation of the predicate MOTHER. In the second we can find it out by applying the function which is given as the value of MOTHER to the interpretation of Janet. This will give us the function {<sam T> <james T> <michael T> <alex F> <hannah F> <janet F> <sue F>}. We now apply this to the interpretation of Sue to get F. We could have made the second model more concise by omitting all the negative entries, and then omitting the T's that mark positive ones since these are now redundant:

{<janet {<sam> <james> <michael>}
<sue {<alex> <hannah>}>}

This is actually more concise than the representation of the standard model, not less. The issue of providing concise representations, however, is not the real reason why we have switched to giving interpretations in terms of functions rather than sets of N-tuples. The advantages of using functions begin to become apparent when we consider the semantics of N-place relations where N is bigger than 2.

(iv) If P is an N-place relation, where N is greater than 2, then V(P) is a function from entities to interpretations of N-1 place relations. This is just a generalisation of the way we dealt with 2-place relations in (iii) above. A 1-place relation is a function from entities to truth values, i.e. a member of $W^{\{T, F\}}$; a 2-place relation is a function from entities to functions from entities to truth values, i.e. from entities to 1 place relations; a 3-place relation is a function from entities to 2-place relations; and an N-place relation is a function from entities to N-1 place relations. The general principle is clear. An N-place relation is something which would turn into an N-1 place relation if you supplied an entity to fix one of its parameters.

Nothing we have done so far does more than provide an alternative way of providing a semantics for FOPC. We can clearly provide rules for compound formulae in terms of what we have just done - the valuation of P & Q, for instance, would be a function which returned T if and only if both V(P) and V(Q) returned T, and the valuation of ∀_xP is a function which returns true if and only if each of the functions $V(P|_{<a,\_x>})$ returns true, but these rules are essentially no more than alternative forms of the standard rules. The interesting point about this form of semantics is that it provides a precise way of specifying the meaning of λ.

(v) Suppose that P is an expression with a free variable _x. Then λ_x(P) is an expression whose valuation is the set {<a_1, $V(P|_{<a1,\_x>})$> ... <a_i, $V(P|_{<ai,\_x>})$> ... }. In other words, it is a function which for any constant a_i returns the valuation of the expression which results from substituting that constant for the free variable throughout the original expression. Suppose, for instance, that we take the expression EATS(sparrow, _x). Then the valuation of λ_x(EATS(sparrow, _x)) is the following set:

{<crumbs T> <meat F> <insects T> ...}

This is a function from W to {T, F}, and as such is just like the interpretation of a 1-place predicate. $\lambda\_x(EATS(sparrow, \_x))$ can be seen as an alternative name for a predicate which we might have called SPARROW-FOOD, with the advantage that its relationships to the general predicate EATS and to the constant sparrow are both accessible. The expression $\lambda\_x\lambda\_y(EATS\_x, \_y))$ has as its valuation a function of the following form:

{<sparrow {<crumbs T> <meat F> <insects T> ...}>
<cow {<grass T> <meat F> <insects F> ...}>
<horse {<grass T> <hay T> <sausages F> ...}>
... }

This is a function which for any item $\_x$ returns another function which tells you about things that $\_x$ eats. The expression $\lambda\_y\lambda\_x(EATS(\_x, \_y))$, on the other hand, has something like the following as its valuation:

{<meat {<horse F> <bear T> <lion T> <sparrow F> ...}>
<grass {<cow T> <bear T> <lion F> ...}>
<salami {<cow F> <person T> <eagle F> ...}>
... }

The difference between this and the valuation of $\lambda\_x\lambda\_y(EATS(\_x, \_y))$ is in the order in which the arguments get fixed. One tells you what each species eats, the other tells you what animals each foodstuff is eaten by. It can be seen as an analogue of the distinction between active and passive sentences in English, though it would be dangerous to assume that the connection between the active and passive is quite as simple as merely changing the order of variables in a λ expression.

This process of picking out particular aspects of an expression need not be restricted to constants. The expression $\lambda\_P(\_P(John))$ is also perfectly well-formed. Its valuation will be a function which takes an expression and returns whatever would have been the valuation of that expression if it were applied to John. Suppose we knew, among other things that V(SLEEPS)(V(John)) was T, and that (V(EATS)(V(John)))(V(spinach)) was F, in other words that John was somebody who did sleep but did not eat spinach. It should be fairly clear that the function which was the valuation of $\lambda\_P(\_P(John))$ would return T for V(SLEEPS), or to be more precise that <V(SLEEPS), T> is a member of its valuation. It would say, in effect, that sleeping was something that was true of John. The way that it would deal with the fact that John does not eat spinach is rather more complicated. We want to capture the fact that eating spinach is false of John. For this, we need some way of specifying the property of being someone who eats spinach. This is, of course, exactly the sort of thing for which λ-calculus is useful. The property we want is $\lambda\_x(EATS(\_x, spinach))$. The valuation of $\lambda\_P(\_P(John))$, then, should contain the pair $<\lambda\_x(EATS(\_x, spinach)), F>$.

The semantics of λ has been set up in such a way that it is captured precisely by the following axiom schema:

$$(\lambda X(E))(t) \equiv E|_{<X,t>}$$

This axiom schema can be used in either direction. It is most commonly used from left to right, in a process known as β-*reduction*. β-reduction removes instances of λ, normally leading to simpler looking expressions. It is a purely deterministic process, and can be done very quickly indeed. It is, in fact, the basis of argument passing in a number of programming languages, notably LISP (Allen 1978) and POP-11 (Barrett et al. 1985). There are also cases where it can be convenient to use the axiom in the other direction, constructing complex expressions from simpler ones. This process of λ-*abstraction* is most often used as part of an overall chain of reductions, where some expression is being applied to something of a type for which it is not parameterised.

Within AI, the most significant uses of λ-calculus have been in natural language processing, where it makes it possible to capture a number of fine distinctions which are difficult to deal with using the other formalisms that have been proposed. Before we pass on to the kinds of task that it has been used for in natural language work, though, we will look at two simple examples.

(1) Arithmetic expressions: consider the expression $\_x = \_y*\_z$. This has three free variables, so that we have six possible ways of constructing λ-expressions from it:

$$\lambda\_x\lambda\_y\lambda\_z(\_x = \_y*\_z), \lambda\_x\lambda\_z\lambda\_y(\_x = \_y*\_z)$$
$$\lambda\_y\lambda\_x\lambda\_z(\_x = \_y*\_z), \lambda\_y\lambda\_z\lambda\_x(\_x = \_y*\_z)$$
$$\lambda\_z\lambda\_x\lambda\_y(\_x = \_y*\_z), \lambda\_z\lambda\_y\lambda\_x(\_x = \_y*\_z)$$

Suppose we take the last of these, $\lambda\_z\lambda\_y\lambda\_x(\_x = \_y*\_z)$, and apply it to three numbers, say 4, 5, 39, in turn:

λ_z(λ_y(λ_x(_x = _y*_z)(39))(5))(4)

β-reduction would apply to this as follows:

(i) λ_y(λ_x(_x = _y*4)(39))(5)

(ii) λ_x(_x = 5*4)(39)

(iii) 39 = 5*4

This is an expression which we can evaluate, either directly in the intended model (namely arithemetic) or from some axiomatisation of basic number theory. However we do it, we should come up with the conclusion that it is false, and hence that the original expression denoted a relation which did not hold in the intended model. If, on the other hand, we had simply applied the same λ-expression to 4 and 5 we would have come up with the expression λ_x(_x = 5*4), in other words, with a way of describing the property of being a number which was equal to 5*4. This is just like any other property. We can use it to make statements about entities, such as the claim that it holds for 39, or to express general rules like ∀_y(λ_x(_x = 5*4)(_y) → _y > 10).

Similarly, if we had applied the first of our six λ-expressions to 4 and 5 respectively, we would have ended up with λ_z(4 = 5*_z), which denotes the property of being a number which was equal to 4/5. Again we could have used it for making specific statements such as ¬(λ_z(4 = 5*_z)(1)) (it is not the case that 1 is a number which you could multiply by 5 to get 4), or for making general statements such as ¬∃_x(integer(_x) & λ_z(4 = 5*_z)(_x)) (there is no integer which you could multiply by 5 to get 4).

(2) If we restrict ourselves to abstraction over ordinary variables, we find that we cannot do all that much more than we could in FOPC. The interesting cases usually involve abstraction over predicates as well. It is, however, a good idea to be wary. Consider the expressions λ_Q(_Q(_Q)) and λ_Q(¬_Q(_Q)). These are perfectly well-formed according to the syntactic rules we have developed so far, and their intended meanings seem reasonable. The first is a property which would be true of any property which was true of itself, the second is a property which would be true of any property which was false of itself. We can perfectly easily supply instances of properties for which each is true. The property of being a set, for instance, is something which is true of itself, since we have defined properties as sets of N-tuples. The property of being RED is something which is false of

itself. If we apply β-reduction to λ_Q(¬_Q(_Q))(RED) we end up with ¬RED(RED), which is clearly true. Only physical objects can have colours, and RED is not a physical object.

Suppose we let E be an abbreviation for λ_Q(¬_Q(_Q)). Since E is the name of a property, we ought to be able to apply it to itself to get an expression of the form E(E). In any model of λ-calculus, this expression ought to have a truth value of T or F. E is a property of properties, so when it is applied to a property we should end up with a truth-valued expression. This is just as true of E itself as of any other property we might have applied it to, such as the property RED. Suppose E(E) is true in our chosen model. If we expand out the first instance of E, we see that E(E) is in fact just λ_Q(¬_Q(_Q))(E). β-reduction will convert this to ¬E(E). But β-reduction does not make any difference to the truth or falsity of the expression it is applied to, so ¬E(E) is also true in our model. This contradicts the very essence of what it means for something to be a model. We just cannot have statements whose negations are true in the same models as themselves, so our original assumption, that we could have had a model in which E(E) was true, must just be wrong. Exactly the same argument, however, will lead to the conclusion that if E(E) is false in some model then so is ¬E(E), and this is again unacceptable. There simply is no way of assigning a truth value to E(E) which does not immediately lead to trouble.

This should not be altogether surprising. E(E) is more or less equivalent to the well known *Liar Paradox*, the sentence *this sentence is false*, which is false if it is true and true if it is false. It is more worrying to find sentences like this in formal languages like λ-calculus than in everyday language. As far as the formulation of the Liar Paradox in English is concerned, people generally just take it as a hint that there are things which we can say whose meanings are rather obscure, but since they do not tend to be things we want to say very often we can just ignore them most of the time. We cannot easily do this in a formal language around which we intend to construct an inference system. If we take the view that E(E) should be regarded as true then we have a formula of the form P & ¬P which we know to be true, and from which † follows. But we already know that absolutely anything follows from †, so that if we take the view that E(E) is true then so is everything else. If, on the other hand, we regard E(E) as false, then we have a formula of the form P ∨ ¬P which we know to be false, and again † must follow, with all its undesirable consequences.

We therefore have a formula which we cannot give a truth value to. It is not the first time we have come across something we could not give a truth value to. We would not, for instance, want to give a truth value to the string of symbols ∀ ∃(p q →). The semantics of formal languages assign meanings to well-formed formulae, and leave anything else uninterpreted. One way out of our problem, then, would be to patch the syntax of λ-calculus to prevent E(E) being a well-formed formula. We would then be under no obligation to give it an interpretation, and hence would not run into the problems we have just been discussing. The usual way to rule out paradoxical formulae like E(E) is to assign types to expressions, and to rule out expressions where a predicate has been applied to something of the wrong type. This approach, which stems largely from Whitehead and Russell's (1925) typed theory of sets, has been widely followed in applications of λ-calculus to natural language (Dowty et al. 1981). It introduces a considerable degree of extra complexity, since we do sometimes need expressions which seem to violate the basic type constraints. The idea of a property which does not apply to itself, for instance, seems to be meaningful in most cases, and there may even be situations in which it is useful to be able to say that RED, for instance, is such a property. The machinery that we need to allow this idea to be used when it is appropriate but banned when it is not is rather more complex than it might seem at first sight.

There are, however, drawbacks with the only alternatives which have been suggested. One approach is to simply ignore the problem except when blatant contradictions are actually derived during the course of attempted inferences. This seems to be roughly what happens in real life, where a property like E might be used wherever it was needed, with paradoxical cases noted and explicitly rejected when they occurred. The trouble with this approach is that it depends on the ability to recognise paradoxes when they occur, and on the construction of an approach to inference that is not based entirely on proof by refutation. It may be that the analysis of *relevant implication* which we will discuss in the next chapter will help here, in that it may help us work out whether the contradiction on which some refutation proof depends is actually related to the conclusion we are trying to derive. Relevance logic, however, is too undeveloped at present for us to be able to pin many of our hopes on it.

The paradoxes arise when we try to combine the pure λ-calculus with the connectives of FOPC. We saw in Chapter 3 that there are no problems with FOPC itself, since we showed there that it is both sound and complete, in other words that it is perfectly well-behaved. The pure λ-calculus, by which we mean a language with constants, variables, functions and predicates, and with the operations of λ-abstraction and β-reduction, and nothing else, is also perfectly well-behaved. The problem arises when we permit abstraction over expressions including connectives from FOPC, particularly expressions involving ¬. Turner (1987) proposes to solve the problem by restricting use of λ-abstraction, so that once having constructed an expression which can be used for saying something is untrue, we are not permitted to use λ-abstraction on it, and hence never find ourselves trying to say that the same thing is both true and false. This theory is also currently too underdeveloped to replace the typed λ-calculus. It may turn out to be possible to provide reasonably efficient algorithms for manipulating its axioms and inference rules, but the semantics Turner provides is so unintuitive that even if this does happen, the theory may fail to gain wider acceptance.

8.2 Montague Semantics

The examples at the end of the last section could almost be taken to indicate the uselessness of λ-calculus. The first one showed that we could use it to do things in arithmetic which we could already do in FOPC, the second showed that unless we are extremely careful we can get into serious trouble when we use it. In the current section we will try to show that it does have applications by sketching the way it can be applied to the interpretation of sentences of natural language. λ-calculus has been used as the basis for some extremely sophisticated analyses of natural language semantics. We will only sketch some of the simpler ideas. The reader is referred to Dowty et al.(1981) for a good presentation of a number of more complex matters, and to Oehrle et al. (1987) for discussion of various extremely subtle points.

Most of the work which uses λ-calculus for natural language semantics falls within the tradition of *Montague grammar*. The aim of these theories is to provide a precise account of the semantics of natural language, and in particular of English. This is done by constructing formulae of some formal language which mean the same as expressions of English. If we can show that some English phrase means exactly the same as some expression of our formal language, then we can give a precise characterisation of the meaning of that phrase by pointing to the meaning of the expression. The argument is that if we knew what expression of the formal language the English phrase corresponded to, we could appeal to the semantics of the formal language for the meaning of the English phrase. This should not be taken to mean that anyone working within this tradition believes that the way that humans process language is by translating it into a formal language. It may well turn out to be convenient for computer programs for understanding natural language to do this, since it seems as though the best way to get programs to demonstrate their understanding is to get them to draw inferences, and this is most easily done at present if their knowledge is expressed in a formal language. It is important to bear this distinction in mind in what comes next. We will often say things like "the meaning of *every student walks* is $\forall\_x(\text{student}(\_x) \to \text{walk}(\_x))$". If we are trying to understand the semantics of English, this should probably be written as "the meaning of *every student walks* is the same as the meaning of ∀_x(student(_x) → walk(_x))". If, on the other hand, we are trying to write a program which will draw appropriate inferences from English sentences, we may well think that a program that could translate from English into some formal language would be a useful tool.

8.2.1 *Compositionality*

The first task that Montague semantics addresses is the problem of finding a way of making the semantics of natural language *compositional*. By this we mean that the rules which tell us what some complex phrase or expression means should be defined entirely in terms of the meanings of its sub-expressions. In particular, if we have taken a view on the syntactic structure of some expression, then the way that we combine the meanings of the constituents should not depend on exactly what the constituents are.

We will illustrate the problem with a well-known pair of sentences. We will take the view that *every student walks* means the same as ∀_x(student(_x) → walk(_x)). We take this view on the grounds that the sentence of FOPC we have given is exactly the one that would sanction the inferences, in FOPC, that we would want to be able to draw from the English. In particular, if we are also provided with the sentence *John is a student*, and we accept that this should be translated as student(john), then we can draw the inference walk(john). It is clear that we have to make a large number of decisions about the formal language which we are going to use for discussing the semantics of English, and about a substantial collection of phrase and sentence types, before we are in a position to make judgements about whether our translations will support all and only the inferences we want them to. In the present case we had to decide that our target language was FOPC, and that the appropriate translations of *John is a student* and *John walks* were student(john) and walk(john), before we could form an opinion about whether ∀_x(student(_x) → walk(_x)) was the correct translation of *every student walks*. We will simply accept these translations of the basic sentences and see where they lead us. The debate on whether or not they are good translations can be found in Dowty et al. (1981), and before that in Russell (1905).

Our other sentence is *some student walks*, which we will translate as ∃_x (student(_x) & walk(_x)). Again we will simply accept this as an appropriate translation, on the grounds that it supports the appropriate inferences when taken with all our other decisions about how to translate things. Our current problem is that we want to find a compositional rule which will enable us to construct these two translations by combining the meanings of the contributing phrases in a uniform way. The contributing phrases seem to be *every student/some student* and *walks*, at least if we follow normal practice in our syntactic analysis of English. We therefore need translations of *every student* and *some student* which will enable us to place the translation of *walks* inside the scope of either a universal or an existential quantifier, and to connect the translation of *walks* to the translation of *student* by either → or &. Furthermore, these translations must each be built out of the translations of *every/some* and *student*.

It is almost impossible to see how this could be done if the formal language we were translating to were in fact FOPC, and if we were to abide by the spirit of the constraint that semantic rules should be compositional. The choice of determiner has to govern the way that all the other meanings are to be combined, yet we are not allowed to refer explicitly to that choice when combining the meanings of *some/every student* and *walks*. We can, however, do what is required if we are prepared to use λ-calculus as our target language. The compositional rules we need are as follows:

S --> NP VP : [[S]] = [[NP]]([[VP]])
NP --> determiner noun : [[NP]] = [[determiner]]([[noun]])
VP --> v : [[VP]] = [[v]]

These should be read in two parts. The first part is a syntactic rule which describes how some expression may be constructed out of sub-expressions. The second part shows how the meanings of the sub-expressions are to be combined to give the meaning of the main expression. Thus the first rule says that an NP and a VP can be combined to make a sentence, and that their meanings should be combined by applying the meaning of the NP to that of the VP. The other rules are similar, and the only comment we will make on them is that the only VP rule we have given is for intransitive verbs.

We now need meanings for *every*, *some*, *student* and *walks*. These are as follows:

[[*student*]] = STUDENT
[[*walks*]] = WALK
[[*every*]] = $\lambda\_P\lambda\_Q(\forall\_x(\_P(\_x) \rightarrow \_Q(\_x)))$
[[*some*]] = $\lambda\_P\lambda\_Q(\exists\_x(\_P(\_x) \,\&\, \_Q(\_x)))$

The meanings of *student* and *walks* are simply taken to be properties that objects might or might not have. The goals of this part of semantic theory are not to work out the conditions under which it would be true to say that somebody was a student, or whether they were walking, but just to see what follows when these basic words are used in sentences. The meanings of *every* and *some*, on the other hand, are given in some detail. It is words like these that glue meaning-bearing words together into sentences, and hence it is these words that should govern the way their meanings are combined. The meaning of a word like *every* is just a set of instructions for working out the relationships between other parts of the texts in which it occurs.

Suppose we now consider the meanings of the phrases *every student* and *some student*. The rule for the semantics of NP's tells us that the meaning of *every student* is [[every]]([[student]]). The specific entries for *every* and *student* convert this to:

$$\lambda\_P\lambda\_Q(\forall\_x(\_P(\_x) \rightarrow \_Q(\_x))(\text{STUDENT})$$

Applying β-reduction to this leads to:

$$\lambda\_Q(\forall\_x(\text{STUDENT}(\_x) \rightarrow \_Q(\_x))$$

We can paraphrase this as saying roughly that the meaning of *every student* is the property of being something which is true of every student. Exactly the same mechanism would give us that the meaning of *some student* is the property of being something which is true of some student:

$$\lambda\_Q(\exists\_x(\text{STUDENT}(\_x) \& \_Q(\_x))$$

The VP rule tells us that the meaning of the VP *walks* is just the same as the meaning of the verb itself, namely WALK. The rule for S now says that the meaning of the sentence *every student walks* is [[every student]]([[walks]]), i.e.

$$\lambda\_Q(\forall\_x(\text{STUDENT}(\_x) \rightarrow \_Q(\_x))(\text{WALK})$$

After β-reduction, this becomes

$$\forall\_x(\text{STUDENT}(\_x) \rightarrow \text{WALK}(\_x))$$

exactly as required. In just the same way we see that the meaning of *some student walks* reduces to $\exists\_x(\text{STUDENT}(\_x) \& \text{WALK}(\_x))$.

There are two important things to note about what we have just done. The first is that since the process of β-reduction does not add anything to what was already present, there is in fact no difference between $\forall x(\text{STUDENT}(\_x) \rightarrow \text{WALK}(\_x))$ and the following unreduced formula:

$$(\lambda\_P(\lambda\_Q(\forall x(\_P(\_x) \rightarrow \_Q(\_x))(\text{STUDENT}))(\text{WALK})$$

Of course the unreduced formula is hard to read, and would be more awkward to use in any automatic inference system, but as far as semantic analysis is concerned that is entirely beside the point. The semantics of the two versions are identical, and hence the unreduced version is just as good as the reduced one. β-reduction should only enter the picture if we want to use our analysis in some automatic language processing system as the basis of inferences. The second point is that the meanings of *some* and *every* have been carefully designed to do exactly what was required in this case. If we were to find later on that this particular design did not work in other contexts, we would be forced to redesign them. But even if it does seem to work in more complex sentences as well, we should be wary of imputing any psychological reality to it. The most we can say is that if we want to do our semantics compositionally, then the fact that we need to use these designs indicates that we must interpret words like *some* and *every* as instructions about how the other, meaning bearing, words in the text are to be organised.

8.2.2 *Type raising*
Suppose we try to continue developing the semantics of English along the lines we have followed so far. We will start by supplementing our grammar with the following innocuous looking rule:

NP --> proper-name : [[NP]] = [[proper-name]]

In other words, if you come across a proper name you can treat it as a noun phrase, with the meaning of the noun phrase just being exactly the same as whatever the name itself meant - probably the person or place that the name belongs to. What happens if we use this rule, together with our existing grammar, to try to interpret the sentence *John walks*?

We see that the new NP rule gives us an NP whose meaning is [[*John*]], while the VP rule gives us a VP whose meaning is [[*walks*]]. We now have an NP followed by a VP. The S rule says that we can combine these to get a sentence whose meaning is [[*John*]]([[*walks*]]). This does not seem to be what we expected.

It seems to say that the meaning of *John* is a property, and that the meaning of the sentence is that this property holds of whatever is denoted by *walks*. Surely what we wanted was that *walks* denotes a property which is true of the individual denoted by *John*, i.e. [[*walks*]]([[*John*]]). To see how we resolve this, we need to look again at what [[*John*]]([[*walks*]]) might mean, if we assume that [[*walks*]] is indeed a 1-place relation (we are more or less forced to assume this, given our earlier analyses of *every student walks* and *some student walks*). The situation seems to be that the meaning of the NP is a function which can be applied to 1-place predicates to get a truth value. What truth value? Presumably the one you would get if you applied the predicates themselves to the individual denoted by the name. It seems as though when we move from the name to the NP, we are raising the type of the original meaning. We therefore use the following *type-raised* version of our apparently innocuous rule:

NP --> proper-name: [[NP]] = $\lambda Q(Q([[\text{proper-name}]]))$

In other words, the NP denotes the property of being something that is true of the object denoted by the name. If we try this rule on our example, we see that the meaning of the sentence comes out to be $\lambda Q(Q([[\textit{John}]]))([[\textit{walks}]])$. Applying β-reduction to this converts it to [[*walks*]]([[*John*]]), which is what we wanted in the first place.

The next obvious extension to the grammar is to try to deal with transitive verbs, i.e. verbs which take an object. The usual syntactic rule for dealing with such verbs is the following:

VP --> verb NP

This is the traditional rule for transitive verb phrases. It is possible to argue about whether it is the right one, but the linguistic grounds for accepting it are fairly convincing. Suppose we supplement this rule with a semantic rule as follows:

VP --> verb NP : [[VP]] = [[verb]]([[NP]])

In other words, that the meaning of the VP is what you would get if you applied the meaning of the verb to the meaning of the NP. The intuition here is that the meaning of a transitive verb is something like a 2-place relation, and that we are trying to instantiate one of the arguments with the object of the sentence, to get a 1-place predicate to combine with the subject.

We will try this rule out on the sentence *John likes Mary*. This is just about the simplest sentence it is possible to construct using a transitive verb, so the least we can ask of our theory of semantics is that it must account for it. With the rules we have given so far, we see that the phrase *likes Mary* is a VP whose meaning is $[[likes]](\lambda Q(Q([[Mary]])))$. If we combine this with the meaning of the subject NP *John*, we get $\lambda P(P([[John]]))([[likes]](\lambda Q(Q([[Mary]]))))$. Applying reduction to this gives us $[[likes]](\lambda Q(Q([[Mary]])))([[John]])$, which again seems to be the wrong sort of thing to be the meaning of *John likes Mary*. If we try a type-raised version of the rule for VP's, things seem to come out rather better:

VP --> verb NP : $\lambda Q(Q([[verb]]))([[NP]])$

With this version of the rule, the meaning of *likes Mary* comes out as $\lambda Q(Q([[likes]]))(\lambda R(R([[Mary]])))$. β-reduction converts this first to $\lambda R(R([[Mary]]))([[likes]])$, and then to $[[likes]]([[Mary]])$. This can be paraphrased as "the property of liking Mary". When we combine it with the meaning of the NP *John*, we get $\lambda S(S([[John]]))([[likes]]([[Mary]]))$, which β-reduction converts to $([[likes]]([[Mary]]))([[John]])$. This final expression says that the property of liking Mary is true of John, which is very much what we would expect this sort of account to provide as the meaning of *John likes Mary*.

We have not got very far in our attempt to give a formal analysis of the semantics of English. All we have managed to cover are some very simple sentences with simple quantifiers, and a single example of a sentence containing a transitive verb. There is rather more to Montague semantics than this - if there were not, it would hardly have been worth our while mentioning it. Our reason for considering it here, though, was more to illustrate the fact that λ-calculus does indeed have applications than to give a detailed account of how the semantics of English noun-phrases works. The lessons to be drawn from our presentation here are that you can do things with λ-calculus which would be more or less impossible in FOPC; but that for problems where λ-calculus does have advantages over FOPC, you are going to have to do quite a lot of work. This is fair enough - if something were easy in λ-calculus, it would probably be possible in FOPC. Readers who are intrigued by the tiny fragment of Montague semantics we have covered here should read Dowty et al. (1981) to see how orthodox Montague semantics treats a rather wider range of phenomena. Once you have read Dowty et al., there is a large body of work reported in Oehrle et al. (1987) and Buszkowski et al. (1986) which sheds light on a number of very subtle points about language.

8.3 Theorem proving in λ-calculus

We have considered theorem proving techniques for first-order languages at considerable length. For a formal language to be any use in AI, it must be possible to construct a program which can manipulate expressions of that language to work out what follows from what, and in particular to uncover facts which are entailed by what is already known explicitly. The first thing to note is that λ-calculus, as we have already seen, is inconsistent. You must ensure that you impose suitable constraints on what you allow people to say, or at least on what you are prepared to regard as meaningful, or you will find any program you write for manipulating expressions of λ-calculus trying to work whether formulae such as λP(¬P(P))(λP(¬P(P))) are true or false.

Once we have found some way of circumventing the problem of the inconsistency of λ-calculus, we immediately run into another negative result. λ-calculus is undecidable. Whereas FOPC was semi-decidable, in that it is possible to write programs which are guaranteed to find a proof if one exists at the risk of possible non-termination in cases where there is no proof, λ-calculus is fully undecidable. You cannot write a program which is guaranteed to find a proof that some expression of λ-calculus is entailed by some collection of other expressions if it indeed is. The trouble is that there is no general way of telling at a glance whether or not two expressions have any connection with one another. Both the major theorem proving methods we developed for first-order languages depended on the fact that unification enables you to tell whether there is some way of binding the variables in a pair of expressions which would make them inconsistent with each other. You can then carry these constraints on variable bindings around until you have managed to establish that whatever you do you will derive a contradiction. Theorem proving techniques for FOPC depend on the fact that there is a decision procedure for telling whether or not one atomic expression is inconsistent with another, so that theorem proving for complex expressions is 'just' a matter of trying out lots of ways of applying this basic operation. For λ-calculus, the basic operation of seeing whether two atomic expressions are mutually contradictory is itself a semi-decidable problem. We can see this if we consider just what is involved in working out whether or not ¬P(b) follows from P(a) and ∀_Q(_Q(a) → ¬_Q(b)). This is a pretty simple problem, and it ought to be obvious that the conclusion does indeed follow from the premises. It ought also to be clear that although ¬P(b) and P(a) are literals, there is no simple way of telling whether or not they clash with each other. In the present example it was easy enough to see that the rule ∀_Q(_Q(a) → ¬_Q(b)) was exactly what was required to get a contradiction between the target expressions, but in general we might have needed to prove an arbitrarily complicated problem of FOPC just to see whether or not P(b) and P(a) were mutually contradictory. In other words the most basic step of our theorem prover would itself be potentially non-terminating.

The argument above is just an argument, not a proof. It is conceivable that someone could come up with some magical proof method for λ-calculus which did not require us to be able to make up our minds about whether specific pairs of literals were mutually incompatible. Rather than go through the sort of proof we gave at the end of Chapter 3 to show that FOPC was semi-decidable, we leave it as a challenge to the reader to come up with an approach to theorem proving for λ-calculus which does not have either exactly the flaw we have just outlined or one which has the same effect. Theorem proving in λ-calculus is extremely difficult. The only approaches that are going to produce any results at all are ones which attempt to provide a first-order description of the semantics, and to do first-order reasoning about this description. In specific cases it seems likely that we will be able to perform something like Bibel's database reduction technique to show that the problem is in fact solvable using ordinary first-order methods. There is very little work in this area so far, and it is not clear just how difficult it will be to find ways of recognising special cases of problems which seem to be expressed in λ-calculus but for which first-order reification will produce solvable problems. It is clear that either something along these lines will have to be produced or that the approach to the semantics of natural language via λ-calculus or other intensional languages will have to be abandoned, at least as far as computational linguistics and natural language processing are concerned.

CHAPTER NINE

ALTERNATIVE VIEWS

All the logics we have seen so far have accepted that the standard analysis of the truth functional connectives &, ∨ and → is correct as far as it goes. The extensions to FOPC suggest directions in which the standard theory does not go far enough - it may be necessary, for instance, to make finer distinctions, introducing analyses of necessity or time, or to account for inferences based on defaults or on falsifiable assumptions. In all of them, however, the analysis of the basic connectives is adopted unchanged. There are a number of puzzles about the standard analysis of FOPC. We will therefore end our discussion of the application of logic in AI with a look at two alternative approaches to the basic connectives themselves. *Constructive logic* provides a reinterpretation of FOPC as an explanation of the construction of valid arguments, rather than as an investigation of some set of timeless truths. *Fuzzy logic* attempts to adapt FOPC for reasoning about propositions whose status is given in terms of how strongly they are believed, rather than as a black and white statement to the effect that they are definitely true or definitely false. We will see that constructive logic provides a precise, well-defined semantics for FOPC, for which meta-results such as soundness and completeness can be proved. Fuzzy logic, however, has not yet attained the degree of rigour which we would like for any language which is to be called a *logic*.

9.1 Constructive logic

Constructive logic is concerned very largely with arguments. The aim is to explain the nature of valid argument, and to provide tools for constructing and checking arguments. The roots of constructive logic lie in a debate in the late 19th and early 20th centuries on the nature of mathematics. For a very long time, it had been thought that the aim of mathematics was to uncover hidden truths about such things as the set of numbers and the nature of space. Euclid's axioms for geometry, for instance, were taken to be timeless truths about the ways that lines and planes behave, and the aim of geometry was to use valid inference rules to discover yet more interesting facts about lines and planes by investigating the consequences of the axioms. This view of mathematics was upset by two important discoveries. The first was that, in various branches of mathematics, it was possible to make changes to the established axiom sets. Probably the first place where this happened was in geometry itself, where it was discovered that you could drop or alter some of Euclid's axioms, and that if you did so the theory that resulted was perfectly coherent, and indeed that such altered geometries often had very natural interpretations. The second discovery was that certain other apparently well-formed statements of mathematics did not seem to have meaningful interpretations at all. The most famous example of such a statement was Russell's description of the set P of all sets which are not members of themselves. It is perfectly possible to write down a description of this object, using the language developed for set theory around the beginning of the 20th century. It is impossible to give it an interpretation. If you suppose there is such a set, you are forced to decide whether you think it is one of its own elements. If you decide to believe that it is, then you are forced to accept that it does not fit the characterisation of members of P. If, on the other hand, you decide that it is not a member of itself, you are forced to accept that it does fit this characterisation, and hence must be a member of itself after all.

These puzzles in the foundations of mathematics led to a number of major developments in mathematics itself, and also to the formation of a variety of views on what mathematics was really about. The view that concerns us here is that of the *intuitionists*. The intuitionists argued that mathematics was about people making up objects in their minds, and then studying the properties that those objects had. There is, of course, plenty to be said about what minds are, and what sort of objects they can contain, but fortunately we do not need to get involved in that part of the debate here. The critical point for us is that this view of mathematics as a whole led to a specific view of the role of logic. The function of logic is to make it possible for people to describe the objects they have created in their minds, and to enable them to *argue* about their properties. It seems that we can say very precise things about about what you can describe, and how you can argue, even though the idea of "constructing an object in one's mind" remains rather obscure.

Constructive logic, then, initially proceeds by specifying the conditions under which particular inferences may be made. We will develop a language called *constructive first-order predicate calculus* (FOPC$_C$). This has the vocabulary of ordinary FOPC, with the symbols &, ∨ and ∃ included as primitives, but with ¬A still defined as an abbreviation for A → †. The inferences that are allowed for each connective are described by a specific set of conditions:

FOPC$_C$-&: you may infer P & Q if you have proofs of P and Q individually.

FOPC$_C$-∨: you may infer P ∨ Q if you have a proof of P or one of Q. Note that this rules out, in general, the assumption that A ∨ ¬A is always true. In the three blocks problem, for instance, we have no way of telling whether B is green or not green, so we cannot conclude green(B) ∨ ¬green(B). FOPC$_C$ would not be much use to us, however, if we could not solve problems as easy as the three blocks problem in it. We will see later how the proof can be constructed despite the fact that we cannot conclude green(B) ∨ ¬green(B).

FOPC$_C$- →: you may infer P → Q if you can show how to turn any proof of P into a proof of Q. As a simple example, consider the formula p → (q → p). Suppose we had a proof P_p of p. Then we could turn any proof P_q into a proof of p by simply appending P_p to it. We thus see that if we had a proof of p we could turn it into a proof of (q → p), which is exactly what is required to show that we have a proof of p → (q → p).

FOPC$_C$-∀: you may infer ∀_xP if you can show how you would prove P|$_{<b,\_x>}$ for any possible b.

FOPC$_C$-∃: you may infer ∃_xA if you can find a constant b for which you can prove P|$_{<b,\_x>}$.

The striking thing about these inference rules is that they appeal to the notion of turning one proof into another. You may infer P → Q if you can show how to turn a proof of P in a proof of Q; you may infer ¬P if you can show how you would derive a contradiction from any proof of P; and you may infer $\forall\_xP$ if you can show how you would prove $P|_{\ll a,x\gg}$ for any a. To realise our goal of giving a precise formal specification of constructive logic, then, we will have to provide a precise description of this notion.

There seem to be a number of ways we could proceed at this point. It is possible to write down a set of axioms that correspond to the inferences that the intuitionists want to allow. We could, for instance, choose the following set of axioms for propositional calculus, taken from Robbin (1969):

$$A \rightarrow (B \rightarrow A)$$
$$[A \rightarrow (B \rightarrow C)] \rightarrow [(A \rightarrow B) \rightarrow (B \rightarrow C)]$$
$$(A \, \& \, B) \rightarrow A$$
$$(A \, \& \, B) \rightarrow B$$
$$A \rightarrow (B \rightarrow (A \, \& \, B))$$
$$A \rightarrow (A \lor B)$$
$$B \rightarrow (A \lor B)$$
$$(A \rightarrow C) \rightarrow [(B \rightarrow C) \rightarrow ((A \lor B) \rightarrow C)]$$
$$\dagger \rightarrow A$$

As it happens, if we use modus ponens with this set of axioms then we do get all and only the conclusions that the intuitionists would like. It is easy to see, for instance, that if we use the axiom $(A \rightarrow (B \rightarrow (A \, \& \, B))$ to derive A & B then we must have had proofs of A and B individually, as required by our definition of the permissible inference rules. Nonetheless, this set of axioms does not seem to be a very natural characterisation of what is meant by *constructiveness*. We would prefer to try to come up with a direct description of constructiveness in terms of permitted operations on formulae. The literature on constructive logic and mathematics contains two approaches to this task. One, Martin-Lof's (1982) *theory of types*, seems to have considerable potential as a programming language within which proofs that program specifications are satisfiable can be turned directly into programs. The theory of types in fact provides a constructive alternative to λ-calculus. As such it contains rather more machinery than we need if we just want a characterisation of constructiveness for first-order theories. Indeed, it should be noted that since the theory of types makes it possible to derive correct programs directly from proofs of satisfiability, it is highly likely that constructing proofs of satisfiability will be more or less as difficult as writing correct programs: the two tasks are just about equivalent.

9.1.1 *Game theoretic semantics*

The characterisation of constructiveness which we shall use for $FOPC_C$ was developed originally by Lorentz (1961) and Lorentzen (1959), and has been used extensively to account for phenomena in natural language by Hintikka and Kulas (1985). We are primarily concerned here with $FOPC_C$, so that we cannot use Hintikka's presentations directly. The work on which we shall base the current discussion is Stegmuller's (1964) proof of the completeness of various axiom systems with respect to specific variants of the semantic framework.

Game theoretic semantics explicitly treats logical languages as being about winning and losing arguments. The aim is not the construction of proofs for one's own satisfaction, nor is it the investigation of absolute timeless truths. What you have to do is win an argument. Sometimes the argument may be with another person, sometimes it may be with yourself, sometimes it may be with "nature". It doesn't really matter who you perceive your opponent to be. What does matter is that you must try to beat them, whilst sticking to the rules of argument which make up the rules of the "game".

The basic structure of a game is very simple. There are two players, who Stegmuller calls W and B by analogy with chess. The game starts with both players agreeing on a set of permitted moves and an initial set of assumptions. W then proposes a statement. B has to try to show that W's proposal might not follow from their initial set of assumptions. B does this by making challenges, in accordance with the rules that the players agreed on before starting play. W can defend against a challenge either with an explicitly permitted defence, or by counter-challenging. W wins if B runs out of challenges and B wins if W fails to defend against a challenge. It is quite possible for neither player to win.

The attraction of game theoretic semantics is that it provides several different points at which we can choose to accept or reject moves. Classical semantics simply specifies that things are true or false by virtue of their form and the truth or falsity of their components. In game theoretic semantics we can make fine distinctions by making specific moves legal for B but not for W, or by allowing W to make a move if B has already made it but not otherwise, or by making use of other facets of the *dynamic* and *asymmetric* nature of games. Before we look in detail at the rules proposed by Stegmuller, we will construct a hypothetical argument between Wendy and Boris about the three blocks problem:

Wendy: OK, we've got three blocks. A is green, C is not green. A is on top of B and B is on top of C.
Boris: OK.
Wendy: I think there's a green one on top of one that's not green.

Boris: I don't.
Wendy: Perhaps A is a green one on top of a not-green one.
Boris: Well A is green, and it is on top of another one. But I think B is green as well.
Wendy: But if you think B is green, then it's a green one on top of a not-green one itself.
Boris: Well perhaps B's not green after all.
Wendy: Which way do you want it - is B green or isn't it?
Boris: I'm bored with this argument. Let's go and play catch instead.

The argument started with both players agreeing on the background assumptions. Wendy then made her claim, which Boris countered with a flat denial (*I don't*). Wendy then came up with a more specific claim as a defence against Boris's denial. Boris challenged this by making a claim of his own (*B is green as well*). Wendy then used Boris's counter-claim to construct her next defence. It is important to note that Wendy did not assume that B was green until Boris had used this assumption as part of his attack, and that when he subsequently tried to deny it she refused to allow him to take it back. The formal rules for arguments come in three parts. The *logical rules* specify the forms of attacks and defences:

Formula	Attacks	Defences	Notes
A & B	?A	A	Attacker can attack with ?B if
	?B	B	?A is successfully defended.
A ∨ B	?	A	Defender can choose which
		B	defence to use, and can switch if the first one fails.
A → B	A	B	The only defence is to claim the consequent is true.
¬A	A		
∀_xA	?A|_{<a,x>}	A|_{<a,x>}	Attacker chooses a.
∃_xA	?	A|_{<a,x>}	Defender chooses a.

The *basic rule* restricts W's use of prime formulae (ones containing no connectives). W is never allowed to use a prime formula unless B has already used it or it is one of the agreed assumptions. This holds both for defence moves and for possible counter-attacks. This rule can prevent W making a defence, for instance if W has posited P(a) → Q(a) and B has responded by attacking with P(a), W cannot defend with Q(a) unless B has already used it (and hence implicitly conceded it).

The *structural rule* places restrictions on when particular moves are allowed. It corresponds to conversational rules like the one that prevented Boris from retracting his concession about the colour of B. In order to be able to state the structural rule, we have to first define the notion of a *round* in a game. A round consists of an attack-defence pair. The attack opens the round, the defence closes it. There is no need for the defence to follow immediately after the attack. The structural rule is as follows:

(i) B may attack *once* any formula that W has put forward in any earlier round.

(ii) W may attack a formula that B has put forward in an earlier round *as many times as he or she wants*.

(iii) Either player may defend against an earlier attack, so long as all intervening rounds are closed. In other words, arguments have to be nested - you are not allowed to go back to an earlier attack until all the points raised subsequently have been dealt with. W is allowed to redefend any formula at any time, but B can only defend a formula once.

Finally, we note that W wins a game if it is B's turn to move but B has no legitimate moves available. We will illustrate these rules with an annotated game aimed at establishing the goal of the three blocks problem.

Open round 0 (W): Wendy starts by stating her goal (the players have already agreed to accept the premises).

∃_x∃_y(green(_x) & ¬green(_y) & on(_x, _y))

Open round 1 (B): Boris just flatly disagrees.

?

Defend round 1 (W): Wendy responds by choosing a specific instantiation of her original goal.

   green(a) & ¬green(b) & on(a, b)

Open round 2 (B): Wendy could defend against either of the attacks ?green(a) or ?on(a, b) by appealing to the agreed assumptions, so Boris' only useful attacking move is to ask her about ¬green(b).

   ?¬green(b)

Defend round 2 (W): Wendy says that as far as she is concerned, ¬green(b) might well be true.

   ¬green(b)

Open round 3 (B): Boris attacks this by saying that he thinks green(b) is true.

   green(b)

Redefend round 1 (W): Wendy has no defence to this, so her only option is to redefend round 1.

   green(b) & ¬green(c) & on(b, c)

Open round 4 (B): ¬green(c) and on(b, c) are in the agreed assumptions, so there is no point in attacking either of them. Boris is forced to attack by questioning green(b).

   ?green(b)

Defend round 4 (W): Wendy can counter this with green(b), thanks to Boris's own introduction of green(b) in round 3.

   green(b)

It is Boris's move, but there is nothing he can do. Wendy wins.

The argument given above corresponds fairly closely to a classical proof using something like the connection method. With the rules as given, however, we have extra flexibility about what moves are allowed when. We can, for instance, alter the structural rule by forbidding W to redefend formulae. If W's first defence of a formula is the only one he or she is allowed, we find that the only goals which W can successfully defend are the ones derivable from our collection of axioms for FOPC$_C$. The point is that W has to be able to pick a defence which will work no matter how B tries to attack it. In other words, W's defence must be such that it can be adapted to deal with any attack - it must lend itself to *constructive extension*. Since all W's permitted moves are specified by the rules of the game, this restriction does provide us with the precise definition of constructiveness that we required. It does not, of course, tell us what W's defence ought to be. Choosing a defence which you will be able to sustain no matter what B does next is likely to require considerable ingenuity. It does, however, give us a clear criterion for judging whether a proof was constructive or not, namely did it correspond to an argument in which W was able to avoid having to redefend anything.

It is clear that Wendy could not have won the argument given above if she had been forbidden to find an alternative defence for round 1, since there were no other points at which she had any choice to make. With this restriction on Wendy's moves, the only way she can solve the three blocks problem is by arguing that it would be absurd for the goal not to hold.

Open round 0 (W): Wendy's first move this time is the weaker claim that the negation of her real goal is itself impossible.

$\quad\quad$ ¬¬∃_x∃_y(green(_x) & ¬green(_y) & on(_x, _y))

Open round 1 (B): The next couple of rounds consist of Boris challenging Wendy's initial claim and then Wendy counter-challenging.

$\quad\quad$ ¬∃_x∃_y(green(_x) & ¬green(_y) & on(_x, _y))

Open round 2 (W):

$\quad\quad$ ∃_x∃_y(green(_x) & ¬green(_y) & on(_x, _y))

Open round 3 (B): The game is now in the same state as the earlier version, and proceeds just like the earlier version for a few steps, starting with Boris' denial of Wendy's basic goal.

$\quad\quad$?

Defend round 3 (W):

$\quad\quad$ green(a) & ¬green(b) & on(a, b)

Open round 4 (B):
>   ?¬green(b)

Defend round 4 (W):
>   ¬green(b)

Open round 5 (B):
>   green(b)

Re-open round 2 (W): Wendy has no defence to this, and she is not allowed to redefend anything which she has already defended. She is, however, allowed to *re-attack*.
>   ∃_x∃_y(green(_x) & ¬green(_y) & on(_x, _y))

Open round 6 (B):
>   ?

Defend round 6 (W):
>   green(b) & ¬green(c) & on(b, c)

Open round 7 (B):
>   ?green(b)

Defend round 7 (W): As before, Wendy has Boris's concession (at round 5 this time) of green(b) to use in her own defence.
>   green(b)

It is quite common for a constructive proof to be available for ¬¬P even though one is not available for P itself. This should not be too surprising. A constructive proof of an existentially quantified statement should not just show you that the goal statement is true, but ought also to supply you with constants for which it is true, or at least with some way of working them out. That would seem to be part of the essence of what it means to be constructive. A constructive proof of a doubly negated existential statement, on the other hand, simply has to show that it is absurd to suppose that the existential statement is false. There is no onus on the person providing the proof to actually point out an instantiation for which it is true. This is exactly the situation in the current problem - it is absurd to suppose that the goal is false, but we have no idea how to instantiate it.

Game theoretic semantics was proposed to provide an interpretation for intuitionist logic, which had previously only been given in terms of its proof theory. The problem was that classical model theory required the interpretation of $\rightarrow$ to be given in terms of the way it combined the truth values of the antecedent and the consequent. There was very little scope for making subtle distinctions between its use in different contexts. Suppose, for example, that we wanted to provide a truth functional account of the meaning of $\rightarrow$ which would make $p \rightarrow \neg\neg p$ valid but not $\neg\neg p \rightarrow p$. We would have to be able to imagine a valuation for which $[\![\neg\neg p]\!]$ was T but $[\![p]\!]$ was F. It is extremely difficult, if not impossible, to see how we could manage it. The advantage of game theoretic semantics is that it provides a very fine grained account of the circumstances in which formulae entail one another. Since it is fine grained, there are places where we can make small changes, and hence fine distinctions between valid and invalid formulae.

We can, in fact, adapt this framework to a variety of axiomatisations by making appropriate changes to the rules governing legal moves. We have seen rules corresponding to classical logic and orthodox intuitionist logic. There are a number of other proposals concerning the nature of the basic connectives, particularly the connective $\rightarrow$. The interpretation of $\rightarrow$ as denoting *material implication*, that $P \rightarrow Q$ is true so long as it is not the case that P is true and Q is false, has struck many people as being an inadequate account of implication. Even if we draw a distinction between implication and cause, there seems to be something unsatisfactory about an account of implication which simply reports on what happens to be true, without any seeming connection between the antecedent and the consequent. If, for example, it is raining and I am looking out of the window, then if $\rightarrow$ denotes material implication both the sentences *it is raining $\rightarrow$ I am looking out of the window* and *I am looking out of the window $\rightarrow$ it is raining* are true. We will not get into any trouble if we accept these as true statements, so long as we remember that all we mean by $\rightarrow$ is material implication, but it seems unsatisfactory that we cannot distinguish between this rather casual kind of implication and cases where there really is some connection, such as *there are no clouds in the sky $\rightarrow$ it is sunny*. There have been two notable attempts to provide alternative notions of implication which will make it possible to make these distinction. The first of these is *strict implication*. This is normally presented by regarding the difference between the two cases as reflecting exactly whether the implication is necessary or merely coincidental, in other words by defining strict implication between P and Q, written $P \rightarrow_s Q$, as a modal operator equivalent to $\neg\Diamond(P \,\&\, \neg Q)$. P strictly implies Q if it could not have been the case that P was true and Q was not. By contrast, P materially implies Q if this just happens not to be the case. It does, however, seem unfortunate that we are forced to move to modal logic in order to explicate this difference. Stegmuller suggests that altering the structural rule to forbid either player from attacking or defending a formula more than once provides an interpretation for strict logic without having to appeal to any modal operations. This is a tempting suggestion, since it enables us to account for an interesting extension to classical FOPC without making radical changes to the semantics.

Strict implication is not, however, the only alternative form of implication which has been discussed in the literature. The axiom A => (B => A) is valid whether you read => as being the material implication operator $\rightarrow$ or the strict operator $\rightarrow_S$. For some authors, there seems to be something counterintuitive about this axiom. Suppose we assume that strict implication is supposed to embody the fact that there really is a connection between the antecedent and the consequent. Why, they ask, should there be any connection between B and A simply because A is true? Belnap and Anderson (1975) provide a very detailed discussion of possible axioms for what they call *relevant implication*, which we will denote by $\rightarrow_R$. They eventually derive a set of axioms which seems to support the inferences they want to accept, and which do not entail the so-called paradoxes of implication. Unfortunately the semantics that Belnap and Anderson provide is extremely unintuitive. It seems likely that the structural rule might also be adapted to provide an interpretation for $\rightarrow_R$, as well as for classical and intuitionist logic and for $\rightarrow_S$.

Having a semantic framework which can be adapted to such a wide variety of logics provides valuable reinforcement to the notion that logic is not some absolute study of properties of things in general. It is rather a detailed analysis of ways of constructing arguments. Game theoretic semantics brings home the fact that there are a variety of different rules for argument, and that any participant in an argument is at liberty to choose the rules they want to abide by. Logic tells you about the consequences of your choice. It cannot, however, tell you whether or not you were right to make that choice.

Constructive logic, strict logic and relevance logic have not as yet had a great deal of influence within AI. Hintikka (1985) has used game theoretic semantics as the basis for a considerable body of work on natural language semantics and pragmatics, but this work has not yet been widely taken up by people working on computer interpretation of natural language. It does seem well worth trying to use the metaphor of game theoretic semantics as the basis for automatic theorem proving. The classical version of the theory corresponds closely to the method of semantic tableaux which lies behind Bibel's connection method. The more constrained versions may well provide constraints on the search space for the connection method which will make it easier to solve certain interesting classes of problem such as the problems of inference involved in natural language processing.

9.2 Fuzzy Logic

The final topic we will consider is Zadeh's (1975) *fuzzy logic*. A large number of AI workers have been faced by the problem that either their data or their background knowledge is in some sense "uncertain". This can occur for a variety of reasons. It may be that they are working with data obtained from unreliable or imprecise sources, e.g. from measuring devices that are known to occasionally produce faulty readings. It may be that their background knowledge has been obtained from an expert in the field whose knowledge has been compiled on the basis of their own experience, and can best be expressed in terms of the strength of the expert's belief about a phenomenon. It may be that the concepts which are used for specifying the data or the background knowledge do not have sharp boundaries. This can happen with simple concepts such as colours. We might, for instance, have a rule which said that litmus paper dipped in acid turns red, but be unsure of whether the particular piece of paper that we have just dipped in the liquid in our test-tube had in fact turned red or not, since the concept of being red does not have sharp boundaries. It can also happen with intensional concepts such as size - the concept of being big, for instance, has no boundaries at all until we know what category of object we are applying it to.

These problems are pervasive in AI. They are particularly significant for people building expert systems, since the rules that they glean from their tame experts are nearly always riddled with vague concepts and judgemental rules. The standard approach is to replace the simple two-valued truth functions we have been using by numerical scores between 0 and 1, representing something like degree of conviction or estimated probability, and manipulate these numbers by some variant of probability theory. Systems taking this pragmatic approach can be very successful indeed. Most of the classical expert systems, such as MYCIN (Shortliffe 1976) and PROSPECTOR (Gaschnig 1982), have done something like this. It seems to be very difficult to do anything else. The information you have available is couched in terms that look rather like probabilities, but it is clear that the appropriate conditions for applying statistical theory reliably do not hold. What can you do other than to use something like statistical theory, with little bits tacked on to compensate for the most glaring sources of error, and with no great degree of faith in any numbers that may accompany the results of chains of inference?

Before we proceed any further, it should be remarked that systems of this kind are among the best, most effective systems currently available. Virtually all the current showpiece expert systems use data and background knowledge with certainty factors attached to them, and inference rules which manipulate certainty factors more or less as though they were genuine probabilities. Nonetheless, the underlying theory of how certainty factors interact, and what they really mean, is so under-developed that there is very little we can say about them in the context of formal logic. The only serious attempt to clarify how they work and what they mean is Zadeh's fuzzy logic. This comes in two parts, fuzzy set theory and fuzzy truth values.

Fuzzy set theory is an attempt to account for concepts such as colours and sizes which do not have precisely defined boundaries. Earlier on we gave an extensional view of the concept *red* by saying that it was in some sense the same as the set of all red things. We can give a fuzzy extension to *red* by saying that it consists of all those things which possess the property of being red to some non-zero extent. We want to be able to talk about the extent to which each of them possesses the property. We do this by interpreting *red*, for instance, as being a set of pairs, where the first element of each pair is some object and the second element is a number greater than zero. We can develop the theory of fuzzy sets perfectly coherently by mimicking the development of simple set theory. Membership becomes a function which returns the value associated with an item in a fuzzy set, or 0 if the item is not in the set. Any set S has an associated characteristic function $CFUN_S$. The only difference is that characteristic functions now return numerical values between 0 and 1, rather than the truth values F and T. One set S1 is a subset of another S2 if every item whose degree of membership of S1 is greater than 0 is a member of S2 to an even higher degree, i.e.

$$\forall\_x(CFUN_{S1}(\_x) > 0 \rightarrow (CFUN_{S2}(\_x) \geq CFUN_{S1}(\_x)))$$

Intersection and union of sets can be defined similarly. We take the degree to which an item is a member of the intersection of two fuzzy sets to be the lesser of its degree of membership of each of them individually:

$$CFUN_{(S1 \cap S2)}(x) = min(CFUN_{S1}(x), CFUN_{S2}(x))$$

The definition for the union of two fuzzy sets is similar:

$$CFUN_{(S1 \cup S2)}(x) = max(CFUN_{S1}(x), CFUN_{S2}(x))$$

These definitions seem to behave sensibly. At the very least they fulfill the criteria that if all values are in fact either 1 or 0 then they behave exactly like classical sets; and that most of the standard relations such as $(A \cap B) \subseteq A \subseteq (A \cup B)$ hold. It is worth remarking, however, that if we take A* to denote the *fuzzy complement* of A, i.e. the set such that $CFUN_{A*}(x) = 1\text{-}CFUN_{A}(x)$, then $A \cap A*$ $\neq \varnothing$, and $A \cup A*$ is not a set such that $CFUN_{(A \cup A*)}(x)$ is 1 for every x.

Fuzzy set theory, then, seems to be reasonably coherent. Whether it is in fact the best way of dealing with concepts such as size, colour or typicality is open to debate. Cohen and Murphy (1982) argue strongly that it is not, in fact, at all appropriate for dealing with a number of concepts to which it seems at first sight to be well-suited. They are concerned about the analysis of complex noun phrases in terms of intersections of fuzzy sets. A typical example concerns the notion of a *pet fish*. Classical set theory suggests that the correct way to deal with this is to regard it as denoting the intersection of the two sets *pet* and *fish* - something is a pet fish if and only if it is a member of the set of pets and also of the set of fishes. If we take this idea over into fuzzy set theory, we see that for any x, the value of $CFUN_{pet\ fish}(x)$ ought to be the minimum of $CFUN_{pet}(x)$ and $CFUN_{fish}(x)$. This immediately runs foul of the fact that goldfish are pretty poor examples of both the contributing concepts *pet* and *fish*, yet are completely archetypal as *pet fish*. Its value as an instance of the compound concept is notably higher than its value as an instance of either of the more basic ones, in direct contradiction to the suggestion that a compound concept should be dealt with as the intersection of its contributors under fuzzy intersection. Cohen and Murphy offer other problems of this kind. There seems little point in repeating them at length here. The problem we have seen indicates that although fuzzy set theory seems to be internally coherent, it is not a theory that can automatically be used in place of classical set theory wherever the concepts involved seem to be fuzzy. We leave it to the reader to choose whether or not fuzzy sets are appropriate in any particular case, trusting that the one example we have seen will warn them to be wary, and turn next to the extension of fuzzy set theory to fuzzy logic.

Fuzzy set theory can be used with a fairly simple logic which simply associates a real number between 0 and 1 with each formula. The choice of how to do this is reasonably free, though it is strongly recommended that the rules for assigning values to compound statements should be constrained to act exactly like the rules of classical logic in cases where the constituent expressions all have either 0 or 1 as their values. The following set of rules (from Turner (1984)) is fairly typical, though almost any of the mechanisms for manipulating certainty factors could be used:

$$[\![P(a_1, ..., a_n)]\!] = CFUN_P(a_1, ... a_n)$$
$$[\![A \ \& \ B]\!] = \min([\![A]\!], [\![B]\!])$$
$$[\![A \lor B]\!] = \max([\![A]\!], [\![B]\!])$$
$$[\![\neg A]\!] = 1 - [\![A]\!]$$
$$[\![A \to B]\!] = \min(1, (1 + [\![B]\!]) - [\![A]\!])$$

These rules do behave exactly like the rules of classical logic in cases where all the primitive formulae have values of 0 or 1, though it is notable that $A \to B$ is no longer equivalent to $\neg A \lor B$ except in this special case. Some set of rules of this kind seems to be safest way to use fuzzy set theory. Zadeh proposes to replace the simple numerical truth values of the above scheme by elements of a fuzzy set of *linguistic truth values*. The elements of this set are the following set of expressions:

{true, false,
very true, not true, fairly true,
very false, not false, fairly false,
very very true, not very true, fairly very true,
very not true, not not true, fairly not true,
...}

In other words the set of linguistic truth values consists of the expressions that can be generated by starting with the basic values true and false, and qualifying each previously encountered item with each of the terms very, not and fairly.

This set itself has a characteristic function $CFUN_{TRUE}$ which indicates how good an example of a truth value an item actually is. The criterion that says that any fuzzy logic should be equivalent to classical logic when there is no fuzziness present indicates that $CFUN_{TRUE}(true)$ should be 1 and $CFUN_{TRUE}(false)$ should be 0. Exactly how the values for other elements of the set are to be computed is left fairly free. We now use these linguistic truth values as the basis of the semantics of fuzzy set theory, and then use something like the preceding set of rules for manipulating the linguistic truth values themselves. It turns out that there are numerous problems with this. A simple example concerns the fact that the set of linguistic truth values turns out not to be closed under the basic operations of propositional logic. Suppose, for instance, that $CFUN_{TRUE}(fairly$ true) was 0.8 and $CFUN_{TRUE}(not$ false) was 0.5, and that we were trying to evaluate $[\![A \to B]\!]$ where $[\![A]\!]$ was "not false" and $[\![B]\!]$ was "fairly true". The rules for combining numerical truth values given above would give us that $[\![A \rightarrow B]\!]$ was min(1, (1+0.5)-0.8), in other words 0.7. It could perfectly easily turn out that there is no linguistic truth value which is an instance of TRUE to degree 0.7, so that we would have taken two linguistic truth values, combined them according to the prescribed computation, and ended up with something which did not correspond uniquely to a linguistic truth value.

Turner (1984) points out a number of other similar problems. It seems that the machinery required for using the whole of Zadeh's fuzzy logic is so cumbersome that it is impossible even to contemplate proving the meta-results we rely on in classical logic to ensure that the system is well-behaved - soundness, consistency, completeness and so on. At the same time, Cohen and Murphy's arguments indicate that the theory fails to capture quite a number of properties of the kind of concepts for which it is proposed. The moral seems to be that if you have to write an expert system which can cope with imprecise data and unreliable rules, it is probably best to make do with some adaptation of statistical theory, accepting that it is not going to be reliable but hoping that it will work reasonably most of the time; but that if you want to construct coherent, defensible arguments you should try to deal with the uncertainties in the skirmishes that precede the debate, and conduct the debate itself according to one of the logics we have considered in the rest of the book.

REFLECTIONS

We have now seen a wide range of formal languages. All of them, apart from the fuzzy logic that we considered in Chapter 9, have had precisely defined sets of inference rules and precisely defined semantics. That was, after all, the way we chose which languages to look at. What else did they have common?

They had, of course, quite a number of technical similarities - the way in which the semantics was always provided compositionally on the basis of the syntax, for instance, or the frequent use of structured sets of worlds as the basis for their semantics. But they also had two common negative characteristics. They are not usually put forward as models of the ways that people actually store their knowledge; and they are not, at least in this book, regarded as infallible.

Consider first the question of whether they should be seen as models of the ways people store their knowledge. Anyone who claimed that they should be seen as such models must surely also claim that the way people deploy their knowledge is akin to theorem proving. To claim that you have a theory of how people store their knowledge, but then to admit that you do not actually know how they retrieve it and make use of it, is an untenable position. It seems most unlikely, however, that people perform anything very like resolution when they are going about their everyday business, or even that they do anything closely resembling connection method theorem proving. The languages we have looked at, then are not theories of knowledge representation in the sense of being theories about how people represent their knowledge.

On the other hand, they cannot really be seen as theories of how the world is. We conceded that the axiomatisations of knowledge and belief were idealisations when we presented them. This was as true of the theory of belief structures as it was of the use of modal logic. We saw in the chapter on time that we could choose different theories to suit different styles of problem solving, but that none of the theories we considered had much to do with the physicists' view of what time is like. It may be, of course, that physicists are also wrong about time, but the fact that none of the theories we have considered even addresses their view indicates that the logic of time is not *intended* as a theory of what it is really like. The point is emphasised by the way game theoretic semantics has been deliberately constructed to make it possible to explore the consequences of small changes.

But if logic is not intended as a theory of knowledge representation or as a theory about the world, what use is it to us in AI? It seems to have two functions. The first is that it provides us with tools for discussing languages, for finding out how they behave, and for ensuring that they mean what we think they mean. This is particularly important to us when it shows us that expressions which we thought were different actually mean the same thing, or that expressions which we thought were identical mean different things. Without the extra precision that is provided when we use the tools of logic, it would be much harder even to talk about the difference between knowing that there is something with a particular property and knowing what object has that property; it would be difficult to argue for the event calculus, say, on the grounds that it enables us emphasise particular facets of what we are talking about; and it would be impossible to see just what the theories of default logic and circumscription have in common and where they differ. The first function of logic, then, is to enable us to talk *about* representation languages, and to see which distinctions can be made in a language and which ones cannot.

Logic's second function in AI is to make the content of AI theories more transparent. A large part of AI is based on the premise that computer programs can be seen as theories of cognition. Unfortunately, when you report a program as though it were a theory, you have to make up a semantics which connects the behaviour of your program to the behaviour you are trying to explain or model. This is a difficult task, and it is a task which people often fail to even attempt. Far too often people just point to a procedure or a datastructure and say "That's the system's representation of how to see if someone's got measles" or "That's its representation of the properties of bicycles", or whatever. It is impossible to test such programs properly, or even to understand what theories they embody, since there is no reliable agreed way of interpreting their inputs and outputs. If the part of your program that embodies your theory is couched in one of the languages that we have looked at in this book, however, then it is easy to find out what knowledge you have given it. We already know what expressions of these languages mean.

If the functions of logic in AI are to make it easier for us to choose appropriate languages for our tasks, and to make the theories we develop more open to testing by our peers, what is the role of theorem proving? Most theorem proving algorithms are definitely not to be seen as models of human cognition. It seems more appropriate to think of them as compilers. The languages of logic are appealing for the reasons we have just discussed, but they would be no use at all in AI if we could not manipulate them to extract implicit knowledge. Theorem provers provide the mechanisms by which we can test our theories, and they make it possible to use these theories in practical systems. We could perhaps sum up the role of logic and theorem proving in AI by remarking that the most advanced work in formal linguistics at the moment presupposes that what we know about natural language is best expressed in λ-calculus or some other higher-order formalism; but that since there are no practical theorem provers for these languages yet, AI work on natural language is still couched very largely in terms of first-order languages.

BIBLIOGRAPHY

Allen J. (1978) *Anatomy of LISP*, McGraw-Hill, New York.

Allen J.F. (1981) "Maintaining knowledge about temporal intervals", Report TR-86, Department of Computer Science, University of Rochester.

Allen J.F. (1984) "Towards a general theory of action and time", *Artificial Intelligence* 23(2), pp.123-154.

Andrew P.B. (1981) "Theorem proving via general matings", *Journal of the Association for Computing Machinery* 28(2), pp.193-214.

Barrett R., Ramsay A.M. & Sloman S. (1985) *POP-11: a practical language for AI*, Ellis Horwood, Chichester.

Bibel W. (1982) *Automated theorem proving*, Vieweg & Sohn, Braunschweig.

Bibel W., Letz R. & Schumann J. (1987) "Bottom-up enhancements of deductive systems", ms., Technische Universitat Munchen.

Buszkowski W., Marciszewski W. & van Benthem J. (1986) *Categorial grammar*, Benjamin, Amsterdam.

Castaneda H. (1967) "On the logic of attribution of self-knowledge", *Journal of Philosophy* 65, pp. 439-456.

Chapman D. (1987) "Planning for conjunctive goals", Report 802, MIT AI lab.

Cohen P.J. (1966) *Set theory and the continuum hypothesis*, W.A. Benjamin, New York.

Davidson D. (1980) *Essays on actions and events*, Clarendon Press, Oxford.

Davis M. (1980) "The mathematics of non-monotonic reasoning", *Artificial Intelligence* 13, pp. 73-80.

de Kleer (1986) "An assumption-based TMS", "Extending the ATMS" & "Problem solving with the ATMS", *Artificial Intelligence* 28(2), 127-162, 163-196, 197-225.

Dowty D.R., Wall R.E. & Peters S. (1981) *Introduction to Montague semantics*, Reidel, Boston.

Doyle J. (1980) "A truth maintenance system", *Artificial Intelligence* 12, pp. 231-272.

Eisinger N. (1986) "Everything you always wanted to knows about clause graph resolution", *Proceedings 8th International conference on Automated deduction*, pp. 316-336.

Fikes R.E. & Nilsson N.J. (1971) "STRIPS: a new approach to the application of theorem proving to problems solving", *Artificial Intelligence* 2, pp. 189-208.

Gabbay D. (1987) "Executable temporal logics for interactive systems", Imperial College technical report 87/5.

Gaschnig J. (1982) "PROSPECTOR: an expert system for mineral exploration", in *Introductory readings in expert systems*, ed D. Michie, Gordon & Breach, pp. 47-65.

Gentzen G. (1969) *Collected papers of Gerhard Gentzen*, ed. M.E. Szabo, North-Holland, Amsterdam.

Godel K. (1940) *The consistency of the generalised continuum hypothesis*, Princeton University Press, Princeton.

Hintikka J. (1962) *Knowledge and belief: an introduction to the two notions*, Cornell University Press.

Hintikka J. & Kulas, J. (1985) *Anaphora and definite descriptions: two applications of game theoretic semantics*, Reidel, Dordrecht.

Hodges W. (1969) *Logic*, Penguin, Harmondsworth.

Hughes G. & Cresswell M. (1968) *Introduction to modal logic*, Methuen, London.

Hughes G. & Cresswell M. (1984) *A companion to modal logic*, Methuen, London.

Jech T. (1971) *Lectures in set theory with particular emphasis on the method of forcing*, Springer, Berlin.

Kleene S.C. (1967) *Mathematic logic*, Wiley, London.

Konolige K. (1986) *A deduction model of belief*, Pitman, London.

Kowalski R. (1975) "A proof propedure using connection graphs", *Journal of the Association of Computing Machinery* 22(4), pp. 572-595.

Kowalski R. (1986) "Database updates in the event calculus", ms., Imperial College.

Kripke S. (1972) "Naming and necessity", in *Semantics of natural language*, eds. Harman & Davidson, Reidel, Boston, pp. 253-356.

Lewis D. (1973) *On the plurality of worlds*, Blackwell, Oxford.

Lorenz K. (1961) *Arithmetik und Logik als Spiele*, PhD thesis, Kiel.

Lorenzen P. (1959) "Ein dialogisches Konstructivitatskriterium", *Proceedings of the symposium on the foundations of mathematics*, Warsaw.

Loveland D.W. (1978) *Automated theorem proving: a logical basis*, North-Holland, Amsterdam.

Manthey R. & Bry F. (1988) SATCHMO: a theorem prover in PROLOG, *CADE*-88

Martelli A. & Montanari U. (1982) "An efficient unification algorithm", *ACM transactions on programming languages* 4(2), 258-282.

Martin-Lof P. (1982) "Constructive mathematics and computer programming", inb *Logic, methodology and philosophy of science VI*, North Holland, Amsterdam, pp. 153-175.

McAllester (1978) *A three-valued truth maintenance system*, BS thesis, Dept. of Electrical Engineering, MIT.

McCarthy J. (1980) "Circumscription: a form of non-monotonic reasoning", *Artificial Intelligence* 13, pp. 27-39.

McCarthy J. and Hayes P.J. (1969) "Some philosophical problems from the standpoint of artificial intelligence", *Machine Intelligence* 4, eds. B. Meltzer & D. Michie, Edinburgh University Press, Edinburgh.

McDermott D.V. & Doyle J. (1980) "Non-monotonic logic I", *Artificial Intelligence* 13, pp. 41-72.

McDermott D.V. (1982) "A temporal logic for reasoning about processes and plans", *Cognitive Science* 6, pp. 101-155.

Moore R.C. (1980) *Reasoning about knowledge and action*, SRI technical report 191.

Moore (1984) "A formal theory of knowledge and action", *Formal theories of the commonsense world*, eds. J.R. Hobbs & R.C. Moore, Ablex Pub. Corp., New Jersey, 319-358.

Oehrle D., Bach E. & Wheeler D. (1987) *Categorial grammars and natural language structures*, Reidel, Boston.

Pelletier J.F. (1982) *Completely non-clausal, completely heuristics driven automatic theorem proving*, MSc dissertationb, Univ. of Alberta.

Reichenbach H. (1971) *The direction of time*, ed. M. Reichenbach, Univ. of California Press.

Reiter R. (1980) "A logic for default reasoning", *Artificial Intelligence* 13(1)

Robbin J.W. (1969) *Mathematical logic: a first course*, Benjamin, New York.

Russell B. (1905) "On denoting", *Mind* 14, 470-493.

Said K.M. (1985) "Axiomatic epistemic logics and artificial intelligence", AISB-85, Warwick, 87-98.

Shoham Y. (1987) *Reasoning about change: time and causation from the standpoint of artificial intelligence*, PhD thesis, Yale.

Shortliffe E.H. (1976) *Computer-based medical consultations*, American Elsevier, New York.

Stallman R.M. & Sussman G.J. (1977) "Forward reasoning and dependency directed backtracking", *Artificial Intelligence* 9(2), 135-196.

Steel S. (1985) "Refinements of operator-based action representation", AISB-85, 98-108.

Stegmuller W. (1964) "Remarks on the completeness of logical systems relative to the validity-concepts of P. Lorenzen and K. Lorenz", *Notre Dame Journal of Symbolic Logic* V(2), 81-112.

Turner R. (1984) *Logics for artificial intelligence*, Ellis Horwood, Chichester.

Turner R. (1987) "A theory of properties", *Journal of Symbolic Logic* 52(2), 455-472.

Wallen L. (1987) "Matrix proofs for modal logics", *IJCAI-87*.

Waltz D. (1975) "Understanding line drawings of scenes with shadows", *The psychology of computer vision*, ed. P.H. Winston, McGraw Hill, New York.

Whitehead A.N. & Russell B. (1925) *Principia mathematica*, Cambridge University press.

Zadeh L.A. (1975) "Fuzzy logic and approximate reasoning", *Synthese* 30, 407-428.

Zadeh L.A. (1976) "A fuzzy-algorithmic approach to the definition of complex or imprecise concepts", *International Journal of Man-machine Studies* 8, 249-291.

INDEX

Printed in the United States
By Bookmasters